The National Physical Laboratory 1995 – 2014

PARTNERING IN PRACTICE

A COMMERCIAL PERSPECTIVE

Alan Mann

Published by New Generation Publishing in 2019

Copyright © Alan Mann 2019

First Edition

The author asserts the moral right under the Copyright, Designs and Patents Act 1988 to be identified as the author of this work.

Photos are Crown Copyright or reproduced courtesy of NPL

All Rights reserved. No part of this publication may be reproduced, stored in a retrieval system or transmitted, in any form or by any means without the prior consent of the author, nor be otherwise circulated in any form of binding or cover other than that which it is published and without a similar condition being imposed on the subsequent purchaser.

www.newgeneration-publishing.com

Front cover – an electron tree produced by NPL scientists

In Memory of
Dr George Gray CBE
1938 – 2018

Founding executive chair, Serco Group plc 1988 – 1999 and chair, NPL Management Limited 1995 – 1996 and 1997 – 2002

A man of quiet but weighty intellect, honesty and integrity who, in 1995, had the vision and confidence to bid the most sophisticated operation yet outsourced in the UK. Despite meteoric business success he behaved with kindness, warmth and humility that generated trust among colleagues, investors, customers and friends alike.

His commitment to taking on the management of national laboratories presented me with the opportunity to be part of a team to deliver the NPL contract which I know was dear to his heart and soon to become so dear to mine.

The Author

Until his retirement in 2012, Alan Mann was a Board Director of NPL Management Limited, a company that he formed in 1995 to operate the National Physical Laboratory (NPL) on behalf of government.

An accountant by profession, he gained wide financial and management experience within a number of service sector companies before becoming Finance Director (FD) of an innovative management buy-out of the direct services organisation from a local authority.

The company was subsequently acquired by Serco in 1991 and he became FD of the division addressing the central government market. As opportunities in this sector grew, he was responsible for leading financial offers within a number of successful high profile bids culminating in the production of the commercial volume of Serco's proposal to operate NPL.

This is where his story begins, inspired by NPL's amazing science, talented and dedicated people and the positive impact that can be achieved by working in a true partnership with government.

Acknowledgements

I'm indebted to my friends and colleagues within Serco and NPL who have taken time out from their busy lives to support me in this venture and, in particular:

Donna Hines (Executive Assistant within NPL)

Dr Brian Bowsher (former Managing Director of NPLML)

David Richardson (former Marketing and Communications Director at NPLML and subsequently Business Development Director within Serco)

But, of course, the real 'stars' are the scientists, engineers and support staff of NPL who inspired me to write this book in the first place.

Newton's Apple Tree – NPL's Teddington Site

Table of Contents

The Author 1
Acknowledgements 2
Preface 6
Introduction 8
Chapter 1 - Serco's Bid: The Successful 'Outsider' 13
    NPL Organisation and Management – Pre-contractorisation 13
    Expressions of Interest – The Serco Consortium 14
    The Invitation to Tender (ITT) – Aims and Obligations 15
    Serco's Core Bid Team 17
    Serco's Commercial Proposal – Risks and Opportunities 18
    Open-book Accounting – a Partnering Approach 26
    Conduct of the Tendering Process 27
    Best and Final – the 'Last' Hurdle (Almost) 29
Chapter 2 - Beyond the Smoke and Mirrors 33
    Contract phase-in 37
    First 6 Months of Operation – Delivering our Promises 39
Chapter 3 - The 'Yellow Brick Road' 47
    Customer Focus – 'Taking Measurement to Industry' 48
    Organisational Change 49
    Our 5-Year Track Record 57
    The 'PFI' – Opportunities and Threats 78
    The First Term Contract – Building a Genuine Partnership with DTI
    81
Chapter 4 - 'A Level Playing Field' 84
    The Contract Extensions 85
    The Extension Period – Other Strategic and Operational Opportunities 90
    Behind the Chinese Wall – NPL during the Contract Rebid Period .. 94
    DTI's Invitation to Negotiate (ITN) 96

    Serco's Proposal for a New Science Contract for Research and Development Services.. 98

    The Commercial Offer – Key Features of Serco's Proposals 100

    New Science Contract – Bid Variants 101

    The Bid Refinement 102

Some of NPL's Highlights 1995 – 2004... 104

Chapter 5 - 'A Game of Two Halves' 107

    The New Science Contract (NSC) – Synopsis.................................. 108

    The New Board and Executive Team.. 111

    The Termination of the PFI Contract – 2004.................................... 114

    Delivering the New Science Contract.. 115

    Continuing Support for the GOCO Model 118

    First-Half Contract Performance (2004 to 2009) 121

    Gathering Clouds on the Horizon 126

    The Second-Half Success and Challenges (2009 to 2014) 132

Chapter 6 - 'The Writing on the Wall' 151

    The Winds of Change 151

    Our Contract Extension Proposal (September 2011) – 'Route to 2019' 153

    Our Follow-Up Proposals (November 2011) – 'A Site Strategy' 160

    The Ministerial Decision... 164

Chapter 7 - End of an Era 168

    Contract Termination.. 168

    The Final Ministerial Decision 169

    Developing a New Sustainable NPLML Organisation..................... 173

    Transition and Transfer Plans 177

    Key Areas of Accounting 'Judgment'.. 181

    The Final Curtain.. 182

Some of NPL's Highlights 2004 – 2014... 187

Chapter 8 – Back to the Future 193

 NPL as a Public Corporation *193*
 Serco's Rise and Fall *196*
 GOCO or No-Go? *199*
 Epilogue *205*
Appendix A 206
 NPLML Managing Directors: 1995 – 2014 206
Appendix B 207
 The NPLML Business Model – An Organisation Structure to Support Government Partnering 207
  Our Partnering Legacy *207*
  Challenges Limiting Success *208*
  A Proven Structure to Support Partnering *211*
  The Service Ethic *215*
Glossary 216
Bibliography 218

Preface

In 1995 I formed a new Company named NPL Management Limited (NPLML). It was to operate the National Physical Laboratory (NPL) on behalf of the Department of Trade and Industry (DTI).

I was a member of a consortium headed by Serco in partnership with AEA Technology and the University of Loughborough. We were bidding for a 5-year contract to run the Laboratory. As Finance Director of the Serco Division focusing on central government contracts, I was responsible for structuring our commercial proposal.

After an intensive competitive tendering exercise the Serco consortium emerged as winners and I became Finance Director of NPLML. All I had to do now was deliver all our financial promises! Little did I know that this new venture would become an important part of my life right up to my retirement in 2012 – and for some time after that!

This book is an attempt to capture the actions and events from a commercial perspective that shaped NPL from 1995 to 2014; its transition from a Government Executive Agency to a thriving business in the private sector, all achieved whilst maintaining and enhancing the Laboratory's scientific standing in the world of metrology and supported by a true partnering approach to working with successive government departments both at a scientific and management level.

Changes on such a scale are never easy. Apart from the inevitable new organisational structure, systems and processes, a more commercial culture had to be engendered over time. By the same token, I had much to learn about NPL's amazing science and technology, and how our talented scientists and engineers were best motivated and programmes of research delivered. It was not long before I was completely captivated by this outstanding institution. A more commercial culture within NPL would take a little longer to evolve!

The views expressed are based on my own experience and knowledge and, of course, from NPLML's perspective, as the organisation and business model developed and political imperatives changed. Where there were gaps in my knowledge or failings in my memory I have relied on help from my then colleagues, now friends. On occasions I have been critical, more usually as a result of rigid or irrational government policies and processes rather than the individuals that had to carry them out!

My story covers one of the most transformational periods in NPL's history; how through all the changes in government, political intrigue, decant to a new Laboratory and economic upheavals, NPL emerged as a stronger, more relevant and fitter organisation ready to face whatever the future may bring.

I make no apology for the passion I had (and still have) for this often underrated (by those who should know better) and always underfunded organisation. I hope at the very least to stimulate your interest in this valuable jewel in the crown of UK's science and engineering capability; how it is possible to combine excellent science, value for the taxpayer and commercial success, and to make a real impact on the competitiveness of UK businesses and economy as well as our quality of life and environment.

Alan Mann
June 2017

Introduction

The National Physical Laboratory (NPL) has a rich legacy of scientific endeavor and achievement since its establishment in 1900. Its history is well documented in the book 'A Century of Measurement' by Eileen Magnello and on its website. There are a number of excellent papers on the political drivers that led to the decision, in 1994, by Michael Heseltine, President of the Board of Trade, to adopt a contractual model for NPL. The consultants' report on which the decision was based is a model of brevity and clarity that puts some current analogues to shame.

As the UK's National Measurement Institute and an important strategic asset, full privatisation was not considered to be a viable option for NPL. The Department of Trade and Industry (DTI) therefore retained ownership of the major assets – the NPL brand, intellectual property, land and buildings and scientific equipment whilst the management of the operation was entrusted to the private sector. The business model was known as a 'Government Owned; Contractor Operated' arrangement or GOCO. It is a model still favoured in the USA for research establishments and has had a successful track record there for more than 50 years.

This book tracks NPL's GOCO story from the award of the first contract in 1995 until the business model changed in 2015, a life of nearly 20 years. In both political and business terms, this is no mean achievement!

For ease of reference the chapters are arranged under the following headings and a brief synopsis of their content is included here:

Chapter 1 - The Successful 'Outsider'
The competitive tendering process was rigorous and exacting for all 5 of the consortia invited to bid. The proposal from the Serco bid team with its 'open book' approach to the commercial offer won the day against all the odds and the resulting 5-year term contract to operate the Laboratory firmly cemented this partnership ethos between owner and operator.

Chapter 2 - Beyond the 'Smoke and Mirrors'
The initial 6 months of transition were particularly challenging as a practical 'modus operandi' was tried, tested and agreed and additional contractual requirements were delivered that were to set a baseline for future operation.

Chapter 3 - The 'Yellow Brick Road'

Serco's bid proposal charted their vision for the future development of NPL with ambitious milestones for every year of the Contract. Amid the inevitable challenges, significant progress was made in meeting our contractual promises, including the delivery of the 5-year business plan, maintaining NPL's science excellence and international standing, growing income from third parties and establishing the first Knowledge Transfer Programme. If that was not enough, the DTI also played their 'wild card' with a successful bid to the Treasury in 1996 for Private Finance Initiative (PFI) funding for a new laboratory building.

Chapter 4 - 'A Level Playing Field'

As you might guess 5 years is not a long time in the life of a scientific research establishment and a re-competition of the Contract was soon upon us all. It turned out to be a very protracted rebid process (3 contract extensions in all) from October 2000 to March 2004. It was first delayed by the hope that the PFI building might be completed before a new Contract was awarded, potentially to a different contractor. With mounting delays caused by issues in meeting the exacting specifications of the new laboratory building DTI resumed the retender process, formed a project team and made the necessary adjustments to a new draft Contract reflecting the on-going PFI. After some time, an Invitation to Negotiate (ITN) was issued. This met DTI's desire to reassure potential bidders that they would not be disadvantaged by the incumbent's detailed operating knowledge of the Laboratory and gave much greater opportunity for shared dialogue during the selection process. During this period of political purdah NPLML, with the blessing of Serco, continued to 'do the right thing' and made major investments in the infrastructure, science capabilities and staff of NPL.

Serco was again successful in securing a new 10 year Science Contract. Unfortunately, some of the contractual changes lent themselves more to ease of procurement than enhancing the quality of science. The ITN had also placed a greater emphasis on generating additional income from third parties, in part to cover the considerable increase in operating costs of the newly built laboratory.

Chapter 5 - 'A Game of Two Halves'

The New Science Contract (NSC) was for 10 years until March 2014 and covered a period of significant business transformation for NPL with impressive evidence of substantial improvement in a number of key science and financial indicators together with greater staff engagement and commercial awareness.

The first half of the Contract was a period of considerable change for DTI, soon to become the Department of Innovation, Universities and Skills (DIUS) and then merging with the Department of Business, Enterprise and Regulatory Reform (BERR) to become the Department for Business, Innovation and Skills (BIS) in 2009. In the same year, BIS transferred the day to day oversight of NPL to a small Executive Agency, the National Measurement Office (NMO), formerly the National Weights and Measures Laboratory (NWML), which occupied the same site at Teddington. The unfortunate consequences of all these departmental 'musical chairs' was that knowledge of the founding principles of partnership and the significant achievements and benefits of the Contract were fast being eroded or eradicated from political memories and knowhow.

Serco had changed considerably as well. Its turnover was only £300M when the first NPL Contract was awarded and by the rebid in 2004 it was £1,600M. By 2008 Serco's turnover had doubled to over £3,000M and in December it had entered the list of FTSE top 100 companies. Although always considered a hugely important and prestigious Contract, NPLML was no longer a 'big fish in a small pond'.

From 2007 - 2009 all this activity was interrupted by the immensely damaging banking crisis and ensuing economic turmoil. Government spending cuts and austerity programmes followed. The repercussions are still affecting us now with budgets likely to be under continuing pressure for many years to come. NPL was not immune to these events, all of them affecting the organisation in different ways, some directly, others indirectly.

With hindsight, it is probably true to say that, by the second half of the Contract, the world was beginning to change for all parties to the NPL NSC. It is testament to the science and business strategy put in place and the 'buy-in' and commitment of staff, that allowed NPL to adapt quickly to these changing circumstances and gave the Company the financial resilience not only to weather the storm but continue to grow its business and invest in its science outputs right up until Contract expiry at the end of December 2014.

Chapter 6 - 'The Writing on the Wall'

There was provision in NSC for a possible 5-year extension to the existing 10 years subject to mutual agreement by both parties. Dialogue was to start 2 years before Contract termination. At this time, NPL was having some of its most successful years in terms of international standing, science outputs and growth in sales. Serco and the NPLML executive team were keen that this momentum was not disrupted unduly by a protracted and expensive rebid of the Contract, particularly at a time of government austerity, and began their engagement with BIS during 2011.

Serco was aware that political sentiment towards the GOCO business model had cooled and recognised the need for possible change. However, the NSC gave little scope for flexibility and NMO were able to offer little direction. Serco's initial outline proposals were submitted to NMO and a BIS review team, chaired by Sir Adrian Smith in September 2011. At their request, a much wider ranging offer including a vision for further development of the NPL Teddington site was submitted in November, with further clarifications provided in January 2012.

The expected detailed negotiations did not, however, materialise. Formally, the future operation of NPL was the responsibility of the Minister of State for Universities and Science, David Willetts. His initial decision was that he was not fully persuaded of the merits of Contract extension and he therefore instructed NMO to consider other options (alongside extension). This was a surprising and disappointing development. NMO were materially conflicted in this undertaking, as its own future was likely to be influenced by the eventual outcome for NPL. The size and complexity of the project grew substantially, requiring increasing levels of additional resource and expertise.

Chapter 7 - End of an Era

In November 2012 a telephone call was received by Sir Peter Williams, NPLML's Chairman, and Brian Bowsher, NPLML's Managing Director, from David Willetts, breaking the news that the decision had been taken not to extend or re-compete the Contract and therefore it would terminate on 31st March 2014.

A new model for NPL was to be developed to include 'strategic partners'. The task was again assigned to NMO. As NPLML prepared a transition and transfer of ownership plan, the true extent of the size and complexity (and cost) of this project was to unravel and slowly become apparent to NMO and BIS …

Chapter 8 – Back to the Future

After a 9 month extension to the Contract, NPLML transferred back to BIS as a wholly owned Company at the end of December 2014. In March 2015 its classification within Government was finally confirmed as a Public Corporation.

So what of the GOCO business model and does it still have a future in the UK? Can a public corporation work as efficiently and effectively? Perhaps the simple insertion of a private sector management team to drive strategic change may be an answer or is this just a short term fix? Full privatisation of strategic national institutions would undoubtedly be politically risky. How would these national assets be valued properly and excessive windfall profits controlled from ending up in the hands of the executive team, employees and advisors?

Well, of course, the jury is out. It will depend on the strategic and business profile of the organisation but most importantly it will be a matter of political will and economic expediency underpinned by smarter procurement that facilitates true partnership between government and the private sector focusing on customer service and added value – and this is where we came in, with Serco's bid in 1995!

Chapter 1 - Serco's Bid: The Successful 'Outsider'

NPL Organisation and Management – Pre-contractorisation

NPL was founded in 1900 and was initially controlled by the Royal Society. The Department of Scientific and Industrial Research was formed in 1916 and assumed responsibility for the Laboratory in 1918. It was transferred to the Ministry of Technology, later to become the DTI in 1965, and in July 1990 became an Executive Agency under the Government's wide ranging 'Next Steps' reforms. Agency status devolved responsibility for operation of the Laboratory to NPL's executive management team with the aim of prioritising and reducing research expenditure while policy functions remained with government. Although this enabled some limited cost cutting and efficiency savings, a far greater degree of commercial freedom would have to be achieved to realise NPL's full potential and remove many public sector operational constraints. As the initiative suggested, further steps seemed inevitable!

With the return of the Conservative Government in 1992 ministerial attention again returned to reducing the level of public expenditure. Michael Heseltine was appointed President of the Board of Trade and quickly proceeded with 'prior options' reviews of all DTI's laboratories. A number of scenarios were considered - closure, merger, privatisation, remaining as an Agency or return to operation within central government. Privatisation itself had a number of variants, from an outright trade sale, to the weakest form where a private sector organisation would be contracted to manage the operation.

Different options were chosen for each of DTI's laboratories: Warren Spring Laboratory was closed; the Laboratory of the Government Chemist was privatised; the National Engineering Laboratory was sold and the National Weights and Measures Laboratory remained an Executive Agency. For NPL, as the UK's National Measurement Institute, there was a strong strategic reason for government to continue to own the Laboratory but entrust its operation to the private sector so as to engender the benefits of best commercial practice. This would be achieved through a competitive tendering process resulting in a Government Owned, Contractor Operated arrangement. However, the National Measurement Accreditation Service

(NAMAS), then part of NPL, was to become a separate non-profit distributing company limited by guarantee.

Expressions of Interest – The Serco Consortium

Serco was already familiar with the National Physical Laboratory site through a 5-year Estates Contract it won in 1990. It had a large number of other contracts with central government customers, predominantly the MOD, but these were generally for individual services. Serco saw great potential to deliver significant efficiencies to Government where these could be combined under a single facilities management agreement, similar to RAF Fylingdales which it had run since 1959. This, of course, would also have the potential of raising Serco's own profile and profit margins. But the company faced the perception among some in and around NPL that it was 'a mower of grass and fixer of taps', rather than having the capacity to manage change in a world class science institution.

In spite of these challenges, when the invitation for expressions of interest from the private sector to operate NPL was issued by DTI in 1994, it was therefore of great interest to Serco. To meet the DTI's contractor selection criteria the search was on for a partner with a strong track record in the management of science and technology and a first class university with excellent experience of working closely with industry.

After approaching several potential partners, Serco identified AEA Technology (AEAT) as a perfect partner and David Richardson joined the bid team on secondment from them in October 1994 to address the opportunity. David identified Dr John Rae, AEAT's Business Development Director for non-nuclear activities (and a former Department of Energy Chief Scientist), as a strong candidate for future MD. John was keen to join Serco and bid this prestigious contract. However, AEAT had just been split from the UK Atomic Energy Authority for later floatation on the London Stock Exchange and there would be continuing uncertainty as to the part it could play in the Contract.

Finding a suitable university partner also proved more troublesome than first thought. Those located close to NPL, Imperial College and University College London had already partnered with competitors. However, Serco had been approached by Loughborough University and although it did not have the scientific standing of some potential partners, it did have a reputation of building strong ties with industry. For Loughborough it would undoubtedly serve to enhance their standing both in academic circles and industry.

After some initial soundings with DTI as to the suitability of their proposed partners, the die was cast, and Heads of Agreement were signed by Serco, AEAT and Loughborough to bid for the NPL Science Contract.

The Invitation to Tender (ITT) – Aims and Obligations

The ITT was issued in December 1994, just before Christmas with submission of proposals requested by the end of February. It set out the aims and obligations of the parties and included a draft contract for review and programme pricing schedules to be completed. Needless to say, there was little time for yuletide festivities that year!

Sustaining excellent science remained at the heart of the ITT. The Laboratory's wide stakeholder community had to be convinced that the GOCO business model would not 'dumb down' its science outputs. There would be a monitoring group from the Royal Society and Royal Academy of Engineering (RSRAE) to provide feedback on NPL's quality of science directly to the Secretary of State. There would also be a list of NPL's key staff drawn up that would prevent the contractor from terminating their employment without prior consultation and agreement with DTI. NPL's scientific reputation and international standing would be a key part of the bid assessment criteria.

However, long term reductions in funding the Laboratory had to be met and DTI saw a number of benefits from introducing private sector management and commercial practices to NPL. Greater commercial freedom would enable new sources of income to be generated from selling a greater proportion of NPL's expertise and services to third party customers resulting in improved asset utilisation and economies of scale. Better value would also come from reductions in government bureaucracy and a greater emphasis on operational efficiency and more effective delivery of its programmes of science.

DTI would, therefore, still maintain ownership and ultimate control over the Laboratory while benefitting from best commercial practice and enhanced performance allowing real reductions in their science and technology budget.

The Term Contract was to last for a period of 5 years with an option of a further 2 years and the contractors would have to adhere to a stringent set of operating principles and requirements. The full economic cost (FEC) of the Laboratory would be borne by the contractor to avoid any complications with UK and European rules on anti-competitive behaviour and 'State Aids'. DTI would therefore continue to charge a rent for occupying the buildings and introduced 'lease fees' for operating the scientific equipment which they would still own. All other costs and existing contractual obligations would transfer to the contractor who would bear any termination costs that may be necessary. Permanent staff would transfer under the 'Transfer of Undertakings, Protection of Employment' (TUPE) rules requiring existing civil service employment contracts to be honoured and, as was considered best practice during that time, a 'look-alike' defined benefit pension scheme was offered.

The most effective way to keep NPL's assets, liabilities and operational activities 'ring-fenced' and separately identifiable was to create a stand-alone private limited company.

For their part, DTI would 'guarantee' to place at least £30M of 'single tendered' research at NPL each year for the period of the Contract. This represented about 80% of the expected overall funding available; the remainder would be competitively tendered with other measurement institutes and contractors. The amount was not indexed but remained flat so effectively the value reduced in real terms over the 5 years. There were two DTI programme 'customers' to satisfy, one in physical metrology, the National Measurement System Policy Unit (NMSPU) and the other in materials technology, the Engineering Industries Directorate (EID). New research programmes were generally formulated on a 3 year cycle.

An ongoing formal tendering process would therefore be required for each new individual DTI research programme with fully costed projects and scientific milestones and these would be subject to final price negotiation with the programme customers. Payment would only be made on satisfactory completion of each milestone. Contractors would have to give fixed prices based on tendered day rates for senior, medium and junior scientists plus direct costs across each research programme for the duration of the Contract.

Serco's Core Bid Team

The DTI selected 5 consortia to bid the Contract – WS Atkins with SIRA and Scientific Generics, EDS with the Defence Evaluation and Research Agency (DERA), Rolls Royce and Associates, Brown and Root with Imperial College and the Serco consortium.

For the size of bid the core team was relatively small with individuals majoring on specific aspects of the proposal – the quality of science and interface with industry, research programmes and delivery, laboratory operation, estate management, business development and communications, and finance, all supported by a dedicated personal assistant/administrator. Other specialist expertise was available from Serco and its partners. Dr George Gray, the Executive Chairman of Serco Group, was to take a keen personal interest in the bid and his support was invaluable throughout the entire process.

The bid team was led by Peter Gange, Business Development Director of Serco's Central Government Services Division. As Finance Director of that division, I was responsible for commercial and financial aspects of the proposal, aided and abetted by a contractor, a very competent modeler and spread sheet 'driver' and there was always reach-back to Serco Group Finance. David Richardson from AEAT had joined the team, majoring on the business development, marketing and communications aspects of the bid. The all-important NPL science and industry interface, making our research relevant and accessible to industry (the 'science exam question' as it became known) was in the experienced hands of Prof John Tyrer at Loughborough University.

The Serco bid team first came together at Loughborough in the late autumn of 1994 for what was to be, I would guess, one of the greatest challenges of our individual working careers – it certainly was mine! Although quite apprehensive as to how the team would work together, I need not have been concerned as we were very quickly at ease with one another and able to concentrate on the formidable task ahead. The lasting recollection I have of that initial meeting is the 'story boarding' session. The level of engagement, commitment and enthusiasm from a group of people who had only just met certainly left me with a reassuring degree of confidence in the experience, knowledge and talent within the bid team and in our ability to produce an attractive proposal both in terms of a management and operational solution and the 'science exam question'. I was just hoping our commercial offering would prove to be equally attractive!

Serco's Commercial Proposal – Risks and Opportunities

Serco was well ahead of the market in seeing the opportunities presented by the government's clear intention to outsource much of its non-core operational work to the private sector. It had developed an effective bidding 'tool-kit' with an extensive library of material that could be adapted to meet specific customer requirements. There was also a skilled graphics department to produce highly professional proposal documents.

The ITT included a large amount of information to assimilate and interpret. In terms of the commercial offer there was a myriad of financial reports, schedules and statements to wade through. One of the most important tasks was to establish an accurate assessment of NPL's financial position. It could then be used as a 'baseline' for all future business forecasts and assumptions for the 5 years of the Contract.

Business risk - contrasting accounting conventions

Unfortunately, in the mid-1990s government and corporate accounting was very different. In the commercial world, the accounting standard requires the 'accruals concept' to be adopted. In essence, income and expenses have to be recognised in the accounting period to which they relate. NPL's finances however, were based on government cash accounting when financial transactions were only recorded in their accounts when cash was either received or paid. Without accruals, the amount of sales turnover, expense and profit and loss in a period would not necessarily reflect the actual level of economic activity within NPL. We estimated that this could amount to well in excess of a million pounds. Although Agencies were meant to maintain two sets of accounts, on both a cash and accruals basis, we only had access to financial information based on cash transactions so it considerably increased our workload and Serco's business risk!

It also became clear that, for different reasons, neither AEAT nor Loughborough would be in a position to take an equity share in a newly formed company but would become strategic partners with subcontracts to deliver specific areas of expertise. The entire financial risk therefore rested with Serco.

Far more complicated was the 'current cost accounting' convention that was used by government when valuing assets at the end of each accounting period. This involved applying the retail prices index (RPI) to the value of all scientific equipment owned by NPL to arrive at an estimated current cost of the asset after allowing for depreciation. When the high inflationary periods of the 1970s, 80s and beginning of the 90s had subsided, most private sector companies had chosen to return to the 'historic cost accounting' convention (i.e. sticking with the original invoice value and depreciating the asset over its estimated economic life) and drop this complicated and often confusing indexing of assets which in NPL's case was likely to have led to over-valuations due to the significant depreciation of high tech instrumentation in the early years of ownership.

The 5-Year Business Forecast

Because of the unhelpful government accounting convention and the amount of change that was going on within NPL during the bid, much of the historic financial data and information received from them was best treated with a great deal of caution and had to be carefully substantiated or simply used as a guide. The most sensible and reliable approach therefore was for a 5-Year Business Forecast to be built 'bottom up' from first principles.

Having formed a new company, NPL Management Limited (NPLML), a pro-forma set of properly audited spread sheets – Profit and Loss, Balance Sheet and Cash Flow – was provided by Serco Group. With some modification to fit the new NPL operation and tender requirements, they could be populated with various financial scenarios and give an excellent high level view of our forecast of business performance over the Contract period. They proved to be an extremely important and invaluable tool not only during the bid process but were later to become the basis of NPLML's future business plan. Of course, to build these top level forecasts involved an extensive and detailed amount of underlying financial modeling work and we still had the complex task of populating DTI's pricing schedules with day rates and direct costs for each research programme.

The bid team had about 9 weeks (including Christmas) from receiving the ITT to bring together all the different work streams and produce a balanced, well structured, coherent and attractive proposal that met all DTI's required obligations and economies. It had to demonstrate how we intended to transform NPL into a financially viable and outward facing company that would be competitive in the private sector and still respected by the scientific community.

Our commercial offer was all about delivering more high quality science for less money. There was a real opportunity to show how this might be achieved now that NPL had been released from many of the public sector operating constraints. In fact, realising NPL's true potential was not rocket science! There were 2 fundamental ways to create better value for money - increasing sales turnover (and thus contribution to overheads) and reducing costs. The former would allow us to spread the not inconsiderable overhead costs of running a measurement institute over a greater customer base and benefit from economies of scale with better utilisation of NPL's resources. The latter would come from introducing best commercial practice with new systems and processes, and professional accounting and procurement skills bringing a whole range of operational efficiencies and improved productivity. Of course, all this was easier said than done!

Estimating Growth in Sales Turnover
One of the biggest commercial risks was pitching the growth in sales turnover to third parties at the right level and judging how much of the 20% of DTI's competitively tendered work we might win. If these targets were set too low our bid might not be competitive; too high and any shortfall would soon put profit margins under pressure.

After adjusting for the loss of income from NAMAS, we estimated that the baseline annual sales turnover from third party customers would start at around £6M. Half of this was from the public sector and European Commission and the remainder, mainly calibration services, was from private sector customers. Because of concerns about NPL having a UK monopoly in some of these calibration services, DTI required future price increases to be agreed with them first.

Relying on the experience of AEAT and some market testing, our best judgment was that third party sales turnover could be increased to £10M p.a. phased over 5 years and that NPL should be able to win two thirds of

DTI's competitively tendered research programmes amounting to £4M p.a. Added to this would be DTI's £30M 'guaranteed' annual spend with NPL on single tendered research. None of DTI's programme spend over the 5 years allowed for inflation, so in real terms their funding would be reducing by nearly 15% (RPI) or £5M between 1995 and 2000. In the year before contractorisation DTI spent £37M at NPL so it is easy to see the depth of Government budget cuts and the sales turnover gap that that had to be filled each year just to stand still.

Of course, this level of growth would also require investment in resources with new skill sets in business development, marketing and communications and their associated costs.

Staff Productivity
There would have to be significant cost reductions right from commencement of the Contract to create a financially viable and sustainable company. First, we had to match scientific resources and direct programme and project costs to our estimated sales turnover.

The largest element of cost was, of course, salaries. Early retirement and voluntary redundancy schemes had been offered to NPL staff prior to contractorisation and it was hoped that this would deal to a large extent with any overstaffing of scientists caused by the cuts in DTI's research programme expenditure.

All permanent staff would have to transfer to NPLML at the beginning of the Contract under TUPE rules which ensured all their existing civil service employee benefits would be honoured. However, there had been a recruitment freeze on employing new permanent staff over the previous year with only temporary contracts being offered. This enabled us to cost all permanent scientific and technical staff into our bid and terminate temporary contracts when they were due for renewal in order to match our assumptions on forward workloads after taking into account anticipated growth in sales, improvements in productivity and normal staff turnover.

Staff utilisation, the amount of all science staff time spent on programme related work, was relatively poor and had remained so over the previous 5 years. One of our key proposals was the introduction of a more consistent and formal system for programme and project management. Our target was an improvement of at least 10% in utilisation and I felt certain that simply ensuring we invoiced our customers in a timely manner for all the work completed would make a real difference.

Based on Serco's extensive experience, we did, however, have a good understanding of the level of management and support staff required to run a commercial undertaking and estate of this size. Like most other public sector organisations at this time there were too many layers of management and administration and with improved business systems and simplified processes, some 30% savings were estimated to be possible. We also built into our estimates a level of redeployment and retraining of staff to keep redundancies to an absolute minimum.

Serco would also have to offer transferring permanent staff a civil service 'look-alike' defined benefit pension scheme. This would be closed to new members as they were extremely expensive to fund. New recruits would be offered a 'money purchase' or defined contribution pension scheme reducing the Company's future pension costs and funding risks.

Improved Procurement of Goods and Services
NPL's annual purchase of goods and services amounted to more than £20M. Government accounting rules meant that NPL suffered from 'annuality' of its budgets which meant that if funding was not spent in year, it was lost. In addition, there was a lack of flexibility between operating (revenue) and capital budgets and funding could not be vired between them. The feast and famine of funding (usually at the end of a financial year) often led to sub-optimal purchasing and waste. Scientific Divisions within NPL also appeared to operate independently of one another so not benefitting from economies of scale and often duplicating purchases. For example, I was astonished to find that there were even different word processing and spread sheet systems between divisions making it difficult for them to share information.

With the introduction of commercial systems and processes together with the development of a professional procurement team we estimated savings of at least 20% could be achieved.

Buildings and Estates Management
The contractor would be responsible for the full economic cost of all NPL's estate and its services. These included a rent for the buildings, property rates, utilities, repairs and minor works (under £3k) and

maintenance. As owner, DTI was responsible for any major capital works. The site comprised 55 building of varying age and state of repair spread over 82 acres of land. Not all the land was Government owned. There was obviously scope for rationalising and improving the building stock with resulting savings in rent, property rates, utilities and maintenance. In fact, under its Estates Contract, Serco had put forward plans to vacate and demolish some buildings. Given the potential for considerable savings, we were keen to work closely with DTI to accelerate and widen these plans. To show our commitment we also proposed a number of 'spend to save' projects potentially financed by Serco rather than relying on the necessary capital budget being available from DTI. We also made it very clear in our proposal what assumptions we had made about rationalisation of the building stock and the savings assumed in our bid. If we were successful, it would be an indication of DTI's support for our plans. The savings would also enable DTI to make much better use of its own capital budgets for the continuing improvement of the NPL site. The benefits demonstrated in our proposal amounted to several £Ms over the Contract period. Of course, DTI's bid for PFI funding to build a new Laboratory was to supersede some of these proposals.

Increased Investment in Scientific Equipment

DTI retained ownership of all scientific equipment over £3k in value. The contractor would be charged an 'operating lease' fee quarterly based on the valuation of the assets using an annuity formula with an interest rate of 6%. NPL's asset register had been verified independently but was still valued based on the existing current cost accounting rules and also included a proportion of VAT. It was therefore likely that the value of scientific equipment and the resulting lease fee would be inflated and from the initial contractor tours of the Laboratory, it also appeared that much was under-utilised or not used at all. If NPL was to be expected to compete on equal terms within the private sector market then this issue would have to be addressed.

DTI were quick to recognise the problem and in order to avoid any delay in the bidding process, contractors were told to assume a cost of £2.5M for lease fees in the first 6 months of the Contract. During this time the contractor would be required carry out a full assessment of NPL's scientific equipment, update the asset register and agree any revisions to valuations with DTI. This would be the new baseline upon which the prescribed annuity formula would then be applied.

Although we believed that, after a detailed assessment, asset values (and lease fees) should reduce by about 20% from the current £22M book value, we built into our model the need to increase investment in scientific equipment to make up for shortfalls in previous years. Of course, this would be dependent on NPL obtaining the necessary capital budget funding from DTI. There was, however, an obligation on the contractor to produce a 3 year rolling capital plan for DTI programmes in the first 6 months of the Contract and annually thereafter so it was hoped that this would enable the appropriate funding to be secured. We also gained assurance that the contractor would be responsible for procuring the scientific equipment and maintaining the assets register on behalf of DTI so as to enable us to improve NPL's poor record of asset management. There would therefore be real opportunities for savings in the short term from the reduced asset valuation baseline but the greatest benefit would be in smarter asset management and professional procurement.

Equipment purely in support of third party work would have to be financed by the contractor, so we would only invest in capital where a formal business case, yielding an appropriate return, had been approved.

In addition, the successful contractor would have to buy all the assets with individual values of under £3k. The value was estimated at £3M affecting our cash flow and incurring financing costs.

Cost Recovery and Day Rates

The costs of maintaining and operating a National Laboratory at the leading edge of science and technology will always be extremely high. In addition, the ITT also stipulated that NPL should deliver a Strategic Research Programme of £1.5M p.a. and a General Activities Programme of £0.5M p.a.

The major proportion of NPL's costs could only be recovered through charging its customers an appropriate day rate for scientists' time. Determining how these costs should be allocated between DTI research programmes and other customers was a key piece of modeling work. In fact, a robust and auditable cost (overhead) recovery policy was essential to ensure that we did not breach European rules on 'State Aids' (government subsidising industry), avoid accusations of unfair competition from other private sector companies (effectively using government cash to under-cut their prices) and still have a pricing policy that was not only competitive for our bid to DTI but was also considered by customers to offer value for money albeit at a premium to reflect the integrity and quality of NPL's services.

Although our proposals would offer DTI substantial savings, the transition from Executive Agency to a private limited company would carry some new or different costs to be recovered. New skill sets would either have to be developed from within NPL, transferred from the bidding partners or recruited from outside the consortium. As we have seen, these would be in areas such as business development, marketing, communications, purchasing, accountancy and IT support and would carry associated on-going operating or one-off set up costs.

Dr John Rae had agreed to be proposed as the new Managing Director of NPLML and David Richardson had also agreed to be put forward as the Marketing and Communications Director. I would be the new Finance Director designate. In addition, Serco would need to provide business support for corporate functions such as treasury management, tax advice, audit, company secretarial services, pension and other advisory services as necessary. DTI also required NPLML to carry fully comprehensive insurance including the buildings and contents that they owned and had previously self-insured. To mitigate some of these costs, NPL would no longer be subject to recharges from DTI amounting to £1M p.a.

The major one-off 'costs of change' would also have to be recovered though our bid price. They included expenditure on Contract 'phase-in', restructuring the organisation - redundancy, recruitment and retraining - and investment in the implementation and development of business information and accounting systems. Most of these costs would be incurred within the first 6 months but realistically, they could only be recovered through the day rates over the 5 years of the contract. This, together with the £3M to purchase the minor equipment would impact our cash flow and would incur financing costs. We therefore had to make sure that DTI's Review Board had a full appreciation of all the costs that made up the day rates we would have to charge in the Pricing Schedules.

The final element to enable us to complete the build-up of our day rates was, of course, Serco's margin requirements. It was now up to Serco's Investment Committee to agree an acceptable profit for the bid and, just as important, the level of the underlying financial information we were prepared to disclose.

Open-book Accounting – a Partnering Approach

As part of our proposal submission I was keen that we included our 5-Year Forecast for NPL – the detailed Profit and Loss, Balance Sheet and Cash Flow - together with our underlying financial bid assumptions. It would demonstrate very clearly that we wished the contract to be a true partnership and that we were prepared to be completely open and transparent about the risks and expected returns built in to our proposal. Why not start as we mean to go on?

Although there was initially some concern within Serco about disclosing too much of our commercial offer to DTI too soon, it was agreed that, on balance, it would be beneficial. It would add clarity to what was a very complex bid and potentially mitigate risks of misunderstanding or misinterpreting our proposal and flag potential issues to DTI. Serco also agreed that they would pitch their required return on the Contract at a very competitive rate of 5% of sales turnover, with a management fee of 2% to cover the services that they would provide directly.

Our commercial offer would therefore include not only the Pricing Schedules required by the ITT but also a 5-Year Forecast showing our estimate of DTI competitively tendered and third party sales turnover, the associated direct costs, and a breakdown of all other expenditure together with the expected 5% profit margin.

Included in the ITT were mechanisms for sharing in the successful operation of NPL. For me, these had 'consultant' written all over them and reflected an old style 'stick and carrot' contractual arrangement rather than a true partnering approach. The first mechanism related to 'saved days'. If programmes were completed in less than the number of days quoted in the tender then they would be shared 50:50 allowing DTI to buy more science and NPL to spend more time working on third party work. Of course, there was no compensation for overrunning time and costs! The ITT also proposed a regime of incentives and penalties relating to overall performance which was subject to a sliding scale of reductions. For example, the contractor would only be paid in full if the delivery of scientific milestones was satisfactory and on time. The mechanisms were not well thought through and impractical to implement, particularly in the context of a working scientific environment and would inevitably introduce an additional layer of administration. They would lead to unproductive time being taken by scientists to micromanage their timesheets so that saved days were only shared where totally justifiable and unavoidable, an unnecessary distraction!

We flagged these concerns in our proposal and explained that we had reluctantly included an additional cost in our bid of £1.5M p.a. to mitigate potential risks to our already slim margin. However, we believed there were more effective ways of demonstrating quality of science and sharing in benefits arising from the successful operation of NPL.

The formation of a separate ring fenced Company, NPL Management Limited, had several benefits for both Serco and DTI. It enabled us to demonstrate our commitment to a true partnership approach. We could offer to go beyond just open book accounting and give DTI full access to all NPL's company and business records. As audited statutory accounts would have to be produced for NPLML each year these would give DTI an entirely independent view of its financial position. The Company would also have a Board of Directors separate from Serco. We expressed a wish that DTI should be represented on the Board together with additional independent members with wide ranging experience of science and industry. A stand-alone company also allowed us to make a much more radical proposal where DTI could share in the profits of the whole of NPLML rather than just savings on their programmes.

Conduct of the Tendering Process

In order to conduct the NPL tendering process DTI set up a Laboratories Unit with a Review Board. There were representatives from both the physical and materials science customers and very able specialists in procurement and finance. In early February 1995 a formal 'plenary session' to which all the 5 bidders were invited, was held at NPL followed by conducted tours of the Laboratory. The bidders were also given access to NPL's divisional directors and other members of the management team at times of their choosing. Again, these were time limited and carefully orchestrated so as not to give unfair advantage to any of the bidders. All this was carefully managed under the watchful eye of DTI's Laboratories Unit.

The plenary session was held in the impressive lecture theatre in the Glazebrook building (now demolished) and presentations were made by DTI and representatives of NPL about the bidding process and some background to the management of the Laboratory and its science. The session predictably didn't provide much additional information but was interesting for another reason; it was a chance for us to see for the first time the other bidding teams. When DTI opened the floor to questions, we eyed one another suspiciously, not wanting to give away any of our concerns! However, the bidders introduced themselves and their company and asked some very polite questions. My lasting memory was when our bid director, Peter Gange, rose to his feet, introduced himself but rather than saying he was from Serco, announced to everyone's surprise that he represented NPL Management Limited – a truly show-stopping 'tumble weed' moment! Perhaps it could be interpreted as a little arrogant, but I am sure others in the theatre were kicking themselves for not thinking of it first! After the initial 'shock' I believe it was taken in good spirit and would guess that it raised a chuckle or two within DTI afterwards. It certainly left them in no doubt that, having already formed a company, we were taking the bid very seriously and were happy to be recognised as NPL Management first and foremost.

The meetings with members of the NPL management team, however, were more informative, not so much for new intelligence we were able to glean, as this was well controlled and scripted but more as an introduction to the NPL management team. Again, I was apprehensive about how we might be received given that we were upsetting their well-ordered world but in fact they were very pleasant and professional. It did reassure me that, if our bid was successful, they would have a strong commitment to work with us to turn around the fortunes of NPL and make it a growing and thriving organisation again. It was very clear that the previous few years with budget cuts, recruitment freezes and uncertainties about their future had been very difficult for everyone at NPL. At least contractorisation would bring a modicum of stability and investment back into the Laboratory. There were still, however, a large number of sceptics to win over. The meetings were also helpful as they confirmed, by inference, that much of the programme and project timesheet bookings and costs were 'managed' and therefore unreliable. Building our financial model 'bottom up' based on reasonable staff utilisation and direct cost assumptions was certainly the best approach.

As far as Serco was concerned, its bidding strategy was straight forward; be easy to work with, ask as few questions as possible, propose the minimum number of changes to the draft contract and get to the negotiating table. As we progressed through the bidding process our confidence grew and we felt sure that we could make a real difference to the Laboratory. NPL was already getting underneath our skin!

All the bidders managed to keep to the timetable. I recollect that there was only an agreed 1 week extension to the 8th March to cover some late TUPE information, perhaps. Our bid was submitted and after sorting out the chaos left after the frenzy of the previous few weeks we all had a well-earned break and awaited the results.

Best and Final – the 'Last' Hurdle (Almost)

DTI took just over a month to assess the bids and we heard a little before the late Easter break on the 14th April that the bidders had been down selected to two: W S Atkins whose partners were SIRA and Scientific Generics, and Serco with AEAT and Loughborough. We were given a tight deadline to submit our 'Best and Final' offers so we would again be working over a holiday break! Both Atkins and Serco were given the opportunity of individual meetings with the full DTI Review Board to receive feedback and be able to raise any final issues.

Of course, I was very much focused on DTI's view of our Commercial Offer. We were keen to receive their feedback on our outline proposals for an alternative to the performance 'incentives and penalties' and the mechanism of sharing saved days so that we could remove the additional cost that had increased our original bid price by £1.5M p.a. The ITT already outlined a regime of independent annual reviews of DTI's research programmes and there would be visits by the RS/RAE Advisory Group to monitor NPL's quality of science. We therefore proposed a far more efficient and effective partnering approach where we would produce a formal annual report which brought together the whole of NPLML's business activities and performance metrics in one document. The report would therefore include key corporate areas such as quality, health, safety and environment, personnel management, procurement, actual performance metrics against financial and capital plans, and business forecasts for the coming year. DTI would then be able to give valuable feedback on any issues and update NPLML on policy changes and future requirements. In terms of sharing in the success of NPL, we believed a better solution would be a more innovative partnering approach which brought together all DTI's proposed mechanisms under a simple cumulative profit share arrangement based on the Company's independently audited statutory accounts. Any profits above Serco's required 5% of total sales turnover would be shared 50:50 with DTI who could then reinvest these sums in extra research.

Dr George Gray attended the DTI Review Board meeting with us, demonstrating Serco's commitment to the success of the Contract. In fact, I remember that in answer to a direct question about this, he replied in his usual reserved and understated way that he would stake the future of Serco on it! It was a truly impressive moment. The Board expressed interest in our proposals for a formal annual performance report and profit share arrangement. They suggested that we might consider removing the £1.5M penalty cost from our final bid as it was their intention to revisit this area. They also suggested that we might want to reconsider our assumptions on future third party sales turnover. This was an immediate 'red flag' as we were concerned that we might have been too conservative in assessing the level of commercial sales growth in our first submission. After a further intensive review of prospective sales we were able to find reasonable justification in increasing our forecast from £10M to £11M (£14M including competitively tendered work) after 5 years. I do believe that giving DTI our detailed 5-Year Forecast allowed them to better understand the assumptions underlying our bid and compare it with their own internal model and raise questions on Atkins' proposal. It also gave them a clear picture of how our proposed profit share would work.

Partnering in Practice
Our Best and Final proposal was submitted at the end of April. After a period of 'silence' DTI's Review Board came back to us on 'clarification points'. I am sure they were doing the same with W S Atkins. They wished to arrange a further meeting on the 25th May and sent us a discussion paper: *'The contracting out of NPL – partnering in practice'*. From my perspective this was an extremely important landmark document where the DTI acknowledged that a partnering approach was the 'only sound basis for a relationship where the definition of an effective future work programme will rely on a close collaboration between the DTI and the Contractor'.

Please forgive me for dwelling on its contents in a little more detail!

The paper stated that there were few practical issues arising from the particular proposals for joint decision making, planning and review and open book accounting and so the note (and meeting) would concentrate on the 'practicalities of the sharing of the financial benefits of better than expected performance'.

The paper went on to say that they were seeking mechanisms for the sharing of additional financial benefits which:
- only come into play once the contractor has achieved the targets agreed by both parties to be legitimate
- broadly offer an even distribution of additional benefits to both parties
- do not provide room for perverse behaviour which might maximise the share of the benefit of one party or other party, but which is irrational in the context of a business-like approach to the development of NPL
- allow the DTI to take its share of any additional benefits in the form of extra research

To this end the ITT had made a number of proposals and it was their understanding that we saw benefits in grouping all these measures under the single umbrella of a profit share. Furthermore, the DTI was, in principle, sympathetic to our proposal as it had the 'prospect of being a simpler mechanism while providing the necessary incentives to both parties and at the same time giving Serco the reassurance that its basic return was not in jeopardy'.

DTI agreed the trigger for activation of the profit sharing mechanism should be the annual profile of profitability which led to the cumulative achievement of 5% on sales over the term of the Contract split 50:50, the contractor keeping the actual cash benefit and DTI taking its share through extra research.

The paper concluded that with Serco's agreement and some joint analysis from both parties on how to make it work in practice, DTI believed that 'we potentially have the basis for a fair and innovatory contract with Serco which might well work as a model for other partnerships between the private and public sector'. (This is discussed further in Appendix B).

It seemed to be a positive meeting but, of course, we did not know what conversations were going on with W S Atkins. We now just had to wait until the announcement!

Chapter 2 - Beyond the Smoke and Mirrors

While we were in our 'bidding bubble' the rest of the world was moving on – and UK politics was no exception. On the 22nd June 1995 John Major announced his resignation as leader of the Conservative Party. It was in response to a deep divide in the Conservative party over Europe. 'Twas ever thus'! John Redwood was the sole contender. It was at this time that Serco heard it had been successful in its bid for the operation of NPL and arrangements were made for us to go up to London for the 'ceremonial' signing of the agreement with the Minister. However, the re-election of John Major and the ensuing cabinet reshuffle on the 5th July followed by a frenzy of activity meant that we had to be turned back from the Minister's antechamber prepared for the meeting which had to be postponed until 13th July.

It was an amiable, low-key meeting attended by the Minister, Ian Taylor, from DTI and Dr George Gray, Dr John Rae, David Richardson and myself from Serco and NPL Management Limited. Unfortunately the only lasting mementos of this historic occasion are t-shirts that were distributed by David Richardson! They carried the following extract of a verse from the Gondoliers by W.S. Gilbert:

'But the privilege and pleasure
that we treasure beyond measure
is to run on little errands for the Ministers of State ...'

Serco: AEA Technology: Loughborough University of Technology
The NPL contract
July 1995

And, of course, NPL Management Limited, under the ownership of Serco, would be focusing on excellence in measurement and running little errands for another 20 years!

When we arrived back at Serco's Head Office, then in Southall, I remember seeing the official announcement board in the reception area and hearing that our share price had jumped significantly. But for us it was back to work! The Contract start date had been agreed as 1st October 1995.

There was a great deal to accomplish in the next 10 weeks and it was right through the Government's summer recess and holiday season (again) for us!

As neither of the other members of the consortium were able to take an equity share in the Company, NPLML became a wholly owned subsidiary of Serco. In reality, this simplified the organisational structure and operation of the Company and a separate Board with independent members ensured a level of 'insulation' from any possibility of an over-zealous corporate parent.

The Board appointments of NPLML and executive positions were quickly confirmed. Dr George Gray became a non-executive director and the first Chair of NPLML and he set about selecting independent members of the Board. Dr John Rae joined Serco from AEAT and became NPLML's first Managing Director. His was the only contract of employment that was with Serco, everyone else joined NPLML. Peter Gange, the Bid Director, became the Support Services Director and I took up the post of Finance Director. Dr Andrew Wallard, who was the existing Deputy Laboratory Director of NPL remained in this role and joined the Board.

Four independent non-executive directors were appointed, two Fellows of the Royal Society, Professors Tony Kelly and Archie Howie, together with Dr Ron Bullough and Dr Bob Whelan. Between them, they had vast experience of the physical and materials sciences, industry and business.

David Richardson was initially seconded from AEAT as the Marketing and Communications Director. An additional person was seconded from AEAT to take responsibility for management of the DTI research programmes and the Serco Buildings Manager already looking after the NPL Estates Contract transferred to NPLML to continue in this role. Finally, Peter's PA and bid administrator, transferred to support him (and the rest of the team) during Contract phase-in. All seven of us had been involved in the bid (John Rae, latterly), thus ensuring continuity and an in depth understanding of Serco's NPL proposal. All we had to do now was deliver it!

The first NPLML Board (from left to right): Dr George Gray; Prof Tony Kelly; Dr John Rae; Prof Robert Whelan; Dr Andrew Wallard; Prof Archie Howie; Alan Mann; Prof Ron Bullough

It felt a little like that western movie with Yul Brynner - the seven of us riding into Teddington to the musical score of Bernstein. We knew we would have to win over the trust of all the transferring NPL staff and work very closely with them to make a success of the venture.

As part of our proposal, a 'Phase-in Plan' had already been prepared. Following the signing of the Term Contract, the DTI Review Board organised regular meetings with Serco, or rather, I should say, NPLML headed by John Rae and progressed by Peter Gange and the executive team. The transitional process required a large number of topics to be discussed and resolved. DTI and Serco quickly identified and agreed their respective task lists and responsibilities.

Of particular interest to DTI in its 'owner' role were staff and assets and their long 'to do' list included such priorities as: decisions on the requirement to refurbish certain laboratories; agreement on future security arrangements for NPL; the valuation and cataloguing of NPL's 'bailed assets' – these were items like furniture, paintings and scientific artifacts of which we would become custodians and that would require to be insured; a fixed and floating charge (debenture) in favour of DTI over the assets of NPLML and a Deed of Priorities signed by our bankers, Barclays; pensions presentations for staff, attended by representatives of the Government Actuary's Department (GAD), to enable decisions on whether to defer or transfer their civil service pension entitlements to the new NPLML defined benefit scheme; firming up on the number of staff who would be transferring on the 1st October; introducing Serco to the representatives of NPL's staff unions; and, finally, identifying any help we could give in mediating to resolve outstanding claims and disputes.

The week after the Term Contract had been signed, a portacabin next to Building 2 overlooking Newton's apple tree was made available for the Serco management and phase-in team to use as a base at NPL until the Contract start date. We quickly built up an excellent relationship with the DTI's Laboratories Unit managing the transfer, working very effectively with them. We were able to complete or resolve many of the required actions before the start of the Contract. As the 1st October dawned, we had a team at the NPL site, painting out the 'Laboratory Superintendent' and other reserved parking spaces to make an immediate impact and emphasise the new 'single status' values of Serco. Staff would also be allowed into Bushy House garden for the first time and on to the hallowed 2nd floor of Building 2 where the directors had their offices and the segregation of executive dining in the staff restaurant was discontinued! In very short order, the NPL site was tidied up, windows cleaned and the Bushy House conference rooms redecorated and refurbished. The Company also reinstated the 'Summer Ball' and began supporting the NPL Sports Club with generous subsidies in return for corporate membership for staff and Dr John Rae became Chair of its managing committee.

Contract phase-in

At the start of the Contract there were 2 activities that had to be managed urgently in parallel. The first was the Contract phase-in – transferring ownership from DTI to NPLML and transitioning all NPL's operations as smoothly as possible. This was mainly carried out by specialist teams from Serco in such fields as personnel, contracts, accountancy, buildings and project management. The second activity was setting up the future on-going operation of the Laboratory and delivering the list of 'promises' that we had agreed with DTI to complete within the first 6 months of the Contract. This was the responsibility of the new management team together with staff transferring from the civil service.

Staff Transfer to NPLML

The most important element of the Contract phase-in was, of course, the transfer of staff to NPLML and implementing the new organisational structure. It was handled by 2 personnel specialists for Serco with reach-back to the parent. Our priority task was to review the curriculum vitae and interview all suitable candidates applying for posts as our direct reports. Once we had the full management team in place we could move on to filling all the other vacant positions in the new organisational structure and remove many of the concerns and uncertainties that NPL staff had endured for too long. There was very little change within the scientific disciplines of NPL. These were now grouped into new Scientific Centres. We wished to play on the idea of 'centres' of excellence rather than the more divisive 'divisions' of old NPL. These had seemed to be managed much more as separate 'cottage industries' rather than an organisation with a unified strategy. The biggest impact came in the 'administrative' area of NPL. With the move to a private limited company and a commercial business, many of the old civil service functions and jobs became redundant.

Just after Contract signature, the 5 unions representing staff at NPL had been introduced to Serco. They had agreed to a single union, the IPMS (now Prospect), to represent NPL staff. This made the transfer of staff more straight forward and we immediately set about agreeing a voluntary redundancy programme and how staff terms and conditions of employment might be unified. Working hours and holiday entitlements were standardised and the myriad of 'allowances' bought out. For example, it seemed to us very '70s' that staff in the engineering workshop were paid weekly and worked 40 hours while administrative staff were paid monthly and worked 36.5 hours a week. Their hours were reduced and from the start of the Contract all staff were on the same terms and conditions of employment except that transferring civil servants would still be entitled to an NPLML defined benefit pension scheme (which was closed to new members).

Civil service redundancy benefits were very generous and so those not successful in securing a post in the new organisation were generally willing to accept these terms and leave. The Company also offered assistance with a placement service to help those staff looking for another job. In all, 53 'administrative' and management staff members became redundant with 52 being on a voluntary basis. As part of the final bid negotiations DTI had agreed to reimburse the initial redundancy costs that we had openly identified in our proposal, in exchange for further reductions in our day rates for the duration of the 5-year Term Contract. It transpired that these costs were well within our estimates and DTI settled the balance due on an 'actuals' basis.

Government staff were paid through the Chessington Computer Centre, itself a government executive agency. We therefore continued to use them as a bureau allowing staff records to be transferred to NPLML seamlessly and redundancy payments and other adjustments to be processed by an experienced provider. We would, however, revisit this service when other priorities had been dealt with.

Completion of NPL's Final Accounts

Another important task to progress with some urgency was the completion of the final accounts of the NPL Executive Agency for DTI. Serco had provided an excellent contract accountant to work with me as part of the phase-in team and he set about preparing these with the help of the new finance team who, of course, already had an in-depth knowledge of NPL before contractorisation. It should have been a relatively easy job identifying and separating income and costs relating to this period and settling any amounts owing. However, given the lack of accurate records showing the progress reached in research programmes and projects, and the cost outstanding to complete them, this proved to be a time consuming exercise.

Old NPL had been slow to raise sales invoices for commercial work and consequently many were queried or disputed. Often, formal sales orders were not in place, particularly for small jobs, so proving what had actually been agreed was a challenge and relied mainly on trust between our scientists and customers. Scientists were also involved in a large number of 'extra mural activities', mainly collaborations with universities. These were generally of mutual benefit involving our scientists' time or sharing of equipment but I can't help thinking that we had always been on the losing side of such arrangements! Nevertheless, if we were to arrive at a true and fair view of the accounts at the 30th September 1995, we had to come up with a reasonable assessment of the future benefits or liabilities so far unrecorded. Other internal arrangements also had to be agreed, for example, outstanding holiday pay (important for a company reliant on charging its scientists' time) and travel expenses. All these records seemed to be handled differently within NPL and with varying degrees of accuracy.

Assignment of Existing Contracts to NPLML

The final major area of phase-in was reviewing all the existing contracts with NPL and agreeing assignment or novation to NPLML together with any necessary amendments or cancelation where appropriate. It turned out to be a very informative exercise where we were able to update the contract database and rectify discrepancies and identify some, but not all, omissions. We then had a much clearer view of our current obligations, costs and the value for money of the transferring contracts. This exercise alone generated savings of more than £0.5M p.a. most of which were on-going. We also identified other areas, in particular, building contracts, where the introduction of greater competition (initially increasing the number of contractors on the select tender list) reduced costs significantly.

First 6 Months of Operation – Delivering our Promises

We've seen how Serco's bidding policy was to meet, if not exceed, all the requirements of the ITT and change as little as possible of the draft Term Contract. All this was accomplished with the Contract only being updated for the proposed cumulative profit share arrangement that DTI were happy to accept. However, the 'saved days' productivity sharing mechanism inadvertently survived and was only deleted from the Contract at the end of 1997 after lengthy negotiations and conceding a reduction in the profit share threshold from 5% to 3.75% of total sales. Right from the start the emphasis was on a true partnering agreement with full access of all the business records of the Company, not just open book accounting, and a real obligation to act in the best interest of the Laboratory and the UK rather than for purely commercial considerations. 'Doing the right thing' for the UK would be a continuing mantra. As Serco had made clear from the outset, their simple financial expectation from the Contract was a 5% return on sales and we were to go on to achieve 4.7% demonstrating our commitment to fulfilling our obligations.

One disappointment was that DTI declined to take up non-executive membership of the Board. I suppose they felt it might serve to compromise their position should there be any future issue or dispute with Serco or change of government policy towards the arrangement. Of course, managing a contract was very different from managing a bid. The DTI team now responsible for the Term Contract probably felt uncomfortable or even compromised by working with us too closely. Virtually throughout the whole of the GOCO period we would have to reiterate and continue to demonstrate the benefits of a true partnering arrangement. One such opportunity arose at the very start of the Contract. Since 1900 the directors of NPL have had their portrait hung in Bushy House on their retirement. To follow this long tradition and to mark the occasion of Dr Peter Clapham's retirement, Serco commissioned a portrait, which, at the end of 1995, was presented to him by Dr George Gray, Chair of Serco Group where it joined the collection in Bushy House.

From left to right are Dr Peter Clapham, former Director of NPL being presented with his portrait by Dr George Gray, Chairman, Serco Group plc, to mark the occasion of his retirement from NPL

My Role as Finance Director

There was an enormous amount of work to get through in the first 6 months of the Contract. This touched every part of the organisation but here, my experience only allows me to major on the commercial aspects of the business. During this time the new management team was interviewing and confirming the appointments of their direct reports and assessing their competences. Many were excellent, perhaps just lacking commercial experience; many were able and keen to be re-trained in new roles. They would have much to learn but applied themselves enthusiastically and their dedication and commitment was vital to our success, particularly during the early months of transition. As well as being responsible for finance which included purchasing and sales contracts, I also volunteered to take on IT as well – yes, really! IT had originally been considered part of Support Services and not Finance. However, there was method in my madness. At the start of the Contract, NPL had no commercial accounting or business systems and I felt that these would be easier to implement if I had full control of the IT function.

Formation of a New IT Support Unit

Internal IT Support had formerly been carried out by staff in the Information Technology and Computing Division combining this function with fee earning research projects and programmes. This was not efficient and lacked transparency especially regarding staff utilisation. To remedy the situation our bid had proposed setting up a separate IT Support Unit (ITSU) and this we progressed urgently. Although quite an upheaval for staff, I believe most saw the wisdom in making this change especially with the introduction of stand-alone business systems dedicated to NPLML. I initially appointed a senior scientist from this old department to run ITSU. I was very fortunate that he was a very able and knowledgeable member of staff and was happy to manage the transition to this new unit before his retirement. Under his leadership we were able to maintain the confidence of the IT user community and, for the first time, create a database of hardware and software being used within the Laboratory. New NPL wide standards were agreed and over time enabled us to make considerable savings by bulk ordering of IT equipment and consolidate software licences under corporate agreements. Clarifying support responsibilities also enabled us to save £800k p.a. by terminating previous contracts and subcontractors no longer required.

Implementation of a Commercial Accounting System
One of the most pressing tasks was to introduce a commercial accounting system. Until this could be achieved, central finance within Serco had to cover any payments required and post cash receipts to our bank. As a government agency, NPL did not have a commercial accounting system and was unable to raise cheques or account for VAT! In 1995, centralised 'enterprise' systems were generally unheard of, so each Serco division or company set up its own accounting system using a standard chart of accounts for financial analysis. NPL already owned one module (nominal ledger) of an accounting system called '*cfacs*'. We had researched this system and found it was used by other UK laboratories and decided to implement the remaining modules including timesheet recording.

The majority of my finance team transferred from the civil service but I did recruit an experienced financial controller. Implementation went smoothly thanks to the new team really getting behind the project which they called 'Beagle'. I guess it **was** a voyage into unknown territory for most of them! Nevertheless we had all the basic ledgers and processes set up within 2 months and were able to produce our first management accounts at the end of December 1995. Cheque payments could be raised and VAT accounted for. In fact, as an executive agency only part of NPL's VAT was recoverable (limited by the amount of 'output tax' from their commercial sales) so there was an immediate saving of £1M for NPL. As we also found out, all scientific equipment was capitalised inclusive of VAT (as it wasn't recoverable under Government operation) so from a commercial perspective our assets were all over-valued by 17.5%! This was an area we would address in the capital asset valuation exercise required in the first 6 months of the Contract.

Verification and Revaluation of NPL's Scientific Equipment
Within the first 6 months of the Term Contract we were required to verify and value the scientific equipment (capital assets) owned by NPL. We were fortunate in that once again we appointed an experienced and knowledgeable scientist who was willing to take on this task before he finally retired. He was able to update the asset register with the scientist ('owner') responsible for the asset, its location, whether it was still required and its estimated remaining economic life. At the same time staff from the finance department checked the original invoice value of each of the assets so that we could exclude the 17.5% VAT and all the adjustments arising from current cost accounting indexation. The appropriate 'straight

line' depreciation charge was then applied based on its estimated remaining life. The opening value of each of the capital assets as at 1st October could then be calculated together with the monthly depreciation charge. As DTI still owned NPL's capital assets we were obliged to maintain and update the asset register on its behalf. All the revaluations had been based on standard commercial accounting practice with original invoice values and generally accepted depreciation policies so the DTI and Treasury were content to accept the revised valuation realising that we now had to be competitive within the private sector. The entire asset register was updated with a valuation of around £17M (from £22M), a not inconsiderable reduction, and this figure would be used to recharge NPLML with a monthly asset lease fee from April 1996.

Under the old Executive Agency, capital and revenue budgets were handled completely separately. This often meant that there was a disconnect between formulating new programmes of research and purchasing the scientific equipment needed to deliver them. Our programme formulation process now brought these together and facilitated the production of a 3 year rolling Capital Plan (required under the Term Contract) which DTI could then use to make the necessary provision for funding in their annual capital budgets. The plan was further improved and refined over the years as new research programmes were formulated.

DTI Research Programmes – The 'Meter-reading' Exercise

Another major task was to agree with DTI the status of all their Research Programmes at the start of the Contract. These were generally formulated for a 3 year period with start dates in different months and years to spread scientists' workloads. This was called a 'Meter-reading' exercise and would confirm exactly how much work there was left to complete. To comply with the new Contract, the work outstanding in these programmes was then costed by project and scientific milestone. The exercise produced a price of £12.8M for the remaining 6 months of DTI's financial year to 31st March 1996 and NPLML's first financial half year. This was almost 4% above its original estimate in the ITT Pricing Schedules as most programmes needed additional scientist days to complete. However, since the new Term Contract offered far better value for money (at least a 10% saving on pre-contractorisation costs) it was not an issue for DTI and, in fact, a Supplementary Programme was introduced to allow full advantage to be taken of the available funding before the end of the financial year.

Under the Term Contract formulating new programmes of research for the DTI was the responsibility of NPL. Having confirmed that the value of the work was within DTI budgets, our scientists could begin to set their minds to future research programmes and projects. Serco was keen to reassure NPL's numerous stakeholders that it remained committed to enhancing and sustaining science excellence and one of the first to be formulated was a new 'Foundation Programme'. This took a fundamental and under-pinning long term view of measurement science needs in the UK and also emphasised Serco's long term commitment to NPL.

Beginning to Win Over 'Hearts and Minds'
By Christmas 1995 the new organisational structure was in place and we had implemented a commercial accounting system which was producing some meaningful business information for management. There was still a long way to go but the financial results of NPLML were exceeding expectations. The meter-reading exercise for the DTI's research programmes had confirmed that they would have more than adequate funding for the last quarter of their financial year and we now had a better feel for all our contractual obligations. Staff uncertainties were further reduced when many who were on temporary employment contracts were confirmed as permanent and some limited recruitment became visible. Although much of the information we had acquired during the bid and on transfer of ownership was not entirely helpful or relevant to a commercial company, no insurmountable issues had been uncovered.

Staff within the Scientific Centres began to gain some confidence in the new organisation and were beginning to become familiar with how they could order goods and materials, arrange travel and claim their expenses based on actual receipts (so we could get the VAT back!) instead of applying civil service allowances. The reduction in purchase orders during the first few months of operation had, however, been a godsend while new systems were set up but now they began to flow through to the newly formed purchasing and finance departments.

The 'Grey' Market!
Getting scientists to involve our sales contracts department in formalising new business opportunities and 'extra-mural' activities was more of a challenge but we had to try and keep our new database up-to-date! The lack of formal orders or contracts for work entered into before contractorisation proved to be one of the most difficult areas for us to fully

resolve and certainly held up completion of the DTI's final accounts. Invoices for work undertaken many months, if not years previously, were coming into NPLML on a weekly basis usually from universities and scientific institutes worldwide. Unraveling the status of contracts with the European Commission where there might be several collaborators also presented its challenges. This long 'tail' of invoices was to continue for another year! In the event we agreed an estimate of the future liability with DTI so the completion accounts could be signed off.

A Revised 5-Year Business Plan

As we began to understand and learn more about the operation of NPL we were in a better position to review the 5-Year Business Plan submitted in our bid and to confirm to DTI, as was required in the Term Contract that NPLML would continue to be a successful, robust and sustainable company over the 5-year term.

We had verified that we had the right mix of resources to deliver DTI's research programmes to the level of their funding. Meanwhile, David Richardson had been engaging with each of the new Heads of Centres to help them take over responsibility for developing their own third party sales plan based on our bid assumptions. Once agreed, they would be accountable for delivering these plans together with generating the necessary 'contribution' towards NPL's operating costs and overheads. In effect we were introducing P&L responsibility to them but at this time we avoided the concept of 'profit'! In true Serco tradition we emphasised the principles of 'we deliver our promises' and 'no surprises'. However, one of the most surprising things was how optimistic the Centres were in their plans for third party sales growth. Even more surprising was that this would be a continuing theme until I was to retire! Perhaps it's just part of a scientists' psyche but the world of business is by no means as 'perfect' as physics. With such a slim profit margin and the high business risks associated with a fledgling company I'm not convinced that our scientists fully appreciated just how critical (and difficult) it was to achieve these plans but they were soon to find out! However, it did allow me the headroom to include a reasonable contingency at Company level in our updated 5-Year Business Plan. The exercise was invaluable for substantiating the majority of our bid assumptions and enabled us to identify new business opportunities and gaps in our marketing and communications plan.

ISO 9000 Registration

One of the key deliverables required by the ITT was the achievement of ISO 9000 registration which was, and still is, a quality management standard that sets guidelines and procedures intended to increase business efficiency and customer satisfaction. The old Executive Agency had already delayed this quite demanding and far reaching assessment twice before mainly because of the disruption caused by contractorisation. I'm sure, like us, they had encountered a fair amount of reluctance and even 'push back' from some of our scientists who felt that it was inappropriate for a national centre of excellence with such diverse work to have to comply with standard quality procedures. However, with the dogged determination of Peter Gange and our Quality Manager, NPL was successful in fulfilling another of our bid promises by gaining registration in May 1996.

I have only mentioned here just the key commercial challenges closest to me in this enormous 'change programme'. I cannot emphasise enough the outstanding work carried out by the rest of the NPLML management team, support staff and DTI representatives during this hugely demanding period. I've talked about 'smoke and mirrors' and, of course, it only appeared like that to me, looking at NPL from the outside and not understanding the mysterious ways of government accounting and the different priorities our civil service colleagues were given but these I would learn to appreciate so that together we could continue to develop many more improvements to our mutual benefit over the years.

Chapter 3 - The 'Yellow Brick Road'

Our bid proposal charted a vision for NPL over the first 5 years of the Term Contract. In one of the graphics we called it NPL's 'Yellow Brick Road'. It showed key scientific and business milestones over the period while emphasising our hope that this would be the start of a long and mutually beneficial relationship spanning many more years into the future.

Our vision included an exciting mix of painstaking commercial systems and process implementation, a plethora of business and ground-breaking scientific projects and financial innovations that would take DTI and even Serco out of their comfort zones. Then, in 1996, DTI were successful in a bid for funding the design, build and operation of a new Laboratory to replace the 50 or so buildings across the 82 acre Teddington site. The only way of securing this amount of cash was through a Government Private Finance Initiative (PFI) which would require changes to the Term Contract and affect NPLML's staff and the operation of the Laboratory all over again. It would entail a large amount of additional work which would once more fall on the shoulders of the relatively new management team who already had an enormous 'change' agenda to deliver. This time, however, there would be limited recourse to Serco as they were also keen to bid for the PFI Contract with John Laing plc in a joint undertaking called 'Laser'. John Laing was responsible for the 'design and build' elements of the PFI while Serco would take on the future 'operation' of the Laboratory.

This was a completely new departure from our Yellow Brick Road. Serco's welcome but untimely participation in the bid meant that there had to be a 'Chinese wall' between NPL staff and Serco during the tendering process. In November 1996, Dr George Gray felt it appropriate to step down from the Board until the successful PFI contractor had been selected.

It is difficult to comprehend just how much was accomplished scientifically, commercially and operationally during the first Term Contract. So many projects of varying length and complexity were managed. New 'not to be missed' opportunities including the PFI, presented themselves and were grasped with open arms. Throughout this period our main priority was to keep disruption to our scientific research and customers to a minimum by forming special 'focus' groups so as to insulate most of our scientists from these activities except where it reinforced awareness of progress towards our goals. I hope to capture here many of the achievements, disappointments and challenges of this hugely transformational period and the essence of the commitment and dedication of our staff and DTI representatives.

Customer Focus – 'Taking Measurement to Industry'

The success of our vision was squarely dependent on how readily our people embraced the GOCO concept and the new way of working. I've said 'customer focus' here rather than 'commercial' because, for the majority of our scientific staff in those early years, the word 'profit' when used in the same context as scientific research, did not resonate well! At this time it would have been fruitless to explain that our business model did not anticipate profit from our DTI research programmes but simply a fair contribution towards operating costs. However, it was absolutely vital that NPL was more outward facing and relevant to industry so we could generate new sources of funding and income. Our model was entirely dependent on generating profit from growth in sales revenue with resulting economies of scale and cost savings through operating efficiencies. Although some of our staff may not have realised, this was, in fact, exactly what we all managed to achieve over the course of the first Contract.

Changing the culture of an organisation (and making it stick!) is hugely challenging. In the case of a well-established research institution like NPL with a long and outstanding scientific legacy it needed to be handled with sensitivity and would take time. There was no 'silver bullet'. Not only did we have to win over the 'hearts and minds' of our employees but also balance the interests of NPL's wide array of stakeholders – including government, industry and academia.

First of all it required us to communicate clearly to our stakeholders the contents of our successful bid proposal and how we, and DTI, believed NPL's commercial development would generate the much needed additional income and investment to benefit the Laboratory as a whole – both infrastructure and science. Unlike the other bidders, Serco was predominantly a task management contractor for government. The company was therefore perceived to be reasonably independent and free from the outside 'vested interests' of an industrial, consultancy or defence organisation. The majority of its employees were, like NPL's, ex-civil servants transferring from other government departments. Serco's values therefore aligned very closely with NPL's – a strong service ethic, customer (government) focus and treating staff fairly and with respect. This could now be adapted and revitalised to bring together the best of both of these worlds; from NPL, there was the emphasis on scientific independence and integrity while from Serco, there was the importance of engendering trust in our relationships and delivering our promises. One further value key to NPLML's future success was fostering an entrepreneurial spirit. In fact, it already existed within NPL but perhaps not until it came to winning more funding from the DTI! Now it was stated explicitly and would be strongly encouraged across all potential income streams.

Having established that our long term vision and objectives for NPL were well aligned with those of the majority of our stakeholders, we could turn our attention to putting in place the building blocks which would provide the necessary working environment and tools for our people. These would help our staff meet their own personal goals while making a real contribution to the Company's longer term success. By living these corporate values we could all demonstrate our commitment to maintaining NPL as a world leading Laboratory.

Embedding a more customer focused culture would take time and effort. For some, we were perhaps seen as being far too 'draconian', for others, we were not taking advantage of contractorisation quickly enough. However, many of our actions would have a lasting impact on NPL, its people and culture. I shall deal with these by category rather than chronologically as most would span a good part of, if not the entire 5 years of the Contract.

Organisational Change

Management Restructuring

There were 2 Board changes in November 1996. Firstly, as we have heard, Dr George Gray resigned as a result of Serco's bid for NPL's PFI and at the same time Peter Gange, who had steered us through the successful bid to operate NPL, also left the Company for a Managing Directorship role within Serco. A new Support Services director was recruited but neither was replaced on the Board immediately. Interestingly, until George's reappointment in October 1997, there would be a greater number of independent Directors on the Board than those directly representing Serco and NPLML – an indication of our mutual trust and shared interest to 'do the right thing' for NPL. A year later, David Richardson was invited to join the Board. Personally, I felt this was long overdue given the importance of growing our commercial sales revenue, however, until this time much of our capacity had been absorbed by additional work won from DTI due to the improved delivery and value of our work.

Our organisational structure followed relatively standard lines as far as the Support Functions were concerned. Marketing and communications remained a central function to engender a more uniform approach to our customer base and take the lead on large bids and new sales prospects. Direct sales remained within the Scientific Centres and were championed by those scientists who showed a stronger aptitude and preference for this work. Soon, each Scientific Centre established the post of Business Development Manager to improve sales growth but with strong oversight from the centre. The Quality, Health, Safety and Environment function was also centralised to give a more uniform approach and was strengthened to enable greater audit independence following ISO 9000 registration and our move to UKAS Accreditation of our laboratory services. The new IT Services Unit had quickly established itself and was successfully supporting the new central accounting and business systems and standardising the myriad of mathematical and scientific software applications used throughout the Laboratory. The savings that resulted from gaining a tighter control of IT expenditure should not be underestimated! The extensive Engineering Workshop facilities were consolidated as far as possible with many of the smaller 'satellites' that had evolved over time being closed. As the site was rationalised and new, simpler and more integrated processes and systems were introduced, support functions could operate more efficiently and absorb additional work-loads from the growing business. There was a greater emphasis on staff training and a more professional approach to their way of working.

The Scientific Divisions, now called Centres, essentially reflected the groupings of the DTI's research programmes and, to a large extent, they had initially been left untouched. It was not until about 18 months into the Contract, after we had been able to appraise the management of the Scientific Centres more closely and had a better strategic understanding of the research programmes that had been formulated or were in the pipeline, that it was an appropriate time to look again at their organisational structure. Some of the Heads of the Scientific Centres were also approaching retirement age. Together with a number of mutually agreed early retirements, we were able to 'delayer' the structure of the Centres, promote 'new blood' into these senior positions and shorten reporting lines.

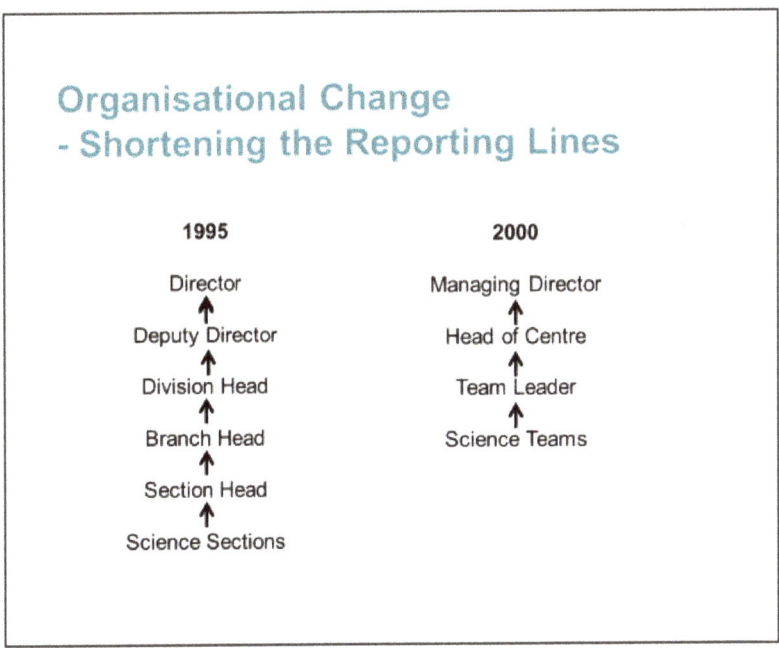

Initially, NPLML's executive had been organised into a Management Committee of 12 members with full and equal representation from all the Scientific Centres. The reorganisation of the these Centres gave an opportunity for the NPL Executive, as it was then called, to be reduced to 7 members, 4 of whom were also on the NPLML Board following David Richardson's appointment in October 1998. The new Centre Heads would now be accountable for financial and planning responsibilities. Centres could now be regarded as individual business units and this led to a number of positive outcomes - managerial recognition of commercial imperatives; greater engagement of staff in programme formulation and delivery; more active resource and asset management. Contrary to what might be thought, our new Heads saw this as a real benefit, giving them greater freedom (within limits!) to manage their Centres strategically and facilitated more rapid operational efficiencies to reduce overhead costs.

Integration of the Malvern 'Outstation'

Additional operational savings came from the integration of NPL's one 'outstation' that had been housed in DERA's facility at Malvern. The small team together with their existing scientific equipment was moved to a specially prepared laboratory within the Teddington site. New equipment replaced that which had been shared.

Strategic Research and Capital Review groups

To further support the integration of the Laboratory's operation 2 specific 'focus' groups were set up. One reviewed 'bids' for new Strategic Research Programmes which, under the DTI Contract, NPLML was responsible for formulating and financing to the tune of £1.5M p.a. index linked. This involved representatives from across the management and research community prioritising research projects submitted by individual scientists or teams. Those that were considered the best fit with NPL's strategic objectives were selected. The transparency of the process and involvement of an acceptable cross-section of the Laboratory added to staff 'buy-in' and awareness of our shared corporate objectives. The other group reviewed 'bids' for capital expenditure on scientific equipment. Again, this group brought together scientists from across the different Centres together with Finance and Procurement, to agree how the sizable budget of around £4M p.a. would be split between the needs of new research programmes and replacing or updating ageing or worn out equipment.

A new Knowledge Transfer Centre

In 1995, each page of our proposal carried the strapline *'Taking Measurement To Industry'*. The importance of technology and knowledge transfer was one of the key areas addressed in our bid which stated:

> 'We are committed to building a much broader range of external relationships for NPL. Our objective is to develop new programmes which are endorsed by industry and achieve the maximum benefit to UK competitiveness'.

Early in the Contract, Serco proposed and DTI accepted the creation of an NPL-wide technology transfer initiative to raise awareness of the value of traceable measurement to business. The concept of a high-level pan-NMS awareness programme was a first for NPL, aimed at breaking the inward focus characterising many of NPL's activities. For NPL to become a more effective NMI and a successful commercial organisation, it needed to develop relationships with industry and intermediaries as a basis for knowledge exploitation.

In late 1996 we formulated a regional awareness initiative, *'Competing Precisely'*, undertaking a series of 24 road shows and publishing 30 case studies. This led to a pilot initiative in April 1998 when some headroom in DTI's funding allowed a new programme called the National Measurement Partnership to be launched by the Secretary of State.

In fact, Knowledge Transfer was identified as a market in its own right and a new Centre was formed under Dr Jerry Benson. It was successful in winning several high profile contracts from a number of Government Departments over the ensuing years that we shall look at in more detail later.

Although all this activity was not considered by our scientists to be 'real' research it nevertheless significantly increased awareness of the importance of the value of metrology to industry and how closer engagement could not only generate new sources of income but also present our scientists with some intriguing problems that could only be solved by higher science!

Staff Management

It is understandable that NPL staff were uneasy about a private sector company being contracted by Government to operate the Laboratory but these fears soon subsided. First of all, there was a strong commitment to core scientific research with the formulation of the Foundation Programme. The scientists on DTI's 'key staff' list had continued to work for NPL and, in fact, the 5-year Term Contract gave a more solid base to plan future programmes of work and increase investment in resource, laboratories and equipment. After a moratorium on recruitment leading up to Contract award and with growth in sales turnover, we were now taking on more staff, predominantly younger scientists and overall numbers were increasing.

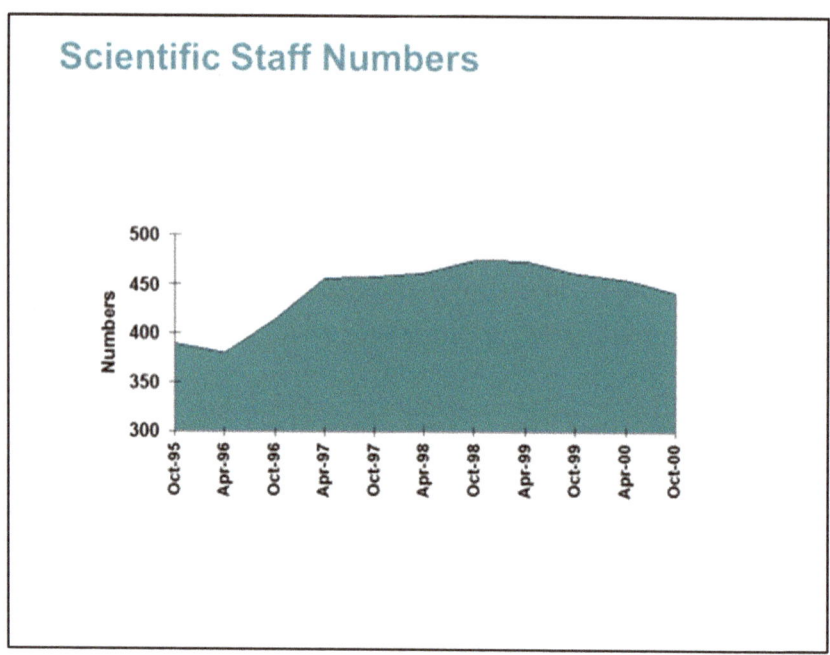

These new recruits had the effect of improving the age distribution of the Laboratory.

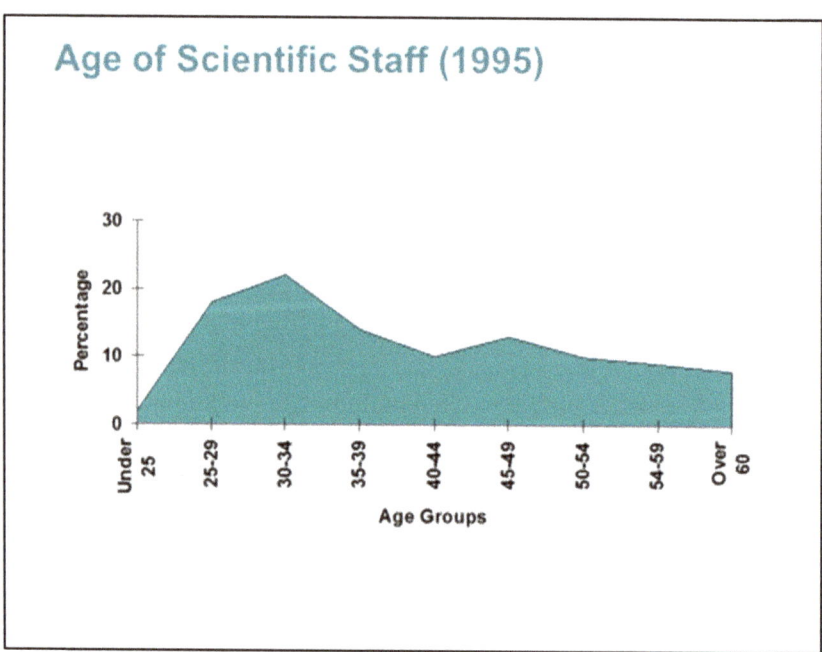

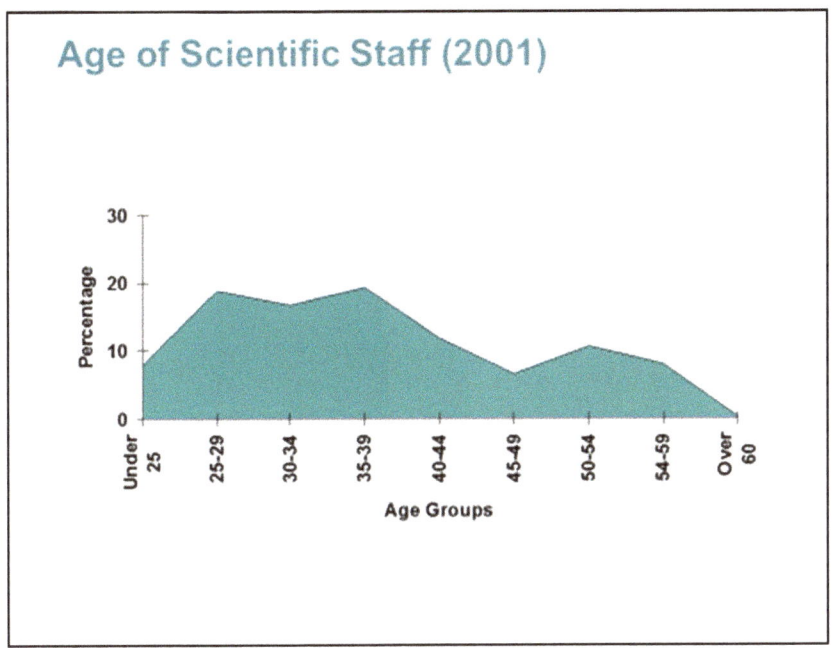

Staff turnover had been very low under government ownership. Contrary to what might be thought low staff turnover for a research organisation like NPL was just as bad as high since it limited the intake of 'new blood'. Although salaries were not necessarily considered high, other benefits, particularly the defined benefit pension scheme, were very generous and tended to act as 'golden handcuffs' for ex civil service staff. However, with all the organisational changes, some staff decided to leave or take advantage of their generous pension entitlement and retire early. There was also a greater emphasis on staff performance with more meaningful staff appraisals and objective setting and the combination of these factors had the effect of staff turnover rates gradually increasing to a healthier 5% by the end of the Term Contract. This was seen by our stakeholders as a positive step forward towards revitalising the Laboratory and did not signify a worsening of relations with staff.

In fact, there were no industrial disputes or tribunals over the Contract period with industrial relations remaining very good. New standard contracts of employment for all staff had been negotiated. Single union representation with IPMS had been established with collective pay agreements. Salary levels had been maintained ahead of the retail prices index.

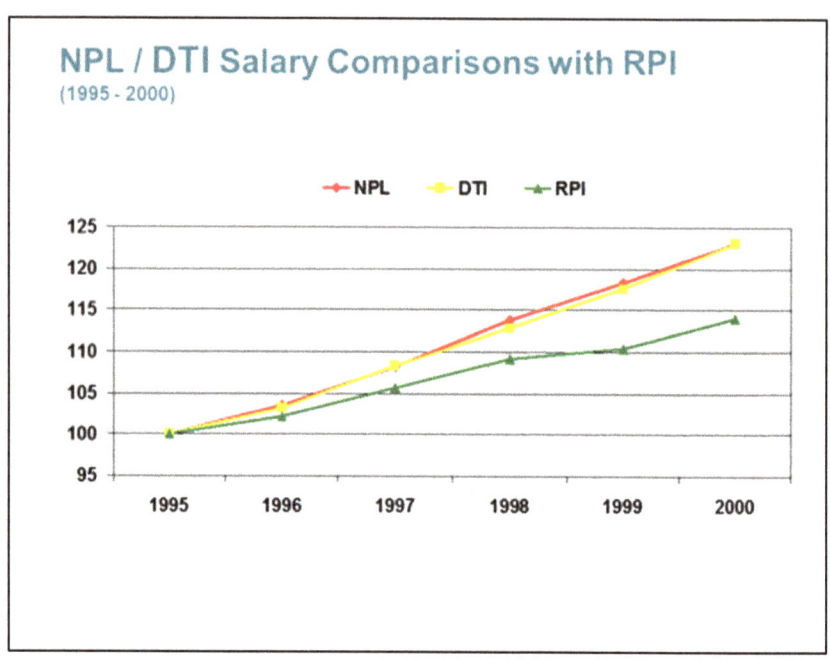

Now that we were outside civil service constraints and rules, we could pay 'market rates' in areas of staff shortage and anomalies could be ironed out.

Staff Development

One of the key ways to win over the hearts and minds of staff is a commitment to supporting them to realise their true potential and career aspirations. Taking over the operation of NPL necessitated a large amount of additional training and retraining, particularly of management and support staff. As this was accomplished we could turn our attention to introducing a formal process of personal development planning.

From the beginning of our Contract, staff management responsibility had been delegated to line managers. This included recruitment, salary increases and performance management. Our ISO 9000 Quality Procedures defined the various processes to be followed with reach-back to the Personnel function for advice and support. Apart from the requirements of 'technical' training across NPL, the Company introduced specifically tailored training including modules on Project Management, Staff Management and Business/Commercial Management to help with these new responsibilities.

Our 5-Year Track Record

As can be seen, establishing our credentials as a competent operator of the Laboratory was of fundamental importance to the success of the first Contract. This meant maintaining our focus on enhancing NPL's core science, retaining key staff and ensuring our vision and values were clearly explained, demonstrated and reinforced by example. We were, however, very cognisant of the fact that our staff were having to come to terms with significant upheaval and change. This affected those in our support functions more than most and there is no doubt that their hard work and commitment to our vision and objectives made a real difference to the level of success we achieved. Wherever possible we tried to 'cushion' our scientists and their research from these changes but with the advent of the PFI for a new building, some of our scientists, including the more senior ones, would quite rightly be drawn into providing Laser with laboratory 'data sheets' specifying requirements for their new laboratories.

However, with all this activity, we could not be distracted from the main requirements of DTI's Term Contract, namely, to improve NPL's performance, both scientific and commercial, and reduce costs. The following is a summary of some of our key achievements although our work could not be considered 'completed' by the year 2000 but still merely 'work-in-progress'. The Contract would be extended from the original term, a further 3 times to 2004, but the facts and figures below reflect for the most part the first 5 years of operation.

Significant Cost Savings to DTI

Many of the areas of cost saving have already been described but it might be useful to understand the overall impact of these from the perspective of the DTI.

I would stress that these savings did not come at the cost of the quality of our science outputs. We were able to maintain excellence with 25% more science per £M than in 1995 by reducing costs and winning more competed DTI work to spread the Laboratory's overhead. The day rates charged for scientist's time in 2000 were 10% below the pre-contractorisation prices (after combining the rates charged to both our DTI customers: NMSPU and EID). Taking into account inflation, this represented a benefit of some £20M which DTI was able to reinvest in additional research programmes and projects over the 5 years of the

Contract. At the risk of sounding like a hard selling TV advert: *'but this was not all'!* The cumulative profit share arrangement also returned £1M to the DTI since the threshold had been lowered from 5% to 3.75% as a result of the renegotiation and retrospective amendment of the Term Contract in 1997 to remove the 'saved days' productivity mechanism which somehow survived best and final negotiations.

We've seen that these savings for DTI were generated from successful delivery of a substantial growth in sales turnover, improved project management, greater operational efficiency and targeted cost reduction programmes. The additional sales allowed us to spread the overhead burden of operating the Laboratory over a greater customer base and benefit from economies of scale. These so called 'overheads' included such things as the cost of the Laboratory buildings: rent, property rates, maintenance, energy and other utilities; scientific equipment 'lease' rentals; scientist's non-recoverable time; selling and marketing; financing; management and support staff costs. In fact, overheads were everything other than scientist's time that was recoverable from our customers and the associated direct project costs. A good way of demonstrating these savings is by looking at the reduction in the overhead rate applied to our scientists' time in each year of the Contract to fully recover our costs. In 1995, to absorb our full economic cost, we had to use a rate of 225% and by the end of the Contract this had reduced to 166% which became the 'norm' for many years to come. This was also helped by increasing the productivity of our fee earning staff with improvements in utilisation rates (time charged directly to customers) of more than 10%.

Finally, it is also fair to mention that Serco required its return which was a modest profit before tax of 5% on sales for the duration of the Contract. Even with of the reduction of the profit share threshold to 3.75% Serco was satisfied with the overall actual return of 4.7%.

Important KPIs

- FEC overhead rate
  252 ➡ 225 ➡ 180 ➡ 166%
- Staff utilisation (after holidays)
  66% ➡ 70% ➡ 74%
- Third Party Sales
  £6M ➡ £16.7M
- Quality of Science

 ✓

Business Growth

Our 5-Year Business Plan was initially relatively cautious in estimating growth in commercial sales but became more 'bullish' in our best and final offer. There were considerable risks and uncertainties associated with the massive change programme which would be running concurrently with the sales push to generate more income for NPL. We were at pains to stay within the boundaries of NPL's core mission and were very sensitive to any accusation of 'diluting' NPL's reputation for science and engineering excellence. Our aspiration was also to become DTI's partner of first choice through which they might realise some of their own policy initiatives.

Our financial performance is best demonstrated by comparing our actual achievement with our bid commitment which was to grow commercial sales from £6.5M p.a. to £14M p.a. (including DTI competitively tendered research programmes). We actually achieved commercial sales of £16.7M by 1999/2000 which represented 33% of total revenues generated and led to an increase in staff numbers of about 120.

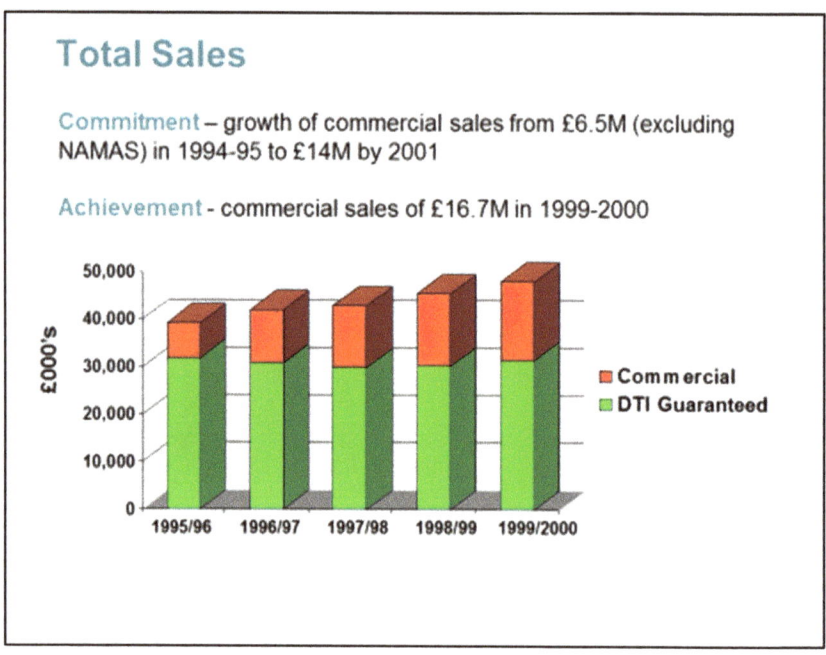

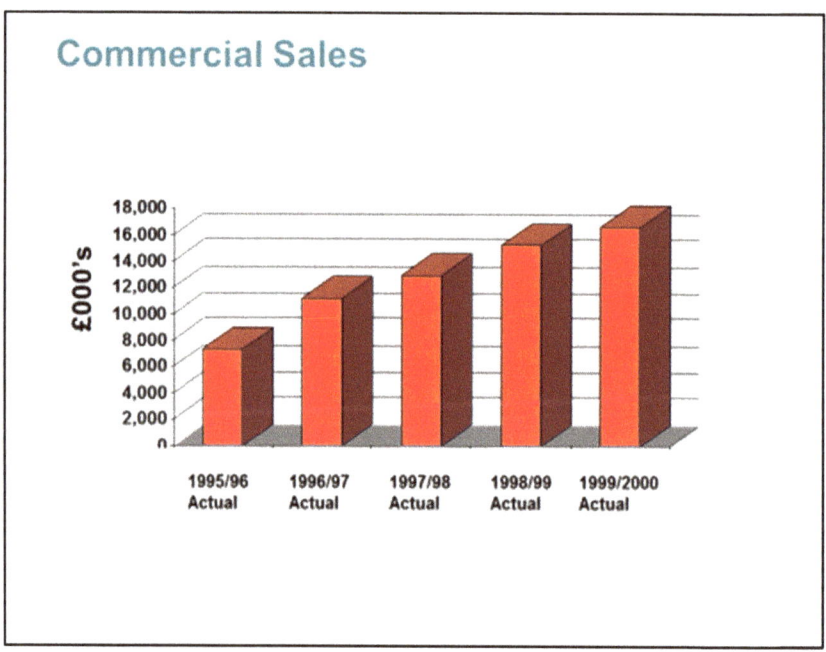

It included competitively tendered business from DTI of £5.5M, £1.5M above commitment. Sales to other Government Departments grew in line with our plan by £1M p.a. to £2M p.a. driven almost entirely by

Environmental programmes, which had been identified as a marketing priority soon after the Term Contract award.

On transfer of the Laboratory in 1995 we carried out a detailed assessment of all the sales contracts that were work-in-progress so that DTI's final accounts could be completed and we fully appreciated the extent of our contractual commitments. The review identified that the majority of EU contracts were not commercially viable when viewed in isolation and so for all future work we decided to bid only for work that was a close strategic fit to our DTI research programmes and enhanced their scientific outputs. This change of policy was agreed with DTI and resulted in a concerted effort started by Dr Andrew Wallard, as part of his international role, to shape the Commission's priorities towards supporting metrology as a real benefit to industry and European competitiveness. As a result, in this period, our sales to the EU only increased from £1.0M p.a. to £1.4M p.a. against a plan of £2M but laid the foundations for significant growth in future collaborations.

Our bid had committed to doubling our sales to the private sector from £2M p.a. to £4M but by 1999/2000 we achieved £6M. The largest part of this market was measurement and consultancy services. Over the period there was a steady growth in sales volume (and margin). Improved systems and processes in this area, however, provided much greater transparency of the true costs of the services. These were gradually reflected in a coherent and consistent pricing policy whilst recognising our sometimes monopolistic position in the marketplace and our desire to avoid any accusations of anti-competitive behaviour. Of course, most price increases were kept to a minimum by our ability to deliver many of our calibration services more efficiently and were subject to DTI scrutiny and approval.

In 1995 we had taken over a heavily loss making contract to build a Force Machine for the Hong Kong authorities. We had encountered problems with achieving the level of accuracy specified mainly due to the lack of climate control within their laboratory. However, as NPL, we were determined to find the best solution and satisfy our customer's requirements. This experience made us much more cautious about international hardware sales and we exacted far more control over potential sales by limiting our bids to those pieces of scientific kit that we had direct experience in building and commissioning. This area of sales had not been specifically addressed in our bid but it nevertheless grew to a business of £1.1M by 1999/2000.

Supporting Industry – Technology and Knowledge Transfer

Recognising the Government's desire for its laboratories to have a greater positive and measurable impact on the UK economy and wellbeing, we gave this a great deal of emphasis in our 1995 bid, promising:

> '… a new culture will be created that is outward looking and determined to maximise **relevance** to industry'.

By 1996 a considerable head of steam was building in Government to 'pump prime' their policy with some targeted funding. We had been quick to identify Knowledge Transfer as a market in its own right, offering considerable additional growth potential to fill the estimated £2M sales requirement created by our best and final bid offer and, at the same time, addressing one of Government's key policy aims. David Richardson had spent a great deal of time positioning NPLML to take on some of this 'promotional' work for DTI and other Government Departments. The first such initiative was called '*Competing Precisely*' which was designed to raise regional awareness of the productivity benefits associated with measurement to thousands of companies around the UK, the majority of them SMEs, through events and related publicity. These events were usually managed in partnership with large firms, such as, BAE SYSTEMS, Courage, Samsung, and Rolls Royce, and local UKAS laboratories. It was very much new business for NPL but was a great success!

This initiative was rewarded with the award of the National Measurement Partnership (NMP) worth £1M p.a. over 3 years. The NMP programme had a number of outcomes including: a National Measurement Conference, attracting over 600 delegates and providing a unique forum for the UK's measurement and instrumentation community; a pan-NMS Newsletter, highlighting key issues and achievements across all NMS contractors; successful best practice guides such as the '*Beginners Guide to Uncertainty*' and a '*Measurement Guide to ISO 9000*'; a framework for improved service for UKAS accreditation, including the web-based directory of UKAS accredited calibration and testing laboratories.

Supporting Industry
- National Measurement Partnership

Uniting:
- NMS contractors
  - NMD, NPL, UKAS, NEL, NWML, LGC with
- Measurement and instrumentation Trade Associations
  - Inst. MC, GAMBICA, WCISM
- Accredited Labs
  - More than 120 commercial UKAS labs

In a partnership approach to serving industry
- First National Measurement Conference in 1999 had 600 attendees
- Calibration NVQ (pioneered with Rolls Royce and Mitutoyo)

Supporting Industry
- Competing Precisely

- 20 regional campaigns
- 1000 companies participating (about 50% SMEs)
- Preliminary studies indicate introduction of measurable change in 20% of companies participating

Some partners/hosts:
British Aerospace - Rolls Royce - ICI - Vickers - Nissan - Mitutoyo - Samsung - Courage Breweries

The campaign targeted SMEs and was based on case studies by commercial companies who could speak from experience about the benefits of good measurement practice.

With the creation of the new Knowledge Transfer Centre under Dr Jerry Benson, NPLML went on to win a number of additional competitively tendered high profile and high value contracts.

Supporting Industry - Some Achievements

"...a new culture will be created that is outward looking and determined to maximise relevance to industry" (Serco bid 1995)

Some achievements 1995 - 2000
- Club membership extended from ~1000 to 1600
- NPL end user data base grown from ~18000 to 26000
- Flagship Faraday programme
- National Measurement Partnership
- 20 Regional campaigns under the Competing Precisely banner
- TCS, Envirowise and QAO contracts
- Creation of one of the world's largest scientific websites (>2 million hits/year)
- Doubling of Helpline activity
- Introduction of cost-shared studio projects in Materials programme

In 1997 we were successful in winning the Environmental Technology Best Practice Programme, Envirowise, for marketing and promotions management which was sponsored by DTI and DETR and was worth £7.8M over 7 years. In the same year NPL and SIRA were awarded a contract by the UK's Engineering and Scientific Research Council (EPSRC) to run one of the four Faraday Partnerships.

Supporting Industry - Flagship Faraday Partnership

1998 NPL and SIRA awarded contract by EPSRC to run one of first four UK Faraday Partnerships

ICI	University College London
British Steel	Imperial College
Unilever	Cavendish laboratory
SmithKline Beecham	Brunel University
Rolls-Royce	City University
Kidde	University of Southampton
BNFL	University of Bath
The Health and Safety Executive	University of Warwick
Glaxo-Wellcome	University of Surrey
BAe	University of Loughborough
DERA	University of Kingston
London Underground Transport Ltd	

This was aimed at increasing the relevance of scientific research projects to industry, particularly SMEs. The partnership involved the setting of research programme objectives and the organisation of knowledge transfer events and mechanisms to improve the flow of information and people between the research community and industry. The following year we won an £8M contract over 5 years for the operation of the Teaching Company Directorate (TCD). TCD's largest activity was the management of TCS (formerly known as the Teaching Company Scheme) on behalf of DTI's Management Best Practice Directorate and ten other government sponsors.

Supporting Industry – Programme Formulation

Growing our sales turnover and expanding our customer base gave us a much greater insight into the requirements and demands of industry from our expertise in metrology. Another key way of ensuring that NPL maximised their relevance to industry was through the formulation of their new research programmes. Over the 5 years of our operation of the Laboratory as part of our revitalised programme formulation process there were 16 major industry consultation exercises. These informed DTI and their own advisory working group how best to prioritise the projects and programmes submitted by NPL's scientists. They involved meetings with more than 1000 UK companies and more than 30 user requirement studies.

In order to aid DTI in their understanding of the priorities of industry and select the most relevant research to sponsor from their limited budget we won funding for the development of an economic impact prediction model called 'Mapping Measurement Impact' in partnership with Scientific Generics, PA Consulting, and London Business School together with input from the private sector and academia. We would go on to improve this impact model over the ensuing years based on our experience and through studies to measure the **actual** impact of our work when programmes were completed.

Cost Management Programmes

We have already looked in some detail at the cost savings that were generated through NPL operating as a limited company within the private sector. Central recharges from DTI were eliminated, VAT could be fully recovered, processes were simplified and support functions slimmed down, the number of subcontractors could be reduced, the building infrastructure rationalised and operations were moved from the DERA site at Malvern. There was considerable investment in staff and systems and corporate policies were unified through formal quality procedures focusing on business improvement. Management was de-layered and responsibilities were passed down the line and staff, both support and scientific, were encouraged to seek professional qualifications. This empowerment of staff actually meant that we had rapidly outgrown many of our systems and processes which were predominantly centralised, initially for good reason!

Business Systems Development

After the implementation of the commercial accounting software at the start of the Contract, the first business system to be developed in 1997 had 'customer focus' as its prime objective. It was called 'MProMS', which stood for 'Milestone Progress Management System', and enabled all the scientific milestones, within projects and programmes to be monitored and updated by our project managers, then invoiced. It was developed with representatives of DTI's NMS and EID contract supervisors and allowed them to have oversight of all their research programmes and track progress. The system offered clear, consistent reporting and traceability. It allowed 250 'project managers' to update their progress which it would summarise and raise around 50 invoices automatically each month for the DTI based on the percentage completed or 'earned value' of each costed milestone. At any one time, records of progress on more than 8,000 milestones were held on the database. The system proved to be robust and helpful to both DTI and staff and was used for several years to come.

The process for invoicing our customers for measurement services was still manual and as many of the calibration services were priced at under £1,000 with packing and carriage, it was very inefficient. We therefore decided to develop a 'Laboratory Information Management System' called 'LIMS'. It was implemented in 2000 and able to raise over 90% of our small value invoices in a far more efficient, reliable and timely manner and highlight un-invoiced work.

By the end of our 5-year Contract we were also considering updating our centralised accounting with a fully web-enabled enterprise business information system. Setting up new work or sales orders could only be carried out by staff in finance. The new organisation structure with devolved management responsibilities for programmes, projects and finance meant that we were ready to 'turn the business on its head' by giving each scientific centre the necessary tools to control all of these processes itself. I personally believed this was the right thing to do for the organisation but it was, I believe, a bold move for many reasons, particularly its timing! Although a 2-year extension to the Contract had been agreed, primarily to allow the PFI building to be completed and give DTI time to organise an appropriate competitive re-tender, there was no guarantee that Serco would be successful a second time. It would also involve investment and additional work across the organisation with some implementation costs not being fully recovered before the Contract end. Because of this I sought the approval of both Serco and DTI. The then chief executive of Serco, Kevin Beeston, gave the project his full support since it demonstrated the company's policy of always taking a long term view in the best interests of the customer and not being unduly influenced by imminent rebids. Serco had been successful in winning more than 90% of their rebids at this time and it might also help support its bid for securing the next NPL Contract. DTI did not object to the project as it promised to deliver additional savings in the future as the systems and processes were fully developed.

Having implemented a number of accounting systems before I knew the risks involved and this was the largest and most complex business-wide application I had encountered. We engaged a firm of specialist consultants to steer us through the procurement process and ensure that we fully appreciated all the pros and cons of the tenders submitted. Dr Helen Anthony, who had managed the implementations of the MProMS and LIMS systems, bravely took on the Enterprise Business Information project. After a great deal of deliberation, we selected the offer from Oracle as it ticked all the boxes. To keep it simple (if that's really possible with an enterprise system!) and control costs, we implemented a 'vanilla' or basic system as far as possible but still meeting our requirements. Further developments could then be made to take advantage of all of Oracle's capabilities in the ensuing years as the Company grew and the system bedded in. We certainly did not want to bite off more than we could chew.

By the time we completed implementation of the system it was 2001 and we were into the first Contract extension for 2 years. The Oracle Business Information System offered us 21st century technology. It was fully web-enabled with built-in workflow to allow far more efficient processes and even greater delegation within a securely controlled framework. It also gave us much improved project and management information. We'll go on to see in the next Chapters the impact that the Oracle system had on the organisation, heralding the next wave of efficiencies. However, it did turn out to be the right time to take on a project of this size, as during the very much protracted period of Contract extensions, it was difficult to progress any new initiatives, science or operational, with DTI. We were entering the rebid period with Chinese walls between NPL's management and Serco's bid team. DTI's attention was now almost completely taken up with the PFI and re-tendering the new NPL Science Contract.

As demonstrated by the Oracle implementation, Serco and the management team within NPLML did not stand still and saw it as an opportunity to use this time as constructively as possible for the future benefit of NPL.

Communications and the 'General Activities Programme'
There are a number of commercial drivers that do not fall within my area of expertise but I shall mention them here as, again, they not only helped us grow our business but also had a positive impact on revitalising and reinforcing our customer facing culture. As we have seen, good communication was key to winning over our stakeholders after contractorisation but it was equally important for us to raise people's

awareness of NPL and the extent of its capabilities, both to commercial customers and the public at large.

The General Activities Programme with an annual spend of £500k was a requirement of the Term Contract. DTI and NPLML had a shared commitment to the public understanding of science and there were a great number of initiatives successfully implemented during this time. I shall mention a few of them here but we were particularly keen to inspire young people at schools and colleges to become the scientists (perhaps at NPL) of the future. The Atomic Clocks exhibition, *'It's All About Time'* at the Science Museum had over 1.5 million visitors. At the 'Tomorrow's World Live' exhibition we organised and presented a *'Physics Facts and Fun'* lecture attended by 1,500 members of the public with our stands being visited by 9,000 people. NPL's 'Metromnia' Newsletter began publication in 1998, issued via the New Scientist and there had been 9 issues with 115,000 being published by the end of the first Contract. It continues to be distributed today and still has a large following. A series of 9 posters were created on the different units of measurement and issued to the 6,000 schools and colleges on NPL's database. And finally, in 1999, NPL took part in the Royal Institution Lecture on 'Time', which had extensive media coverage and an audience of 1 million plus.

General Activities Programme

- Shared DTI/NPL commitment to Public Understanding of Science
- It's About Time
  - Atomic clocks exhibition at the Science Museum – had 1.5 million visitors
- Tomorrow's World Live
  - Physics Facts and Fun lecture to 1,500 members of the public
  - Stands visited by 9,000
- Metromnia
  - Issue 9 this month
  - 115,000 published via New Scientist
- Series of 9 schools and colleges posters (6,000 schools on data base to receive each edition)
- Royal Institution Lecture on Time 1999
  - Audience of 1 million
  - Extensive media coverage

Other indications of our growing outreach to our customers were in the increase of the number of helpline enquiries.

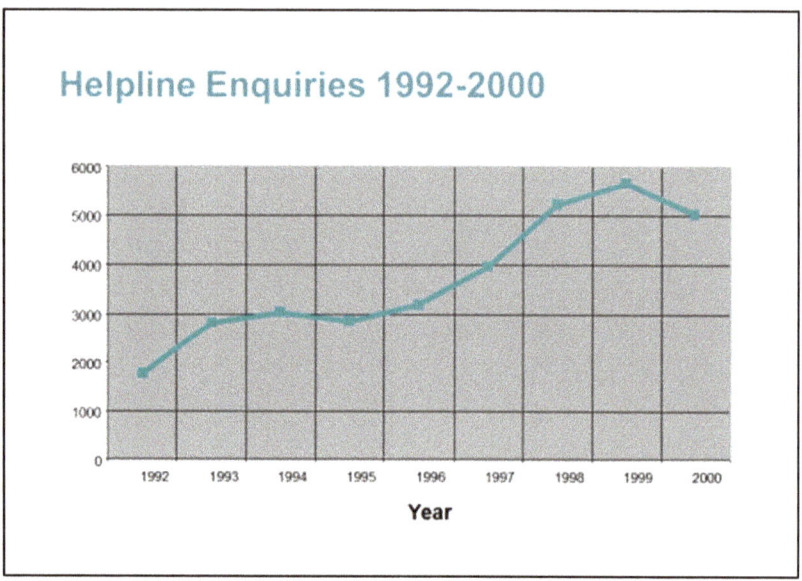

This facility was widely publicised through our numerous clubs, publications, newsletters and, in particular our redesigned and refreshed website.

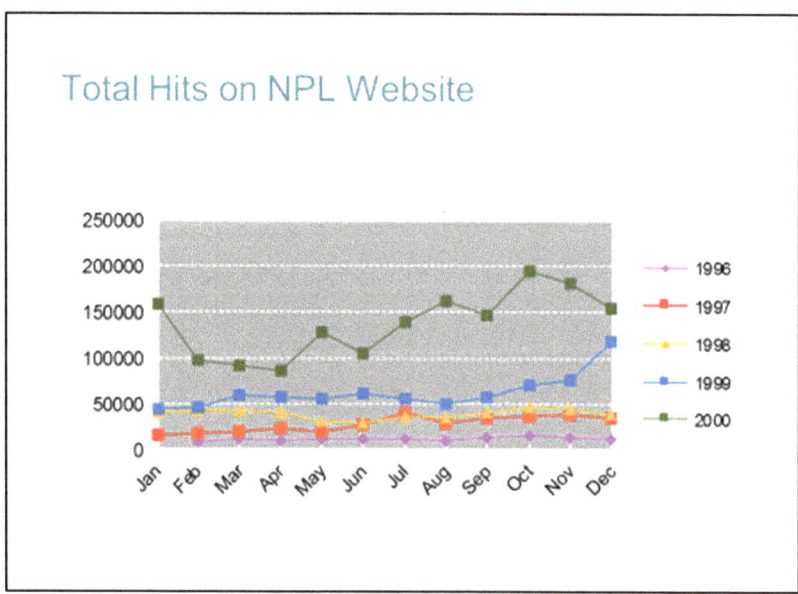

From the start of the Contract we created a new 'corporate' image for NPLML. At its centre it still maintained the original NPL logo which was refreshed and unified all of the diverse formats each Science Division had developed for their own publications before contractorisation. The only evidence of Serco's presence at the Laboratory was the words at the bottom of the letter heading saying: *'NPL Management Ltd. is operated on behalf of DTI by Serco Group plc.'* Although a contractual requirement, in those days Serco was content to maintain a low profile and was happy to be part of NPL's illustrious history. *'Think of us as part of you'* was how it wished to be known to customers. In the City at that time, Serco was known as *'the most successful Company that you've never heard of'*!

Financial Outturn for the 5-Year Term Contract

Against the background of significant Government budget cuts throughout the 1990s, the Term Contract had achieved successful outcomes across all of the main requirements set out in the ITT which stated:

> *'The core requirement is that the contractor should provide specified research, development and related scientific and technical services of the highest standard to and on behalf of the DTI, and disseminate the same for the benefit of UK industry and for regulatory purposes. The contractor will need to maintain NPL as an internationally respected centre of scientific excellence, and represent the DTI in both national and international fora. Subject to meeting these requirements, the contractor will be expected to maximise third party work at NPL'.*

I've only touched upon NPL's science and international standing. My primary objective is to look at the GOCO years from a commercial perspective but it goes without saying that it always remained a priority for us. The RSRAE Monitoring Group was satisfied and positive about NPL's science throughout this period. Our international influence was widely recognised to have increased through NPL staff being appointed or elected as members of the International Committee for Weights and Measures (CIPM) and its committees and our role in the development of the Mutual Recognition Agreement (MRA). A new International Programme was being formulated to act as a focus for our international work across the Laboratory and Dr Andrew Wallard, NPLML's Deputy Director, had been invited to be the next Director of the Bureau International des Poids et Mesures (BIPM) based just outside Paris. Maintaining and enhancing NPL's scientific excellence and international standing ensured the GOCO business model was tried, tested and seen to work well and that a second Contract would be re-tendered, possibly for a longer term.

The success of the GOCO business model was nevertheless reliant on maximizing work from third party customers, a point that had not escaped DTI's notice! There were a myriad of strings attached to the extent and type of work we could take on but as a prestigious National Measurement Institute (NMI) these were fair and reasonable. For example, the ITT went on to state:

> 'The contractor will ensure that all work for third parties does not jeopardise the reputation and independence of NPL as a centre of excellence and its core capabilities to deliver the services required by the DTI. The work had to develop the overall income and cost effectiveness of the Laboratory, increase the skills and capabilities of our staff and make best use of the assets (physical and technical)'.

In developing this new third party income the contractor also had to ensure that:

> 'the core capability to deliver the DTI's guaranteed services was maintained; overheads between third party and DTI guaranteed work were apportioned fairly; any examples of work for foreign governments or organisations which may not be in the national interest were referred to the DTI and the nature and profile of third party work did not compete unfairly with NAMAS accredited laboratories'.

There was also an overriding provision that the value of DTI guaranteed work, taken as a whole, was sustained at the tendered level. At a Company level, there was the additional arrangement to share any annual profits with a return of over 3.75% of sales equally with DTI.

The Financial Performance Chart for the 5 years of the Term Contract gives an overall view of our DTI guaranteed research programmes which were 'designated' as part of the Term Contract. The rest of our sales were classified as 'commercial' and contained work for the DTI which was won in competition with others together with a growing amount of 'decant' costs recovered from DTI to compensate us for the work and loss of income associated with the PFI contract (described later).

Financial Performance

£000's	1995/96 Actual (6 months)	1996/97 Actual	1997/98 Actual	1998/99 Actual	1999/2000 Actual	2000/01 Actual (6 months)
Sales						
- DTI Guaranteed	15,978	30,923	29,988	30,365	31,507	15,832
- Commercial	3,662	11,189	12,979	15,246	16,657	8,412
Total Sales	19,640	42,112	42,967	45,611	48,164	24,244
Profit Before Tax	(828)	1,830	2,760	2,796	2,750	1,132
Return on Sales	(4.2%)	4.3%	6.4%	6.1%	5.7%	4.7%
Cum. Return on Sales	(4.2%)	1.6%	3.6%	4.4%	4.7%	4.7%
Cum. Profit Share to DTI	0	417	522	731	939	1,044

Obviously, it is easier to bid for work from existing rather than new customers and DTI's competitively tendered contracts took up a significant proportion of our commercial business during this period. However, we also knew that Government funding for non-guaranteed work could disappear almost at a moment's notice so we had to be cautious about the number of permanent staff we recruited to deliver our growing workload. As we approached the end of the Term Contract uncertainty grew as to the extent of future DTI work, single and competitively tendered. Together with the increasing disruption caused by the PFI contract this tended to constrain our ability to grow commercial sales in the latter part of the Contract.

The significant costs of phasing-in the Contract could be spread over its lifetime but some had to be written-off immediately giving rise to planned losses in the first 6 months of operation. For the remainder of the Contract our profit before tax was just above the levels forecast in our bid proposal with a cumulative return on sales of 4.7% even after sharing over £1M with DTI. With the considerable savings passed on to DTI through our fixed day rate charges amounting to more than £21M, I believe this could be considered a WIN - WIN - WIN for all parties, DTI (and taxpayer), NPL and Serco.

Cash, Dividends and Tax

To a private limited company like NPLML cash is 'king'. To a Government Department, keeping its spending within budget each year is a priority. This annuality of Government budgets meant that the 'time value of money' within a financial year was not a key consideration for DTI but supporting our customer to meet their budgets at each year-end was a must. With this understanding, we were able to support each other's cash management to our mutual benefit.

At the beginning of the Term Contract the necessary cash settlements resulting from the finalisation of NPL's Agency accounts had to be paid. We then had to turn our attention to the not inconsiderable costs of transition and transformation. In terms of our Profit and Loss account many of the 'phase-in' costs could be spread over the duration of the Contract and the cost of assets were similarly depreciated over their useful lives thus smoothing their impact. These costs were, however, a strain on our cash flow and this working capital had to be financed.

Serco had arranged an overdraft facility of £3M for NPLML to address the Contract phase-in costs. Our aim was to stay within this facility and begin reducing it by the end of the first full year of trading. There was a contractual obligation to pay DTI for NPL's low value assets (under £3,000 each) valued at £2,632k and precious metals and stones with a value of £338k. We agreed with DTI that these could be paid by 5 annual installments thus taking some of the pressure off our cash flow and allowing the overdraft facility to be reduced to £1M more quickly than anticipated. Of course, our expenditure on capital assets was financed through the payment of quarterly lease rentals which again smoothed our cash flow. In 1997 the overdraft was completely cleared and we were able to pay a relatively small dividend of £354k to Serco. By the end of the Term Contract total dividends amounted to just under £6M and NPLML was self-sufficient in cash and working capital. The tax benefits to

Government of a company operating under a GOCO arrangement are often overlooked (as are the costs and cash flow impact to the company). During the first Contract, NPLML's corporation tax paid or payable amounted to nearly £3.5M.

Investment in New Facilities and Capital Assets – Management and Innovation

Outside of the PFI to build a new NPL Laboratory there were 2 additional construction projects completed during the Term Contract. The first was a new building extension to house an acoustic pressure vessel acquired from the USA. This gave NPL the most comprehensive under-water acoustics capabilities in Europe. The other was a building to house a new cobalt-60 facility allowing us to deliver a range of state-of-the-art radiation dosimetry services to the NHS medical community and UK's nuclear industry.

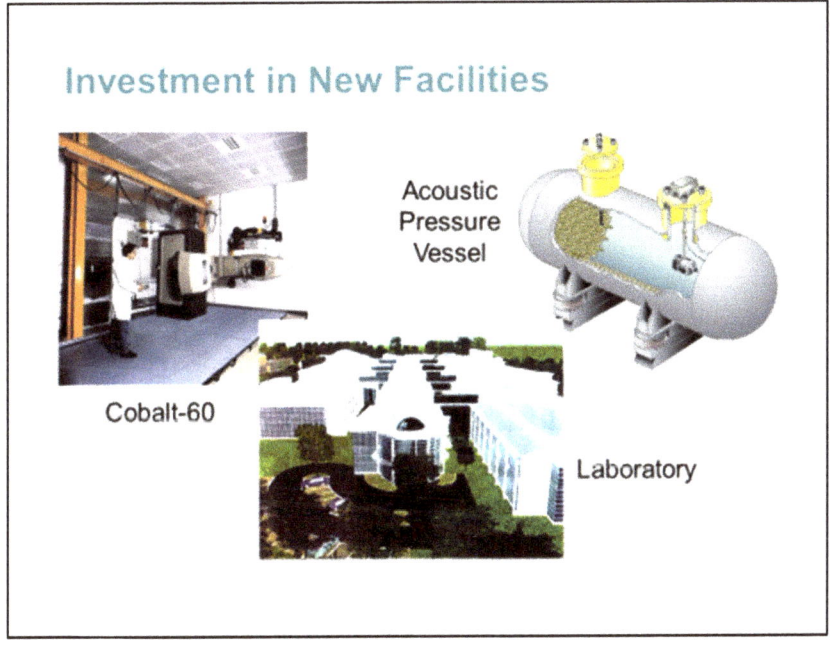

As DTI owned and financed these buildings, NPLML was required to pay additional rental to cover these investments when the new Contract was let. In 2004/05, therefore, the charges for buildings outside the PFI contract were £500k p.a. plus associated insurance. NPLML also paid lease rentals on all existing and new scientific equipment based on a 6% annuity formula. As I've mentioned before the DTI operated two distinctly separate budgets for capital and revenue items and it was not possible to vire between them. When formulating a new research programme it could be difficult to marry up the budgets for the purchase of the capital equipment with the requirements of the programmes. Cuts of more than 50% in capital budgets were not unheard of. The administration around the procurement of capital equipment was also long and arduous for both us and DTI. I had therefore long seen the advantage of taking the purchasing and financing of these assets away from DTI and doing it ourselves. After all, we already had to pay lease fees to DTI so why not pay a bank or leasing company that specialised in providing these services? Of course, NPL's scientific assets were owned by DTI on behalf of the nation and many of them were unique. I would have to convince DTI that they did not have to **own** the assets to still be able to **control** them. In April 1996, while in the process of agreeing the first Capital Plan with DTI I put forward an outline proposal for *'The Acquisition of Laboratory Assets through a tripartite agreement with the DTI, NPLML and [a Lease Company]'*. The proposal included two types of transaction: the first was a single transaction to put in place alternative arrangements for existing assets, the second, a procedure to purchase and lease new assets.

We had already gone through an asset valuation process at the beginning of the Term Contract. Their value was now based on historic cost accounting with new remaining lives and all the original purchase invoices were available for verification. Our investigations with DTI confirmed that the laboratory assets (our asset register) listed in Schedule 15 of the Term Contract would satisfy private finance lease criteria i.e. they were 'movable', durable and identifiable. Moreover, leasing companies were content to accept the net values we attributed to these assets and our assessment of their remaining economic life. The assets would be sold to the leasing company either through NPLML or directly by DTI and immediately leased back to NPLML (a sale and leaseback agreement). Title to the assets would pass to the Leasing Company and rental would be payable to them by NPLML. At the end of the lease period the DTI could enter into a buy-back agreement if required. New assets would be agreed with DTI through the existing programme formulation and capital planning processes and procured by NPLML's purchasing team as agents to the Leasing Company.

For me the advantages of this form of arrangement were overwhelming as 'through life costs' of operating the assets compared favourably with the existing 6% annuity fee charged to us by DTI. My synopsis went on to note the following advantages:

> '*the release of a substantial amount of capital to reinvest in the Laboratory; financing and asset management risks are transferred to those best placed to manage them; demonstrable value for money; transfer of much of the administrative burden [from DTI] to NPLML and the Leasing Company; financing will be provided by the private sector, not, as now, the public sector; effective control over the assets remains with DTI; further evidence that the Laboratory is being placed on a true commercial footing; interest rates and lease rentals compare favourably with those currently offered by DTI'.*

In November 1996, I received a letter from DTI agreeing that *'there are a number of good reasons to pursue this option ... However ... there are a number of difficulties which would be presented in integrating a revised arrangement within the framework of the Contract'*. It went on to say that at that time there was not a compelling enough business case to justify negotiating the changes required to the Contract. This was quite a positive reply and it did go on to *'suggest that we 'park' consideration of this issue for perhaps a year or so'*.

In fact, it was not until 1999 that DTI revisited this initiative and the possibility of an asset sale and leaseback arrangement explored in detail. The timing was more appropriate as the Term Contract would have to be updated for the 2 year extension. Any amendments to accommodate this new financing arrangement could be made at the same time. The PFI was in full swing and, perhaps most important, cash was in short supply!

There is no doubt that from the Government's perspective the 'cheapest' form of financing is through the Treasury. However, when looked at in the context of the whole life costs of an asset within an operating contract, the 'sale and leaseback' arrangement has distinct advantages. The capital assets would be removed from DTI's ownership so there would be no capital charges payable and no recharges to NPLML necessary. Management of NPL's assets, the asset register, capital planning and budgeting and procurement (as agents of the bank) would be squarely the responsibility of NPLML. Capital assets would be purchased as part of programme formulation and through the Capital Review Group to ensure they were properly managed and prioritised and not subject to the spending constraints and vagaries of Government budgeting.

In order for the selection process to be seen to be 'independent' and at arm's length, a capital financing specialist from Deloitte and Touche, the Company's auditors, was engaged to advise DTI and funded by NPLML. A 'beauty parade' of 5 leading banks was arranged and DTI were able to select the most competitive offer. The 'Tripartite Agreement' was signed in 2000. It included 'step in' rights for DTI (in the unlikely event that NPLML were to default on the lease rentals) but this was also advantageous for NPLML as it was an effective Government guarantee and enabled the Bank to offer the most advantageous rates possible to a private company, yet another WIN – WIN – WIN for all parties. The whole arrangement required ministerial approval. The initial transaction was valued at over £14M with an additional £2M tranche the following year (as a major asset was being moved as part of the PFI and could not be valued until recommissioned). New assets would then be purchased by NPLML on behalf of the bank and lease rentals paid quarterly in arrears to them directly. DTI had effectively transferred the risks of ownership of these assets completely to the private sector and as a result of the reduction in administration, were able to redeploy 2 full time posts to more productive work.

The 'PFI' – Opportunities and Threats

In 1996 DTI were successful in obtaining £80M of funding for the design, build and operation of a new Laboratory for NPL at its current location in Teddington to replace the 50 buildings across the 82 acre site. As a result of Serco's interest in bidding for this PFI contract, NPLML's management and staff had to abide by strict rules throughout the process so as not to prejudice the outcome.

The Term Contract had given us the freedom to operate the Laboratory, including all support services in a fully integrated way and gain the greatest economies and efficiencies. PFI funding required that, in return for a unitary fee paid each year by DTI, bidders would design, build **and operate** a new Laboratory for a period of 25 years. To make this work, DTI therefore had to 'carve out' an operational element from our existing Term Contract. Serco was agreeable to this as it cleared their path to bidding the PFI contract. It was our job to negotiate and agree with Serco and DTI the extent of the operational services to be transferred to the successful PFI contractor. According to DTI the annual value of this operational element had to be substantial in order to meet the conditions of funding and be attractive to the bidders.

We had made considerable savings by integrating the support services but with the introduction of contractual boundaries again, some of the benefits already realised would inevitably be lost. However, we fully appreciated that the challenges of maintaining the efficient operation of the Laboratory while transferring more than 500 scientists and their equipment from 50 old buildings into a new facility would be immense and were keen to support DTI through this process. Our principle of 'being easy to deal with', meant that variations to the Term Contract were kept to a minimum and were as straight forward as possible. After much discussion it was agreed that the 'operational' part of the PFI contract should comprise the estate and buildings management and maintenance, security, cleaning, the integrated logistics (good in and out) function and the front of house reception duties. These could be 'detached' from the Term Contract relatively easily without too much disruption to the business (and staff) or loss of efficiency. They had an estimated annual cost of around £4M.

John Laing plc and Serco Group plc were successful in their bid for the NPL PFI. The contract was signed on the 31st July 1998 by Laser, a jointly owned 'special purpose company' and was for 25 years. John Laing was responsible for the design and build of the new Laboratory which in the end was worth £96M. DTI would pay a unitary charge of £11.5M (1998 prices) a year inflated by RPI once the construction was completed. At the end of the contract the Laboratory would be returned to DTI. It would comprise 36,000 square metres of scientific laboratories (around 400 in total), library, conference centre, engineering workshop, offices and meeting rooms arranged over 16 interlinking modules each 2 stories high. The scientific areas were to be designed with built-in flexibility but also meet exacting metrology requirements to give them a 'life' well into the next century. Special attention had to be paid to high environmental stability, low vibration, and minimizing magnetic and electromagnetic fields so that the most advanced scientific standards could be realised. Serco was responsible for the on-going operation of the Laboratory building. The operational staff in those functions affected by the PFI contract transferred to Serco straight away under TUPE rules together with all their associated equipment and a separate office block was provided for the support and management teams. Initially, it was business as usual and we would continue to reimburse Serco for the costs of the original support services that had been transferred. A new 'Science' Contract would be required at the time of the rebid.

I, and probably many others, at this time, were sceptical about the wisdom of using PFI funding to build a new laboratory since, unlike hospitals and prisons, for example, NPL was a 'one-off' highly complex technical project needing a great deal of research and testing to ensure the exacting laboratory specifications could be achieved. However, at this time it was the **only way** to obtain funding for a new Laboratory. To make things more challenging, tight bidding deadlines had to be met to ensure the funding was secured. It is not appropriate for me to go into the rights and wrongs of a PFI for NPL and much has already been written. NPLML was going to be significantly affected by the PFI project and we had to do our utmost to assist DTI in every way to manage the process whilst protecting NPL's science.

For NPLML, the new Laboratory represented the potential of a significant step forward in NPL's business environment and offered both opportunities **and** threats. A new Laboratory was long overdue and it would certainly raise NPL's UK and international profile and reinforce our 'Big Three' global position. It would provide an environment for us to continue excellent science well into the future. From a corporate perspective it provided a far more integrated platform for organisational, business process and cultural change under 'one roof'. However, there were enormous challenges for Laser in meeting the required environmental specifications. Disruption to services and loss of commercial sales were inevitable and potentially there would be a significant increase in NPL's cost base.

New Laboratory – front elevation

New Laboratory – rear elevation

The compensation terms agreed with NPLML for scientists' time spent on the PFI project and loss of third party income caused by decanting of staff and scientific equipment were favourable to DTI. Scientist's time was charged at gross salary plus pension and national insurance costs but with no overhead recovery. Loss of third party income was charged at full economic cost but without a profit margin. Most equipment could be moved and re-commissioned in weeks but because of traceability requirements, in some cases new equipment had to be purchased and run in parallel to enable calibration against the original standards. Large pieces of equipment, such as the 1.2 MN force machine standing 2 stories high would take well over a year to dismantle, move, reassemble, commission and calibrate with significant loss of income to the business.

By the end of the first Contract we had moved into the first 2 scientific modules of the new building together with the interlinking central spine unit which would be for goods in and out and storage. Moves to the new building would take a great deal of time and effort yet!

The First Term Contract – Building a Genuine Partnership with DTI

One of the most valuable achievements of the first Term Contract for Serco and NPLML was building a working relationship with DTI that was based on trust and a genuine partnering approach to the operation of the Laboratory. This was maintained through changes of personnel both in NPLML and DTI and variations to the Contract as a result of the PFI. We had very quickly worked out a modus operandi that was effective and beneficial for us both and in 1998 we were advised that the Contract would be extended for a further 2 years as permitted by the Term Contract.

A number of 'mechanisms' were put in place to cement this relationship still further and to conclude this chapter I shall mention just a few of them here. First of all, despite much initial scepticism, the Company, NPLML, survived in the private sector and was successful. There was no stripping out national assets for profit or dumbing down of our science! NPLML's business records were completely open to DTI and, in fact, by 1998 the financial management system was accessible on line from DTI's offices in Buckingham Palace Road. Profits over a 3.75% return on sales were shared and proceeds ploughed back into the science. The arrangement was robust, transparent and independently verified during the annual statutory audit of our accounts with a signed 'Profit Certificate'.

There were secondments in both directions between DTI and NPLML (6 by the end of the Contract). Our Business Plan was fully disclosed and agreed with DTI who had rights of attendance at key management meetings. Over the period we developed comprehensive performance metrics which satisfied DTI's monitoring requirements and were scrutinised at each of our Annual Performance Reviews. With the advent of the PFI Contract we had a joint commitment to the success of the new Laboratory building.

The partnership also extended to NPL's science with joint innovation in a number of new and exciting initiatives. The programme formulation processes had been simplified but with a much higher degree of consultation with industry to aid DTI and their advisory group and measure the impact of NPL's science. New programmes of research were created not only pushing the boundaries of the fundamentals of metrology in the Foundation Programme, but also in areas of growing interest to the UK, like Photonics, Software and Knowledge Transfer. In fact, knowledge transfer had become an important part of our mission and business during this Contract.

We were working closely with DTI on new methods of capital financing with a sale and leaseback initiative releasing much needed finance to Government and integrating the budgeting for new programmes of research.

We had assisted DTI in their development of a new, much needed review of NMS research programme priorities and had raised the public understanding of science with many exciting events and activities throughout the Contract period. Our excellent working relationship was built on a common understanding of our mutual interdependence. This was to be further demonstrated by the support given during the protracted rebid process.

Chapter 4 - 'A Level Playing Field'

It was now October 2000 and we had reached the end of our first Contract. It had allowed for a possible extension of 2 years subject to agreement by both parties. This option had been exercised by DTI and agreed with Serco. The main driver for the extension was the hope that the PFI for the new Laboratory would be completed thus facilitating a 'clean' contractual agreement for the next term, unencumbered by transitional arrangements and decanting of staff and equipment. There might also have been some limited information for the bidders on the running costs of the new Laboratory but perhaps this was a little too optimistic!

DTI staff and their consultants were already completely preoccupied with managing the PFI arrangements so running a re-tendering exercise at the same time would mean considerably more resource. Nevertheless, a new Science Contract was required to be in place at the end of the 2 years unless there were strong mitigating circumstances which would have to be communicated to the original bidders in 1995 with a revised retendering timetable to ensure 'fair play'. DTI also had to take advice on the whole retendering process to ensure that there was a 'level playing field' for all bidders and that Serco, as the incumbent, was not advantaged in any way.

This chapter will deal with the extensions to the existing Term Contract and rebid for a new Science Contract. It was called a 'Science Contract' this time because facilities management services and maintenance of the new building were now part of the PFI agreement with DTI. In the end, three extensions were required covering the period from 1st October 2000 to 31st March 2004. A level playing field meant that Serco had to set up a separate NPL bid team and a 'Chinese wall' would exist between NPLML and Serco except for normal parent company and statutory reporting requirements which would be shared with DTI and all the other bidders as deemed appropriate. David Richardson, our Business Development Director, resigned from the Board and, together with Dr Jerry Benson, joined the Serco bid team from NPLML. The rest of us remained with NPL to continue to operate the Contract during the rebid and the PFI building works and moves to the new Laboratory.

The Contract Extensions

In these circumstances the DTI team responsible for overseeing the NPL Contract could be forgiven for being distracted from the operation of the Laboratory. For the executive and management team at NPL however it was not only business as usual but much more. We had to ensure that our staff remained motivated and engaged, our research programmes were delivered and we maintained high levels of customer care throughout a period of undoubted disruption.

Most of all, we did not want our programme of business improvements to stall and were determined to turn this period into an opportunity to push forward with a number of performance improvement projects. It demonstrated one of Serco's guiding principles of 'taking the long term view' and might even serve to diminish the impact of competitors' bid proposals. It was also 'the right thing to do' and an obvious priority for us to continue to show a genuine commitment to the successful future of NPL. From NPL's side of the Chinese wall it was our responsibility to support DTI in their rebid process. At the same time, these performance improvement projects would lay the foundations for a new Science Contract and ensured we could 'hit the deck running' if successful.

Implementation of the new Oracle business system was already underway and the final sale and leaseback transactions for NPL's assets were completed. Through the agency agreement with our leasing partner, new equipment began to be procured using a much simplified process aligned to programme and Laboratory priorities. Greater time and effort was also devoted to updating our Personnel, now called Human Resources (HR), procedures under a new Director. This would be an important step towards the development of a more defined career path for scientists and support a review of salaries, particularly of scientific staff, to ensure rates of pay were competitive in the 'war for talent' as it was called in those days.

What we thought would be a 2-year extension including perhaps a 12 month Contract retendering timetable, however, turned out to be far more protracted and complex than ever envisaged.

The 2-Year Extension

As we knew that DTI were preoccupied with the PFI Contract we opened our dialogue on the 2-year extension in 1998 as the Term Contract had prescribed. The Contract was working well so we were happy to continue for an additional 2 years of operation on the same terms subject to 2 main clarification points, namely, DTI's guaranteed and competitively tendered spend on research programmes and agreeing how we should deal with the running costs of the part-finished new Laboratory over that period.

Initially, both of these points proved to be stumbling blocks. A strategy review of DTI research programmes coupled with a decision to merge EID's materials area with the NMS customer, led to delays in finalising funding budgets. Although this was a sensible and positive action for both DTI and NPL, it called for a more fundamental 'rebalancing' of research programmes. These had inevitable resource implications, particularly within the materials area.

In addition, technical issues with some of the laboratories in the new building, particularly those requiring close temperature or climatic control, were affecting commissioning dates and delaying staff and equipment moves. Estimating the running costs of the new Laboratory would become a distant cry!

Nevertheless, as soon as we had solutions to these issues, a supplementary deed of amendment to the Contract would be relatively straight-forward to enact. To assist and speed the decision making process we put forward a number of discussion documents presenting different scenarios and solutions for consideration. Treasury approval for an additional 2 years of guaranteed funding had to be sought. Our input and assistance to DTI was greatly appreciated and helped expedite the process.

Our extension proposals were relatively detailed and set out 3 principles for a successful agreement: a value added commitment, pricing principles and assumptions, and minimal Contract changes.

A Value-Added Commitment
First of all we confirmed that our profit margin assumption would revert to 5% of sales turnover which would, in fact, be a 10% reduction (£480k) from the actual performance level achieved in 1999/2000. DTI were obviously keen to see efficiency benefits arising from the operation of the new Laboratory. We estimated that there would be a reduction of 15 administration and support posts amounting to £400k p.a. after the moves to the new building. In addition, we offered to bear the management costs

of implementing the NMS review and restructuring the EID materials programme (£200k) while any potential redundancy costs would be borne by DTI and phased over the remaining lives of the materials programmes. Any associated savings would be reflected in future day rates. Our proposal also included a commitment to continue to maintain long term investment in NPL's resources and infrastructure resulting from the NMS Review, and pass on additional efficiency savings from implementation of the new Oracle enterprise system. DTI also expected to see gains in the productivity of our scientists from being located in one building rather than being distributed over a 55 acre site and we undertook to consider how these might be realised when formulating new programmes from mid-2001. Finally, we made a commitment to maintain 1999/2000 levels of sales contribution to the NPL cost base despite the disruption and risks caused by the PFI decant.

Pricing Principles and Assumptions

In order to finalise the pricing of the Contract extension we would have to set in train another 'meter-reading' exercise to estimate the position of the DTI research programmes at the end of September 2000. The number of scientist days could then be matched with the new NMS funding for the period and day rates calculated covering different income and cost scenarios. Once a baseline DTI programme spend for the 2-year extension had been established, including the 'guaranteed' and competitively tendered mix, we could confirm our assumptions on the impact of the NMS review and restructuring of the materials programmes on the pricing of new science day rates. It was then possible to agree the pace at which these changes could be rolled out so that DTI's aspirations could be fulfilled while managing our respective budgets and business risk.

As the costs of the new PFI building were still uncertain DTI decided to 'cap' accommodation costs which included 'rent' for site occupancy, rates, utilities and facilities management (FM) services (catering, conferencing, site services and estates) at the then current cost which amounted to £5.5M p.a.

All our workings and planning assumptions were completely transparent and shared with DTI so that there was a good level of confidence in the revised pricing schedules for the period. The day rates continued to include an NPLML funded Strategic Research Programme at 5% of DTI's guaranteed spend and a General Activities Programme of £500k p.a. Inflation over the period was assumed to be 4% p.a.

Proposed Minimal Contract Changes

A Supplementary Deed of Amendment extended the Term Contract by 2 years to 30th September 2002. Apart for revised Pricing Schedules, only 2 principal areas of the Term Contract had to be amended. The Schedule on Leased Assets was revised to reflect the new private sector leasing arrangements and the Schedule of Accommodation had to be amended to reflect the capping arrangements introduced while the uncertainties on the costs of the new PFI building remained. The profit share arrangement was also reset to the original 5% cumulative return on sales but we agreed a 60:40 split in favour of DTI. A new property lease at a fixed annual rental for the 2-year extension was signed and covered the entire site regardless of buildings occupied.

Positioning NPL for post-2002

While the terms of the Contract extension were being negotiated and DTI's requirements for the following 2 years were being clarified, we continued to push ahead with our business improvement programmes with great success. The timing of the merger of the materials area with our NMS customer was fortuitous as it meant that these changes could be incorporated in our overall business plans without too much difficulty. The NMS review gave DTI a clear vision of their mission and strategic objectives for NPL and this, together with our financial forecasts, became part of the Invitation to Negotiate (ITN) for the New Science Contract (NSC). Operating efficiencies in the new building were realised with improvements in scientist and support staff productivity. The Oracle Business Information System enabled us to monitor these performance improvements in the new PFI environment much more effectively and with greater transparency. The new asset management processes and financing arrangements bedded down well and the clean-up of the asset register together with standardisation of equipment descriptions (where possible) gave us far greater visibility of the kit we operated. The new system also enabled the asset register to be shared throughout the Laboratory and line managers could interrogate this before authorising the purchase of new assets to avoid the possibility of duplication.

There was, during this time, the beginnings of a 'war for talent'. Recruiting 'the best of the best' from science graduates was becoming far more competitive and there was an urgent need to review the salary scales that were required to attract new blood to the Laboratory and retain existing staff in areas of particular skill shortage. Under our new HR Director, Paul Gaskin, a huge amount of time and effort went into completely updating our HR processes in full consultation with staff. These included new job evaluations re-defining roles, responsibilities, competencies and accountabilities and researching the market place to identify the competition and required salary levels for new recruits and agree 'market rate adjustments' for existing staff. A much more defined career path was put in place for those wishing to progress within a purely science discipline as an alternative to that traditionally requiring management roles to be pursued. Our timely intervention limited any significant issues with recruitment and retention of our scientists and technicians. It did, however, impact our cost base and, as we were in a rebid situation, we had to obtain the necessary approval of DTI but, again, these changes could be reflected in financial data and forecasts for the ITN.

At this time, we thought we could look forward to a return to growth in sales and margins when the moves to the new Laboratory were finalised and the building works completed. There was some apprehension about the operational and financial implications of a drive within Europe to begin devolution of equipment calibration services between laboratories belonging to the European Association of National Metrology Institutes (EURAMET), but we did know that such things moved at a glacial pace. Most of all, we were keen for the time to return when we could resume 'normal' activities without disruption to our science and business.

The 1-Year and 6-Month Extensions
Our hopes were thwarted when it soon became apparent that technical issues with the build and fitting out of the new Laboratory were continuing to cause severe delays. In the end DTI had to concede that the new Laboratory would not be completed to their satisfaction in the near future and the tender for the NSC would have to go ahead taking account the operational uncertainties surrounding the PFI contract.

Again, we were quick to confirm to DTI that we would be willing to extend the Term Contract for a period of its choosing on the same basis as the supplementary extension agreement subject to the usual confirmation of guaranteed and competitively tendered spends. By February 2002 it had become clear that an extension would be required for a further 1 year. We put forward a number of financial scenarios and by July we had the basis of a commercial proposal. Volumes of work were agreed together with some defined adjustments to the cost base. The General Activities programme was cut from £500k to £350k as a direct result of the building works disrupting Laboratory based activities, giving a £150k saving to DTI. The general inflation factor was reduced to 2.875% but limited increases to our cost base were required. These were confined to 3 areas of business, namely, Company contributions to the NPL Pension Scheme (£400k), Company insurances (£100k) and the salary 'market rate adjustments' noted above (£300k). All other arrangements covering accommodation, the costs of redundancy for the materials area and the moves to the new Laboratory (decant) were to remain the same.

And finally ... one further extension was required. This began life as an open ended 'Contingency Contract' which later became a 6-month extension up until the NSC could be let.

The Extension Period – Other Strategic and Operational Opportunities

The National Weights and Measures Laboratory

During the period, other strategic and operational opportunities presented themselves. In 2000 there was a quinquennial review of the National Weights and Measures Laboratory (NWML) which had remained an Executive Agency after the last review in 1995. Its function was to provide a regulatory measurement infrastructure for the UK that facilitated fair competition, promoted international trade and protected consumers. It occupied the same site as NPL. To an outsider, it was a close 'match' to NPL and indeed its measurement services were very similar. There were undoubted synergies and efficiencies to be gained from bringing the laboratories together to better utilise resources and facilities and reduce duplication of effort. We offered and were permitted to submit a report to DTI on the advantages of merging the two organisations. NWML was a much smaller laboratory with a turnover of just over £3M p.a. and staff of around 60. The report was well received but NWML successfully galvanised its customers to lobby for it to remain independent and with so much more going on within the site, the idea was shelved.

Wraysbury Reservoir

A contractor of the MOD, Neptune Sonar Limited, had been operating an underwater facility based at a reservoir in Wraysbury which was only a few miles from Teddington. They could no longer fulfill their contract and we saw the opportunity to take over the operation of this facility as it was a good fit and enhanced our already leading underwater capability within Europe. Although we were very much in the middle of the Contract rebid, DTI gave their approval for the contract to be novated to NPLML in 2003.

Technology Transfer and Innovation Limited – An NPL Spin-Out Company

I've talked about the significant increase in technology and knowledge transfer initiatives by Government and NPLML's success in winning a number of prestigious contracts. Admittedly these contracts were not our core science but helped us remain closely engaged and relevant to industry. However, the NPL brand could be a blessing and a curse particularly when pursuing opportunities that were not commonly associated with our area of expertise. We therefore formed a new company to continue to pursue this new and growing business stream. We called it, Technology Transfer and Innovation Limited (TTI) which was a wholly owned subsidiary of NPLML. Our view was that the new company would show our commitment to invest in developing expertise in this specialised market place and become a key player.

During the rebid for the NSC, DTI were at pains to demonstrate that they were doing everything possible to create a level playing field for bidders. It was a rebid that was therefore dominated by adhering to strict procurement rules with mechanisms that would simplify the selection of a new contractor whilst keeping the whole process as transparent as possible so as to avoid any potential repercussions about fair play. NPLML's subsidiary, TTI, was seen as a potential complication to the retendering process and we were asked to exclude the company from our business portfolio for the purposes of the rebid. The company had a turnover of more than £3M p.a. and although its profitability was modest it was nonetheless strategically important for NPL. As the company was a good fit within Serco's own central government business it was agreed with DTI that we would spin out the company to Serco before the NSC was signed. If Serco were to be successful in their rebid then NPLML would still have the benefit of being able to work closely with TTI (rather than potentially in competition!).

Serco's bid for the operation of the Atomic Weapons Establishment (AWE)

With the experience gained from successfully managing and operating NPL, Serco decided to bid for the GOCO Contract to operate AWE together with partners, Lockheed Martin and British Nuclear Fuels Limited

(BNFL). A bid team was assembled in 1998 and permission was sought from DTI for a limited amount of support from NPL, rechargeable to Serco. Whilst recognising the high security environment required by AWE it was hoped that there would be some level of synergy in certain areas between the two organisations that might be mutually beneficial.

As part of the proposed executive team for AWE, Dr John Rae was put forward as the new Managing Director (MD) and I was designated for the role of Finance Director (FD). In 2000, the Serco consortium was successful in winning the bid and John transferred to AWE. The process of selecting a new MD for NPL commenced and under the Term Contract, DTI's approval was required. After interviews by all parties including the NPLML Board, Dr Bob McGuiness became the new MD of NPLML in March 2000. John Rae remained as a non-executive director on NPLML's Board until 2005.

From left to right: Richard White, Chief Executive, Serco Group plc, Irene and Dr John Rae, retiring Managing Director, NPLML and Dr George Gray, Chair, Serco Group.

However, DTI were reluctant to see both the MD and FD leave NPL at the same time and I agreed to remain at NPLML, after all, it was my dream job! Serco was more than happy for me to stay at NPL, particularly with the Contract rebid and extensions in progress and I knew that new opportunities would present themselves within the NSC with fresh and interesting challenges facing the Laboratory. In particular, there would be the need to maximise the opportunities following completion of the new PFI building, implement the bid proposals of the successful contractor and continue the development of the Oracle business information system. If a different contractor was selected then it was likely that they would install their own FD and as my employment contract was with NPLML there might be new career choices at that time. Of course, as it turned out, I was to remain with NPLML for another 13 years!

Financial Performance during the Extensions

The three and a half years of Contract extensions were difficult times for NPL. The decant of scientists and equipment was taking far longer than anticipated with planned moves continually being pushed back. Our measurement services were badly affected and although there was an agreed mechanism for DTI to reimburse loss of third party income, it was limited to the full economic costs of scientists' time without any profit margin. The disruption to our operation meant that our revenue growth and profitability suffered, remaining virtually static over the period. In fact, much of our time was taken up managing customer relations, offering discounts for rescheduling their orders, for example, rather than marketing and selling our services. As we were not able to grow our business during this time we paid particular attention to our costs and limiting expenditure so as to maintain margins. As a result, we were still able to deliver an additional £522k in profit share to DTI over the period. In the last financial year, our performance was particularly affected by supporting DTI in the retendering of the Contract as it took an enormous amount of management and administrative time and effort across the Laboratory. The uncertainty during the prolonged extension and rebid period was undoubtedly a distraction for all parties and a constraint to further developing NPL's science capabilities and profile internationally.

The table below shows our financial performance over the three and a half years of extensions.

Financial Performance

£000's	2000/01 (6 months)	2001/02	2002/03	2003/04
Total Sales	25,661	49,484	51,197	49,057
Profit Before Tax	1,417	2,874	2,902	2,447
Return on Sales	5.5%	5.8%%	5.7%	5.0%
Cum. Return on Sales	5.5%	5.7%	5.7%	5.5%
Cum. Profit Share to DTI	75	224	373	522

Behind the Chinese Wall – NPL during the Contract Rebid Period

For those of us in NPLML behind the Chinese wall, the conduct and progress of the rebid remained an unknown. The executive team and senior managers of NPLML had to sign a 'non-disclosure' agreement prohibiting us from communicating with Serco on pain of disqualification (death!) apart from normal business and statutory reporting which would be shared with bidders. In anticipation of Dr George Gray stepping down from the NPLML Board at the end of the 2-year Contract extension, Sir Peter Williams was appointed as an independent non-executive member of the Board at the beginning of 2002 and elected as Chair. He was to be a great asset to and supporter of NPL and was to remain as Chair until the end of the GOGO era in 2014.

I shall summarise the content of Serco's bid proposal and the key differences of the NSC later but these were not known to us until after the Contract had commenced in April 2004. DTI engaged a team of external consultants and lawyers to help them through the whole rebid process from expressions of interest, agreeing a preferred contractor short list, drawing up the ITN, conduct of the tendering process and final contractor selection.

The DTI representative given responsibility for managing the process was also a procurement specialist.

It is not surprising therefore that in their quest to ensure a level playing field for all bidders, DTI and their consultants and lawyers made the process as watertight as possible and as a result, it felt excessively rigorous. We were asked to set up a 'data room' for bidders with files of hard and soft copies of information. Rather than it being just information that was relevant for the bidders to produce their proposals it consisted of virtually every output that had been produced in the eight and a half years of our Contract. We soon realised that this was a 'belt, braces and piece of string' approach and any query about the necessity of some of the information was construed by the lawyers as unhelpful.

We were also keen to help DTI in their discussions on the appropriate financial and pricing mechanisms to be included in the new Contract. NPLML was in an ideal position to express opinions on proposals or options that would be suitable and workable for NPL in the future Science Contract. The final choice would always be DTI's in consultation with their advisors. However, we were precluded from input to any part of the new Contract. With the best will in the world, it would be difficult to expect DTI's advisors to fully understand and appreciate the intricacies of the successful operation of NPL, particularly at a practical level. I was concerned that the unsuccessful mechanisms that we argued against and changed in the first Contract might reappear. I did, however, understand DTI's concern about the perception that NPLML (Serco) might be influencing the content of the future Contract to their advantage.

For my part, I had to content myself with being as helpful as possible and refrain (as much as I could) from expressing any opinions! Although frustrating I believe we did an excellent job in supporting DTI and their advisors throughout the rebid, filling the data room and ensuring no stone was left unturned. At the height of this activity one member of staff spent almost all his time verifying and feeding these data and information through to DTI's advisors. Of course, some of this was commercially sensitive (prices and charge out rates, for example) and some of the bidders were in direct competition with NPLML. We flagged this issue to DTI and marked this information accordingly but it was up to DTI whether it was disclosed or redacted.

Before I move on to Serco's rebid proposal I do need to acknowledge the outstanding resilience and dedication of NPL's staff during this period. Operating a National Laboratory and producing excellent science is exacting enough in normal times but with the disruption of the moves to the new Laboratory together with DTI's onerous rebid requirements, our staff remained engaged and committed to the wellbeing and continuing success of NPL. There had been three and a half years of Contract extensions and, as we were not party to the content of the ITN, our staff were, out of necessity, completely in the dark about their future personal situation but reassured, to an extent, by DTI's commitment to NPL and the construction of the new Laboratory.

DTI's Invitation to Negotiate (ITN)

The success of the GOCO business model in operating NPL made DTI's decision to tender for another term Contract relatively straight forward. DTI would continue to maintain ultimate control over the operation of NPL although a PFI contract for maintaining and servicing NPL's buildings would now be in place. Having followed the European Union's procurement rules, 5 contractors were selected to bid for the Contract; Serco with SIRA; W S Atkins; QinetiQ; Scientific Generics and Babcock. Rather than adhering to the strict tendering rules of an ITT with no opportunity for bidders to negotiate terms individually, DTI chose to issue an ITN. This streamlined the bidding process and enabled dialogue between DTI and the contractors. It also acknowledged that Serco, as the incumbent, had greater operating experience and this was another mechanism to reassure bidders that there would be a level playing field.

DTI's requirements in the ITN followed much the same lines as the original 1995 ITT. Excellent science remained at the heart of the NSC together with maintaining NPL's international influence and standing. The refreshed NMS Review set the future science agenda and completion of the new Laboratory would present significant new opportunities for enhancing NPL's science outputs and growing its business. DTI would be looking closely at bidders' proposals to see how they would take advantage of operating in this new, state-of-the-art Laboratory. There was inevitably an emphasis on commercial sales growth over the period.

Having proved the robustness of the GOCO business model, the NSC was to be for a term of 10 years with the possibility of a 5-year extension subject to mutual agreement to be flagged within 2 years of the Contract end date. As feared, the pricing mechanism for the NSC was changed. This made the financial element of the bid criteria transparent but in terms of clarity of the real costs of DTI programmes and subsequent monitoring it was useless and required a parallel set of costing schedules to be maintained.

The actual pricing mechanism comprised a single day rate for all DTI's research programmes irrespective of technical area, including every grade of scientist and all associated direct programme costs. The contractor was then asked to estimate the retail prices index excluding mortgage payments (RPIX) for the 10 year period and apply an additional inflation factor which could be a *plus or a minus*. DTI guaranteed a 'minimum research commitment' (MRC) of 56,500 scientist days each year. In the first year, for example, if the contractor's day rate was £670 then DTI's MRC would be £37,855,000. In year 2, the RPI inflation rate together with the adjustment factor would then be applied. Because of the ongoing building works and disruption to business continuity, DTI undertook to maintain this MRC but only until the new Laboratory had reached a level of completion known as the 'Planning Commitment'. It would then be entitled to reduce the MRC by up to a cumulative 5% each year. This was to reflect the need for greater productivity and the generation of more commercial sales income once the new building was fully operational. Rather than reducing the funding commitment, it would have been more advantageous for DTI to plough these savings back into NPL in the form of increased science outputs but there was a value for money requirement for Treasury to be fulfilled. In effect, the Planning Commitment took longer to exercise than expected and so funding remained available for DTI to pass on to NPLML until budgets ran out.

Apart from ease of assessing the bidders' financial proposals, the new pricing mechanism had little to recommend it. From an operating perspective, it was a simple way to invoice DTI each month for the number of scientist days worked but bore no relationship to the actual cost of individual research programmes. Those with high levels of direct costs or requiring the use of NPL's most senior scientists would be significantly undervalued whilst those with low levels of direct cost and using junior scientists would be overvalued. The mechanism necessitated the production of separate schedules to show the real cost of the research programmes but the fact remained that the headline cash DTI paid for the work was the value that was most evident to DTI's science community and advisory groups who remained mystified by the prices invoiced for the programmes of work. It did nothing to demonstrate the excellent value for money offered by the NSC. Furthermore, this mechanism was a potential disincentive for the contractor to improve the quality and scope of the science, as neither the premium for employing additional senior staff nor the incremental subcontracted cost of a greater level of collaborations would be reflected in the price paid through the single day rate.

From a procurement perspective this appeared to be an elegant pricing methodology but, in my opinion, was a retrograde step with unforeseen consequences. With some timely input from NPL these pricing issues could have easily been resolved. As a fundamental part of the NSC, it was not possible to change and would take several years of discussion before agreeing an acceptable modification to our modus operandi with DTI. The inflexibility it introduced to the Contract probably contributed to the decision not to extend the NSC after 10 years.

Serco's Proposal for a New Science Contract for Research and Development Services

Being part of the NPLML executive team during this period meant that I could take no part in the Serco rebid but I summarise its contents below.

In some respects the commercial proposal was more straight-forward than the original bid. The data room contained all the latest management and statutory accounts together with financial forecasts. They had been prepared on a consistent historic cost accounting basis for 8 years.

The major challenge in the rebid would be the 10 to 15-year timescale of the Contract and setting out a package of attractive and deliverable proposals both scientific and operational, taking full advantage of DTI's investment in the new Laboratory. The potential reduction in DTI's research programme funding by the cumulative 5% each year following completion of the PFI building made commercial sales growth an imperative.

Although Serco's track record in operating the Laboratory had been impressive and plain for all to see, this rebid would be all about the future of NPL and there was no room for complacency. Serco's proposal had to demonstrate how the pace of change at NPL would be maintained while always giving priority to DTI and the NMS. It had 4 key objectives:

Improving the Quality of Science
Serco's proposal put forward an ambitious long-term vision with DTI of generating high quality science not only within existing fields of expertise and demand but also new areas vital for the future of the UK. The strategic challenge for NPL and DTI was one of choice within a limited budget, moving focus away from standards that addressed past needs to this new science and technology. To aid these discussions Serco had developed a 'roadmap' for discussion with DTI.

Science leadership would be strengthened under a Director of Science with accountability for quality, the alignment of science planning with the NMS strategy and formation of key alliances at national and international levels. The Director of Science would also act as the 'head of profession' for all scientific staff at NPL and, together with a new post of Chief Scientific Advisor, would lead the enhancement of NPL's capability through the development of its people. Accelerating the move to new areas of science would entail extending the scope of collaborations and partnerships to secure gearing on funds from DTI and NPL's own Strategic Research Programme.

NPLML would also invest £50M in new equipment and support DTI in the establishment of an Advanced Metrology Laboratory which was part of their longer term strategy.

Maintain NPL's International Status
NPL's status as one of the three world-leading National Measurement Institutes was of paramount importance. It would be accomplished by protecting and developing the independent NPL brand, building on a platform of scientific excellence and playing an integral part in the process of international devolution. NPL would also be taking the Chair of EUROMET, a European collaboration in measurement standards.

Extend the economic and social impact of metrology
A 'measurement impact' team would be created to track industry requirements and establish a foresight process to anticipate the needs of emerging technologies. To accelerate knowledge transfer Serco would also

promote a new NPL 'kite-mark' called Technology Applied and set up partnerships with Regional Development Agencies (RDAs).

Deliver Value for Money

Applying its private sector management skills and building on the strategic platform created over the previous 8 years, Serco would reduce costs to DTI by an overall 12% achieved through cutting overheads by 30%, growing third party revenues by 150% to £27M by 2013/14 and improving scientist utilisation by 8%.

The Commercial Offer – Key Features of Serco's Proposals

Serco's financial proposals were based on the same principles and methodology that it applied in 1995 and that underpinned every Serco contract. These were: value for money – based on improvement through change and good management practice, but never losing sight of the need to deliver the customer's mission; credibility – building programmes upon robust financial assumptions and professional risk management; transparency – by provision of open book accounting to the customer (and in NPLML's case, much more) and therefore, no surprises; willingness to accept risk – recognising that this is a primary driver for Government outsourcing and a central tenet of Serco's business.

In compliance with the ITN a single day rate of £680 was submitted together with an inflation adjustment factor giving a composite RPI rate of 2.15%. (The Government's target for the Bank of England at this time was an inflation rate 2.5%). It delivered an overall 12% saving to DTI, equivalent to £5.4M in year 1, achieved through significant growth in sales turnover and further cost reductions. The third party revenue growth amounted to 9% compound over the ten year period and would require substantial investment in the sales and marketing team. The cost reductions came from the restructuring of NPL's Scientific Centres into 3 Directorates and further reductions in support staff as a result of operating in the new PFI building and efficiencies brought about by the continuing development of the new Oracle business information system. Investment in capital expenditure was forecast to amount to £5M p.a. and financed through the new DTI approved leasing arrangement which had the advantage of matching more closely the profile of NPLML's revenues. The same profit sharing threshold of 5% return on sales shared equally between NPLML and DTI was proposed.

The forecast Balance Sheet as at the 31st March 2004 was available from the data room and could be used as the baseline for the next 10 years. In the first year there would be a significant outflow of cash of £5M to deliver the change programme that would lay the foundation for a successful second term Contract.

Charges for the new building and FM services (PFI Contract) would be considerably higher with the rental payable monthly in advance. Restructuring (transition) costs amounted to £4M in the first year. They were amortised over the 10 years of the Contract and recovered through the day rate in response to DTI's wish to avoid front end loaded expenditure but the cash-flow would nearly all be in the early stages of the first year. Investment in the considerable sales growth plan was estimated to cost in the region of £1M p.a. and covered a substantial reorganisation of the sales and marketing function.

New Science Contract – Bid Variants

As well as a compliant baseline bid, DTI were also open to considering additional proposals. Serco made a number of value enhancing variant proposals to DTI. The first two variants offered 15-year contracts which would provide DTI with the basis of a longer term strategic partnership without the distraction of a rebid in year 10 and with a guaranteed price for a 15-year term. The full 15-year proposal had an increased business risk especially over the later years and carried a higher cost reflected in a less favourable inflation adjustment factor element of the price. The other had a 'break clause' after 10 years. This innovative variant contained the same price as the baseline bid and therefore represented better value for DTI but required both parties to consent to contract extension after 10 years. Both these 15-year proposals were influenced by Serco's Atomic Weapons Establishment bid which was extended from 10 to 25 years for reasons of capability enhancement rather than budget reduction.

Another variant proposed that the small NPL defined benefit pension scheme be merged with the much larger but similar Serco scheme to benefit from economies of scale. This would generate long term savings for NPLML so the inflation adjustment factor could be improved. A further 2 variants involved some cash contribution from DTI. During year 1 of the NSC, Serco would incur transition (restructuring) costs of £4M recovered by an increased price over the 10 year Contract period. DTI was given the option of reimbursing this cost directly in year 1 so that the day rate could be reduced as well as improving the inflation adjustment factor. It was estimated that the NPLML Pension Scheme would have a small deficit at the beginning of the NSC. Serco offered to share any gains made as a result of savings if DTI were able to remove this deficit from the NPLML pension scheme. The reorganisation process for redundancies involved a consultation period with staff of 3 months. Savings had been offered in the baseline bid if this could start 3 months earlier at the beginning of January instead of the Contract commencement date of April 2004 and included as a variant in case this was not acceptable to DTI.

Serco was keen to support DTI in the expansion of the Teddington site and one opportunity proposed was for the establishment of an 'Innovation Centre'. On the basis that DTI wished to proceed with the funding for such a proposal, Serco confirmed that their day rate and inflation adjustment factor would remain identical to their baseline bid.

The Bid Refinement

The bid proposals were submitted to DTI in July 2003 and down-selected to two contractors – Serco and QinetiQ. I understand that there was next to nothing to differentiate the two bids so the DTI instigated a 'best and final' bid refinement stage to the process. The data room was updated with the very latest financial information including the phase II pay award (salary rate adjustments for scientists) agreed with DTI mentioned earlier in this chapter so the final 2 bidders were asked to take into account DTI's comments during the final round of negotiations and look once more at their prices and submit a refined bid.

Serco's Refined Bid
Three pricing elements actually increased the original day rate. To take account of DTI's concerns at the level of sales in year 1 together with market conditions and the latest forecast revenue performance of NPLML for 2003/04, prices were reduced for third party revenue across the board by 4% (but not volumes of work). The additional phase II salary increases also had to be reflected as well as reversing the start date assumption for the staff consultation period for redundancies (back to 1st April 2004) as this was not accepted by DTI.

To reduce costs (and the day rate) Serco had to effectively take on more risk. They reduced their salary inflation assumption to 1.5% above RPI and their contribution rate to the NPLML Pension Scheme. In addition, electricity consumption estimates (for the new building) were reduced and equipment lease costs restated.

The net result was an overall fall in the day rate by £10 and an improvement in the inflation factor adjustment to *minus* 0.98%. The DTI single tender revenue line in the 10 year business forecast was accordingly reduced to reflect the saving. These refinements then had to be fed through into all the 7 bid variants and the final submission was made in November 2003.

It still seemed that there was little to choose between the 2 bids. This was certainly Serco's 'Waterloo' and it was a near run thing. In the end I believe it inevitably came down to the price and the final reductions offered by Serco won them the NSC for 10 further years.

Just before we leave the first Term Contract and extensions perhaps it is timely to look back at some of NPL's Highlights 1995-2004.

Some of NPL's Highlights 1995 – 2004

1998

Work starts on NPL's new laboratory

In 1998, the foundations are laid for the world's largest and most sophisticated measurement facility. Almost 100 years of sporadic growth and demolitions have resulted in a mixture of buildings spread over much of NPL's existing 82-acre site. The new scheme was an opportunity to consolidate the laboratory and provide more up-to-date, efficient facilities whilst greatly improving the setting of the laboratory.

2000

NPL starts biotechnology research

Responding to the changing demands on measurement, NPL opens a new biotechnology laboratory to support measurement challenges experienced in the biomedical and pharmaceutical industries.

2000

Europe's largest underwater Acoustics Pressure Vessel arrives at NPL

A facility of strategic importance at the National Physical Laboratory provides vital measurements demanded by manufacturers and designers of sonar equipment used in the oil and gas, oceanographic and defence industries. The facility also strengthens fields as diverse as the identification of fish stocks, seismic measurements and the location of buried artefacts under the seabed.

The purpose-built unit is the only such commercially available testing facility in Europe. It can simulate sea conditions at depths of up to 700 m and at temperatures of between 2 °C and 35 °C. Previously, trials and acceptance tests had to be undertaken in the USA or involved expensive sea trials.

2002

NPL helps Formula 1 racing

NPL provides materials expertise to the Federation Internationale de L'Automobile (FIA) to ensure teams respect the rules of F1 racing without compromising the safety and competitiveness of the sport.

2004

New method for measuring time developed

NPL announces results for a new technique to measure time using optical frequency, which could provide a ten-fold improvement in time measurement accuracy.

The technique involves freezing a single strontium atom to about -273 °C by bombarding it with billions of tiny packages of light. The atom then moves precisely between two energy states, like the ticking of a clock. A laser beam is then locked onto this 'ticking', which provides an optical frequency that can be measured.

Chapter 5 - 'A Game of Two Halves'

Securing the 10-year NPL Science Contract had been hard fought. Serco's proposal included substantial restructuring and reorganisation of the Laboratory. The bid refinement process had forced down the pricing of the day rate for DTI's research programmes by a further £10 to £670 for a Minimum Research Commitment of 56,500 days.

For me, it felt nothing like the original 1995 bid. I had not been involved in putting together the commercial offer and all of us in NPL's executive and management team would have to spend time understanding and interpreting the contents of Serco's proposal. We did have the benefit of David Richardson's return from the bid team with his detailed knowledge of the proposal. He took up his old role as Marketing and Communications Director and his Board appointment again. During the rebid process, Dr Bob McGuiness had also been allowed special dispensation to 'straddle' NPLML and Serco so that he could continue to perform his duties for both organisations. Obviously he was precluded from divulging any intelligence gained to either party but now it was possible for him to reveal his thoughts about the bid and his vision of the future.

It was agreed within Serco that the bid proposal would be more effectively implemented by NPLML's existing executive team with reach-back for additional resources as and when required. However, they would be monitoring our progress very closely to ensure close adherence to the proposal and delivery of the promised change programme and efficiencies both for DTI and within NPL. After careful examination of Serco's proposal it was clear that the level of savings could be achieved but with some relatively minor adjustments. Any changes, however, had to be clearly justified and signed off in blood!

So why was it a 'game of two halves'? After the initial period of understanding and implementing Serco's bid proposal there were a few years of reasonably 'calm waters' only disrupted by the on-going completion of the new Laboratory building works. NPLML's relationship with DTI remained positive despite the termination of the PFI contract in 2004 (see later). Our scientific and business performance steadily improved in line with and in some areas exceeding Serco's bid expectations. The early years helped create the foundations of a financially strong and resilient Company better prepared to meet the future whatever it may bring.

But it was the calm before the storm. What was to happen between 2007 – 2009 shook the world to its very core – the global banking crisis. In the second half of our Contract, the ensuing economic turmoil, recession and Government austerity programmes were to test NPLML, DTI and Serco. In March 2007, DTI was reorganised and became the Department of Innovation, Universities and Skills (DIUS). Like all other Government Departments they would be subject to even deeper cuts to their budgets. All but 'front line' services in health and education were affected. Serco did not escape unscathed either since the majority of its contracts were in the global public sector. Because of its relative financial strength and the underpinning NSC, NPLML was able to weather the storm better than many but the economic and political landscape would be changed forever.

For NPL there were 4 significant challenges. Apart from the NMS Contract funding cuts and economic recession affecting our commercial sales, energy consumption within the new Laboratory proved to be far greater than estimated and much more difficult to control, but one of the most intractable problems would be funding the increasing deficit within the defined benefit pension scheme following the market crash. Thoughts turned from growth and prosperity to a more defensive outlook and even purely survival.

The New Science Contract (NSC) – Synopsis

There were a few key areas in which the NSC was updated from the original Term Contract. The facilities management agreement under the PFI contract with DTI had to be incorporated in the NSC as well as the Schedule of Leased Assets which now consolidated this arrangement as the accepted process for procuring NPL's scientific equipment. The largest change was to the pricing and billing mechanisms which would eventually be modified to everyone's benefit.

Once again, Serco was entrusted with the management and enhancement of NPL, a critical (inter)national asset, still **G**overnment **O**wned and **C**ontractor **O**perated. NPLML continued to be the operating company which remained a wholly owned subsidiary of Serco with a partnering agreement with Sira.

Operational Requirements

NPLML was required to operate *'in a manner as in the opinion of the DTI is best calculated to maintain and enhance the image, reputation and position of the Laboratory as a world centre of excellence'* ... *'in the fields of measurement science, materials metrology and related standards'*.

It could not do any work for third parties *'that is likely to impair the image, reputation, or position of either the laboratory or the DTI'*. We were permitted to use the NPL name but had to look after it, recognising it had *'substantial reputation and goodwill'*. We were required to *'develop, maintain, protect, repair and replace the Laboratory assets ... in order to maintain the laboratory's status as a world centre of excellence'* and *'exercise all reasonable endeavours to maintain an international presence'*.

Capability

Underpinning nature of measurement science requires that we maintain a very broad capability including (not a comprehensive list!):

- Acoustics
- Advanced Materials
- Air Quality
- Biometrics
- Biotechnology
- Corrosion
- Dimensional metrology
- Environmental measurement
- Lasers
- Mass and force
- Micro/Nanometrology
- Neutron measurements
- Photonics
- Photometry/Colour
- Pressure
- RF/Microwaves
- Radiation Dosimetry
- Radioactivity
- Radiometry
- Scientific Software
- Sensory metrology
- Statistics
- Surface analysis
- Thermal measurements
- Time & Frequency
- Electrical Standards

Constraints

There were 2 potential sales and income areas that we were not permitted to market. We could not *'actively pursue or solicit custom for calibration services of a kind which are offered as standard services by UKAS accredited laboratories'* and were required to devolve to them any 'routine' services. We were also barred from bidding directly into the Government's main research budget held by the Research Councils. In addition, work for third parties could not be allowed to *'impede or be likely to impede the proper performance by the Contractor of its obligations to provide services to the DTI'*

Features of NPL contract

Delivering four outcomes

Excellent science World-class metrology	Real & demonstrable impact on Economy & QoL
(Inter)national status and influence	Growing and sustainable business

Enduring capability and national asset

NPL's independence and integrity had to be retained as *'it is of utmost importance to the DTI and a fundamental condition to this agreement that conflicts of interest should not be allowed to arise'*. We had to *'take all necessary steps to avoid such conflicts'*. Any contracts or agreements with Serco had to be arranged *'on fair and reasonable arm's length terms'*.

We also repeated our original bid commitment that *'if there was a conflict between maximising impact of our knowledge, and commercial benefit, we will always choose the former'*.

Governance and Quality Assurance

The same regime of governance and quality assurance was incorporated in the NSC. NPL's contractual performance was monitored through a comprehensive annual review. The report included all aspects of NPL's science and business. Research programmes were supervised by DTI staff and external working groups. An Advisory Group comprised of Fellows of the Royal Society and the Royal Academy of Engineering continued to inspect the quality of our science 4 times a year. NPL maintained its certification to ISO 9001 and accreditation by UKAS. NPLML's Annual Report and Financial Statements were externally audited and published together with an independent certified profit statement and internal control review produced exclusively for DTI.

Maintenance of an 'Independent Entity'

The NSC covered in great detail, the instances that might arise and procedures to be adopted if or when the NSC was to be terminated. In general, however, there were some key obligations to which Serco had to adhere.

Serco had to return to DTI: a going concern, a fully functioning independent entity with its knowledge, people, experience, scientific assets, systems and processes. Hence, we could not strip out capability, business or support functions, for example HR and finance, without the express approval of DTI. All transactions between NPLML and Serco had to be on an arm's length commercial basis and we could not and, of course, would not 'export' profit margin.

At this time we did not imagine that NPL would go back 'in house' at the end of the NSC. Nevertheless, we were particularly aware of these terms and were at pains to remind Serco of them when, quite understandably, recommendations of further integration of support functions arose from time to time to improve margin.

The New Board and Executive Team

The NPLML Board

The role of the Board was to ensure that the strategy and direction taken by NPL enabled the organisation to realise its vision and that the Company fulfilled the requirements of corporate governance.

One of Serco's first actions was the appointment of an NPLML Board of Directors drawn from the management team at NPL, senior directors from Serco Group and Non-Executive Directors from academia and industry. During the period of the first Contract extensions and rebid a greater industry focus had been brought to the Board with the appointment of Sir Peter Williams, former Chair of Oxford Instruments, as Non-Executive

Chair and Prof Richard Brook, President of Sira, as a Non-Executive Director.

The new Board was:
Sir Peter Williams FRS (Chair, non-executive)
Dr Bob McGuiness (Managing Director, NPLML)
David Richardson (Marketing Director, NPLML)
Alan Mann (Finance and Support Services Director, NPLML)
Dr Seton Bennett (International Director, NPLML)
Prof Richard Brook (non-executive)
Dr Clive Marsh (non-executive)
Dr John Rae (non-executive)

In addition, Serco, as part of its commitment to continue to improve the quality of science, also appointed Prof (later Sir) Peter Knight FRS from Imperial College, as NPL's Chief Scientific Advisor and with rights to attend NPLML Board meetings.

A place on the NPLML Board was again offered to DTI and once again refused. A representative of DTI did however agree to attend meetings after the conclusion of business to meet the Board members and discuss any issues face to face.

A full list of NPLML's Managing Directors and the dates of their tenure can be found in Appendix A.

The Executive Management Team

The NPL Executive (NPLX) was the decision-making team responsible for delivering the mission of NPL. Its organisational structure was changed to reflect Serco's bid strategy for NPL and improve the delivery of DTI's NMS Research Programmes.

The new NPLX brought together the 3 new Science Directorates, the key functions of Finance, Marketing and Human Resources, and strategic Science and International areas under the Managing Director.

The Finance Director was now also responsible for other Support Functions and had 3 direct reports – a Financial Controller, Head of IT and Head of Support Services covering commercial contracts, procurement, the engineering workshop, library, printing and graphic design, and building services.

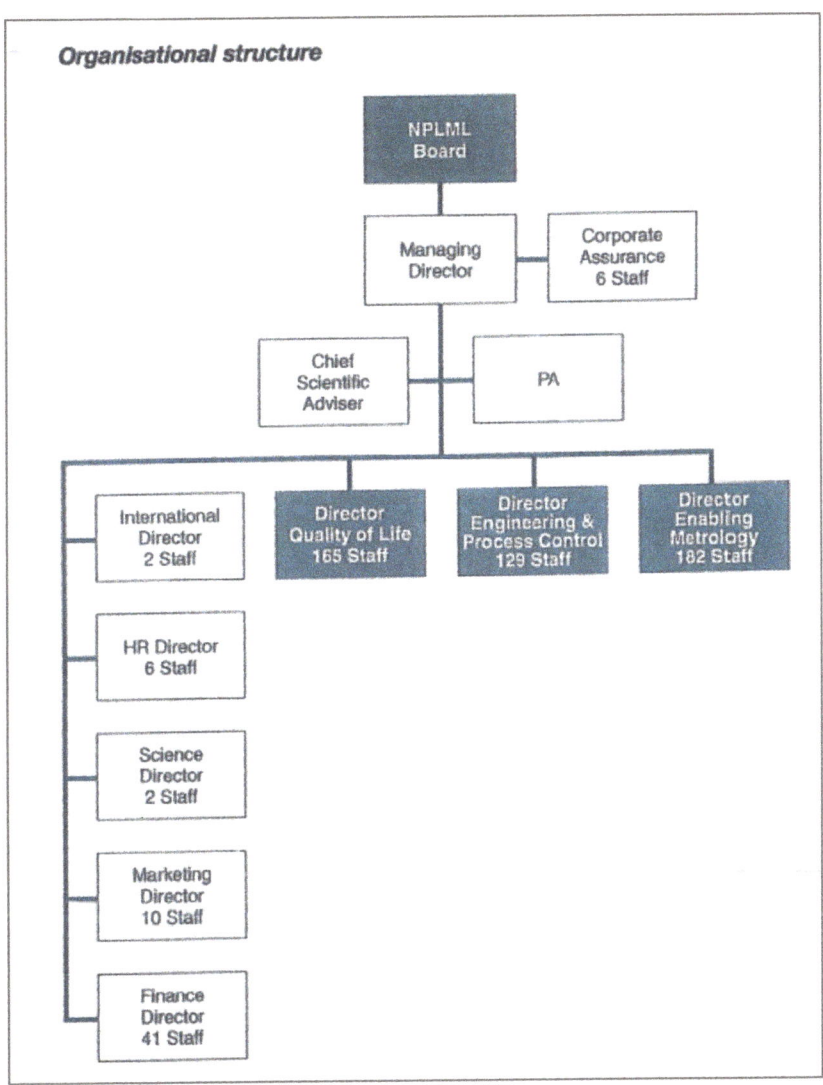

This new structure enabled NPLX to balance science and operational drivers more effectively and improve decision implementation and communication throughout the whole business. It was a real improvement which was to be further enhanced with reorganisations in 2007/08 by Steve McQuillan and in 2009/10 by Dr Brian Bowsher.

The Termination of the PFI Contract – 2004

The PFI project had been suffering considerable construction delays for a number of years due to difficulties in achieving the specification of some of the laboratories within the building. In December 2004, DTI and Laser finally agreed to terminate the PFI for the new Laboratory due to non-performance of the contract. Laser's shareholders had divided the main contract between John Laing who was responsible for a fixed price contract for the design and build of the new facilities, and Serco who would manage them when completed.

The high specification of some of the laboratory spaces proved to be an intractable problem for John Laing. By July 2004 Laser recognised that it could no longer complete the project and John Laing was also slipping into serious financial difficulties. DTI therefore agreed effectively to 'buy out' the PFI contract. It paid Laser £75M for its interest in the new buildings and took over responsibility for completing some outstanding works. John Laing suffered severe financial losses on their part of the PFI contract from which they never recovered. Serco continued to manage the new facilities at NPL but this remaining part of the contract would be competitively tendered again when the new build and retrofitting of NPL had been completed.

As the PFI project had been deteriorating DTI had been forming an in-house building management team and retaining a number of expert consultants. From an NPL operational point of view it now meant that we, and particularly our scientists, could communicate with DTI on the new building and help expedite its completion. We could also make reasonable modifications to the specifications of laboratories where particular 'control' problems had been encountered while still ensuring that our fundamental scientific requirements were met without too much compromise.

In 2007 Serco lost the Facilities Management (FM) contract to another bidder. It seemed to me that the successful company had submitted an unrealistically low bid which it then subsequently struggled to deliver to the required standard. The NSC was amended to take account of the termination of the PFI and the reversion of ownership of the buildings to DTI (then DIUS). Although NPLML did have some input into the level of services required under the FM contract it was let and managed by DIUS.

The NSC therefore also had to include a Schedule of their obligations to NPLML and service level agreements. It would have been advantageous for us to have managed the FM contract directly but our approaches requesting this operational simplification were always refused. This contractual 'triangle' was eventually rectified but not until NPLML had returned to Government ownership in 2015.

The new Laboratory was not officially opened until 'World Metrology Day' in May 2008.

Delivering the New Science Contract

The New Organisation

Serco introduced a fundamental change in NPL's organisation structure by reducing the 6 Scientific Centres to 3 new clearly defined and outwardly focused Science Directorates each addressing a core cluster of technologies, a discrete set of business sectors and a key policy outcome of the NMS. They were the Engineering and Process Control Directorate, Enabling Metrology Directorate and Quality of Life Directorate. The realignment of the science teams and change of roles and responsibilities reduced the number of 'project management' roles within jobs by 80%, increasing productivity and time to spend on science outputs.

A new Marketing Directorate was tasked with delivering third party sales that reinforced the NMS mission and met the growth requirements of the bid.

Finally support functions were rationalised and the existing structures were consolidated and simplified, releasing savings from the new organisation structure and from operating in the new building.

Serco and NPLML had established good rapport with Prospect, NPL's trade union, over the previous 9 years of operation and they were fully consulted over our restructuring plans. The development of clear role profiles across the whole of NPL during the rebid period facilitated the selection process for redundancies and enabled us to produce a tight and efficient structure for the Laboratory. The redundancies, involving both scientific and support roles, were dealt with respectfully and professionally and our HR Director was commended by Prospect on the way the whole process had been handled. Whenever possible employees were redeployed into vacant posts in the new structure and voluntary redundancy arrangements were agreed where appropriate. Of course, those staff members who were originally civil servants retained their entitlement to enhanced benefits.

Serco's organisation plan was closely adhered to, with just a handful of changes being agreed but only where they had a beneficial impact on our delivery of science. For example, a building services manager had not been included in Serco's proposal but, as the new Laboratory was still some way from completion, it was vital for us to maintain this role to act as interface between the scientists, DTI and their contractors.

Financial Drivers and Initial Impact
As noted in the previous chapter the NSC guaranteed a Minimum Research Commitment (MRC) of a 'designated' number of programme days (56,500) each year at the day rate tendered (£670), inflated by RPIX but deflated by Serco's adjustment factor (0.98%) which served as a pseudo-efficiency target. The number of designated days broadly reflected levels of activity in the previous Term Contract. Any improvement in performance would therefore have to come directly from further operating efficiencies or profitable sales growth. As in the first Contract, DTI also funded additional competitively tendered (non-designated) work and as we had established a reputation for delivering high quality outputs, a growing proportion of this work was placed with NPL. Although not always recognised, this additional budget was a powerful incentive to maintain the highest levels of overall service and value. During the first half of the NSC it amounted to between £6 - £8M p.a. but would reduce significantly year on year from 2009 as a result of the Government's austerity programme.

NPL continued to be fully involved in the formulation of designated programme work. The NSC again required NPL to invest £1.5M p.a. (RPI indexed) in its own Strategic Research Programme and £400k p.a. (RPI indexed) in a General Activities (Outreach) Programme.

As the new Laboratory progressed to full operation the running costs of NPL had increased considerably. These additional costs for property rent, rates, facilities management services, utilities and insurance were all recovered through the scientist day rate. The principle still prevailed that the contractor should pay the 'full economic cost' for the Laboratory to avoid charges of unfair competition and 'state aids'. As such, our rent increased to £5.6M p.a. payable monthly in advance and subject to an annual inflator of RPIX. The facilities management services were delivered by Serco (now as part of Laser) with an annual baseline fee of £2.97M. These were charged monthly in arrears and inflated annually by RPIX plus 1% as these services were more people intensive and wage inflation was running higher than general inflation at that time.

NPLML continued to take the revenue risk of non-designated and third party work as well as the inflationary costs of staffing, pensions, direct project costs and all other business expenditure. Technology Transfer and Innovation Ltd. (TTI) had also been spun out from NPLML before the NSC was granted leaving a 'gap' of about £3M p.a. in turnover to be recovered.

Finally, NPLML's business information, accounts and systems remained accessible and available to DTI as they had been since 1995. Serco continued to take a 2% management fee and profits of up to 5% return on sales turnover after which they were shared on a 50:50 basis.

Unlike the original Term Contract the profit share arrangements were not based on cumulative actuals and forecasts of turnover and profit over the duration of the Contract but were calculated on an individual year basis. While the operation of the business was in 'steady state' there was no issue. However, if substantial costs were incurred restructuring the business in one year with resulting benefits increasing profits in the future, NPLML could 'pay' twice – once for incurring the costs of change and again when sharing the increased profits in subsequent years. DTI recognised that in normal circumstances costs of reorganisation would be financed from future benefits and this profit sharing mechanism would be a disincentive to performance improvement. When such a reorganisation was proposed in 2007 we worked closely with DTI to agree an amendment to the NSC and effectively moved back to a cumulative arrangement that had served us so well under the original Term Contract!

The NSC 'Step-Change' in Revenue and Cost Baseline
In the original Term Contract NPLML's sales turnover in the 2003/04 statutory accounts had amounted to £49.1M. The increasing accommodation costs had been temporarily capped during the construction of the new Laboratory buildings. In the NSC, the total cost of the new buildings had to be fully recovered through the single scientist day rate in Serco's bid proposal. This caused a 'step change' in the costs charged to

NPL and recovered from DTI with a resulting increase in turnover to £58.3M in the 2004/05 statutory accounts.

DTI's guaranteed single tender spend on NMS Research Programmes in the original Term Contract was around £31M in the period before the NSC and rose to £39M (the MRC plus some residual contract commitments) in 2004/05 primarily to cover the build and running costs of the new Laboratory noted above. Of course, DTI made substantial annual savings in maintenance costs of NPL's old, now demolished, building stock. However, during the bidding process, these significant increases certainly focused attention on maximising the operational benefits of the new Laboratory and growing new streams of business revenue.

Interestingly, the profit before tax in these two years was almost identical at £2.4M and £2.3M respectively so Serco's bid and NPLML's management teams must have been doing something right! Restructuring and reorganisation costs came in under the estimated £4M and were spread equally over the 10 years of the NSC so as to lessen the impact on profit in the first year.

However, NPLML still had to manage the 0.98% annual deflator on designated NMS programmes which meant that efficiency savings of £0.4M p.a., equating to a cumulative £18M over the 10 years of the NSC (even more in real terms after inflation) or the equivalent profit margin on additional sales, had to be generated. The mechanism certainly achieved the objective of maintaining downward pressure on costs throughout the Contract. Given NPL's enormous positive impact on the UK's economy it is perhaps regrettable that improved performance could not have been rewarded with additional funding for science rather than below inflation pricing of NMS work. The savings from the 0.98% annual deflator might have been better used to accelerate our research in key areas or augment the Strategic Research programme, for example. Just think what additional positive social and economic impact to the UK our metrology might have generated over the 10 years of the Contract!

Continuing Support for the GOCO Model

The benefits of the GOCO business model for NPL remained attractive to Government at this time and there were distinct additional advantages for DTI/DIUS.

The 10-year Contract meant that Government had made a long-term commitment to funding NPL and the NMS. This was further reinforced by the building of the new state-of-the-art Laboratory for NPL. The official opening in 2008 was attended by many notable representatives from Government, academia and industry including past Laboratory Directors from 1990 and the UK Government Chief Scientific Advisor, Sir John Beddington.

Left to Right: Steve McQuillan, Dr Bob McGuiness, Sir John Beddington, Dr John Rae, Dr Peter Clapham

The uncertainty and annuality of government spending had been removed and there was transparency of a consistent level of funding year on year albeit with the possibility of prescribed reductions. The NSC enabled DTI to defend the budget for NPL when others were under annual pressure. It enabled NPLML to plan more strategically and gain DTI support for longer-term business investments as the financial 'payback' could be spread over several more years into the future.

NPLML was now an established company with many years' track record. The NSC with its Minimum Research Commitment together with the commercial freedoms of a private company gave it a level of security and stability that was the envy of other National Laboratories. The organisation had been placed on a sound commercial footing adopting the concept of continual improvement and 'best practice' in all aspects of its operation. With the support of DTI it had invested strongly in new business information systems bringing greater levels of management control and efficiency to the organisation with our goods and services being more competitive in the market place. NPL's overhead costs were spread over a far broader and growing revenue base offering far better value for money to DTI.

As a private limited company, NPLML had adopted UK GAAP (Generally Accepted Accounting Practice) which covered not only accounting but also law and tax. As such it could take advantage of tax allowances and incentives available for investment in scientific equipment and applied research. It meant that more cash was available for investing in growth and funding increasing costs, in particular, the NPLML pension scheme which, from 2008 onwards, was costing more than £2M p.a. over that estimated by the actuary during the bidding process for the NSC.

In 2006, with the agreement of DTI, NPLML changed its accounting reference date from 31st March to the 31st December which was co-terminus with its parent, Serco Group. Having a different financial year-end from Government was advantageous to both NPLML and DTI as it allowed the high work-loads at this time to be spread over two quarters and facilitated better financial forecasting particularly for cash outturns over these crucial periods.

Revenue growth was an imperative of the NSC. The status of many government bodies precluded them from expenditure on selling or marketing and forming business collaborations and strategic alliances. NPL was able to take advantage of all these for the benefit of government and DTI. NPLML had a dedicated sales and marketing resource with a clear remit to expand business in areas aligned to the NMS and NPL was free to work closely with other strategically important businesses and organisations.

Through our parent, Serco, and NPLML's classification as a private company, we had access to additional sources of funding and financing options not available to government departments. We were able to benefit from Serco's close relationships with banks to source the very best financing arrangements for NPL's scientific equipment. Following the 'sale and leaseback' initiative the cost of NPL's assets were fully subsumed into the pricing of the NSC. This removed the need for DTI (or NPLML) to have cash available for the purchase. Investment in NPL's scientific equipment was therefore no longer dependent on DTI's capital budgets and expenditure could be maintained at levels consistent with the requirements of the Laboratory. NPL's asset base was much more rigorously managed through the Capital Review Group who ensured that purchases were closely aligned to the Laboratory's strategic requirements and new programmes of research. As a result scientific equipment had much higher levels of utilisation. We were also able to access grant funding that would have been unavailable to DTI, for example, from the Technology Strategy Board (TSB) [now Innovate UK]. The potential for additional funding or financing through Serco was always available to DTI.

One of the greatest benefits for NPL was the flexibility we had in attracting, recruiting and retaining scientific talent to work at the Laboratory. There were no civil service constraints on remuneration and we were able to negotiate financial packages to recruit best in class. We could engage students, post doctorates and arrange secondments on a mutually agreeable and flexible basis.

High performance could be incentivised whether for science or business and we were keen to reward and recognise individual achievement and celebrate success. Over time we were able to build clear staff succession plans and a pipeline of talent. Scientists now had credible career paths and personal development targets. Over the years, our recruitment policy had gradually evolved and by the time the organisation had been restructured at the end of 2004 we had reduced our recruitment of permanent staff to about a 50:50 split with fixed term contracts. This was much more in line with universities and other research organisations, reflecting both the cutting-edge science and the project nature of our work.

First-Half Contract Performance (2004 to 2009)

The first half of the NSC was challenging but significant progress was made on several fronts thanks to a number of key factors. The continuing strong and supportive partnership with DTI/DIUS was crucial to the long term development and success of NPL and the new Laboratory. The improvements and foresight brought about by Serco's rebid proposals created sound foundations on which to deliver NPL's scientific and business strategies. The 10-year NSC together with the new Laboratory buildings reassured employees of Government's commitment to NPL. Staff were broadly enthusiastic and supportive about their new working environment and our plans for the future. Relative economic stability until 2008 helped us to take full advantage of our increased investment in marketing and sales resources.

At the beginning of 2005, Dr Bob McGuiness resigned as Managing Director having steered us successfully through the NPL rebid.

Dr Bob McGuiness' portrait hanging in Bushy House

As part of our emphasis on supporting industry and growing non-NMS third party turnover, Stephen McQuillan gained DTI approval and was appointed his successor. He had immense business experience within the high tech sector as MD of Oxford Instruments for more than 6 years. The Serco bid proposal had given us a new mantra, *'Science with Impact'*, where NPL exists to deliver benefit to the UK economy and Quality of Life. Stephen McQuillan's appointment would be a boost to the more entrepreneurial culture that was beginning to produce real results in both our commercial and scientific performance. In fact, an internal report by

DTI estimated that its investment in core NMS work had an impact of as much as £2B p.a. on the UK's Gross Domestic Product (GDP).

Real Impact

To gather evidence of the very positive impact NPL was having on the UK's economy, a number of studies were undertaken. DIUS economists estimated that from an additional £6M investment in NMS research, the UK economy would benefit by £400M. In fact, a typical return on NMS research projects was 10 to 30 times the initial funding. In a survey of 500 private companies, they reported additional profitability of £634M in one year as a direct result of NMS funding.

NPL was also impacting 'quality of life'. Through its work with UK's radiotherapy centres it was providing the most consistent and accurate radiation dose in the world, with estimates of saving 200 lives a year. Our work in environmental research and development on low carbon technologies and climate change together with contracts with the Environmental Agency to provide such services as air quality monitoring would enable us to make real impact on the UK's carbon footprint into the future. NPL's work on low carbon technologies was estimated to save 8 Mtonnes CO_2 over the projects' lifetimes.

Each of our NMS Research Programmes had a specific knowledge transfer element to deliver. These would bring us closer to the UK's regions (Regional Development Agencies until the 31st March 2012), industry and academia.

Excellent Science

Maintaining and improving NPL's scientific standing was a key objective since our operation of the Laboratory commenced in 1995. There was now a greater emphasis on the formation of more formal strategic partnerships and by 2009 there were agreements with Surrey University, Imperial College, the Engineering and Physical Sciences Research Council (EPSRC) and the British Standards Institute (BSI).

The appointment of a Science Director and Chief Scientific Advisor and their impact on improved programme formulation saw greater emphasis on specifically allowing quality time for the publication of scientific papers as part of an important knowledge transfer deliverable. From a baseline of just over 100 peer-reviewed publications per annum at the beginning of the

NSC they had increased by 64% by December 2008 and were to rise to over 300 by 2014.

International Reputation

Following the distractions of the NPL Contract rebid we were again able to focus attention on enhancing our reputation within the international, and in particular, European metrology arena. NPL continued to be one of the top 3 National Measurement Institutes and world leading in terms of real and measurable economic impact. Through our International Director and his small team we were able to grow our influence within EURAMET working towards the first European Metrology Research Programme (EMRP) in 2009 worth 400M Euros over 7 years. It embodied the concept of pooling resources across Europe and developing joint metrology programmes. NPL played a key part in the first phase launched in 2007 which entailed aligning and enhancing national programmes (called iMERA-Plus). The EMRP Programme was managed through NPL by a very talented member of staff who was later to become the director of International Liaisons and Communications with BIPM in Paris.

Having been the driving force behind the EMRP, NPL was well positioned to win a sizable proportion of this work, growing our income and adding great value to the existing and future NMS research programmes.

Growing a Sustainable Business

NPLML was operated as a 'stand-alone' entity supported by Serco and underpinned by substantial parent company guarantees. It incurred the full economic running cost of the Laboratory and the business was sustained by charging DTI/DIUS the pre-determined competitively tendered day rate for their research programmes and attracting income from sources other than the NMS. The vast majority of costs were fixed or semi-fixed making it essential that we managed those areas where we had some control in the most efficient manner.

The 2004 rebid had set out a new more efficient structure, a refreshed vision and refocused marketing strategy. In the first five years of the NSC our turnover from 'non-NMS' customers doubled from £11M to £22M, a laudable achievement, and testament to the investment in additional marketing and selling resource during the beginning of the NSC and the growing entrepreneurial culture amongst our scientists. NPL continued to increase its non-NMS third party turnover by over 10% year on year right through the recession period and until the end of the Contract, particularly with grant and co-funded European Union work.

Greater Efficiency; Greater Effectiveness

Over the first half of the NSC we continued to made great strides in reducing our overheads and improving our productivity. We implemented 3 new fully integrated Oracle systems. These replaced existing aging systems; one managing and invoicing our measurement services and small orders work; one controlling the delivery of our numerous NMS research programme milestones and invoicing earned value each month; and a new Customer Relationship Management system for our restructured marketing and sales function. The implementation involved extensive redesign of processes and re-training of staff and, although scientists and support staff were fully consulted in specifying their requirements, the systems and their operation took some time to bed in. For example, our measurement services had been handled within scientific directorates and this led to inconsistencies in standards of customer care. These services were brought together under a dedicated team and experienced manager. It was a cultural shock for some scientists to 'let go' primarily of the management of this work but eventually the benefits of a professional customer-facing function was to pay dividends for all concerned. Although the Operations Directorate and users of the systems and processes were fully involved in their design, some proved to be too time-consuming for low value transactions and a 'lite' version was later introduced.

Apart from major systems updates we encouraged 'Continuous Improvement Initiatives' to ensure we kept up with latest best practice. These were based on 'Lean 6 Sigma', a methodology that relies on collaborative team effort to improve performance by systematically removing waste. It was specifically adapted for our laboratory environment and after a slow start in gaining scientists' interest and commitment, the benefits to internal organisation and resulting working conditions told their own story and it proved to be an on-going success.

By the end of 2007, pressure was again growing on our cost base. The NMS Programme Portfolio was being re-structured with the threat of budget reductions and the economic outlook was at best uncertain. With the support of Serco, the decision was taken to restructure the business again to reduce costs and create headroom to recruit the new staff and skills required to deliver the NSC and the emerging NMS programmes.

The 3 Scientific Directorates were reduced to 2 with the merger of Engineering & Process Control and Emerging Metrology together with associated support staff and the centralised Measurement Services function began to be phased-in. Again, this was a difficult and costly exercise but was to prepare us for the full repercussions of the banking crisis and resulting recession.

Gathering Clouds on the Horizon

The New Laboratory – Energy Costs

Since the termination of the PFI contract for the building of the new Laboratory at the end of 2004, DTI took control of retrofitting poorly performing laboratories and completion of the fitting out of those remaining. The Laboratory had not been designed to be energy efficient (by present day standards) and, although the running cost of the new Laboratory had been queried by NPLML with the architect at a very early stage and then repeatedly during construction, at that time, it was not considered a high priority. DTI and their expert consultants now had the unenviable task of ensuring the laboratories met scientists' requirements. This involved installing or upgrading effective systems of environmental control for the whole Laboratory building and carrying out for the first time, the necessary tests on energy consumption. To their credit, this was achieved with a certain amount of compromise in the specification of some laboratories.

As the new building was occupied, energy consumption (both gas and electricity) did, however, rise substantially. In addition, between 2007 and 2009, the prices of both commodities increased significantly. DIUS acknowledged that the new Laboratory's actual energy costs could not have been foreseen at the time of the bid and agreed a 'subsidy' until ways could be devised to develop a more sustainable, energy efficient building. Within a year of the official opening of the new NPL building in May 2008, energy costs had risen by more than £1M over the bid estimate even after the subsidy. With the coming uncertain economic environment and following the inevitable withdrawal of the subsidy in 2009, the energy costs of the Laboratory became a major concern and risk to the business's financial performance. Investment in energy saving measures remained a high priority for both our Government customer and NPL through to the end of the Contract.

NMS Strategy Review - Funding Priorities

During 2005, the prospect of severe Government spending cuts prompted DTI to commission another detailed strategy review of the NMS. NPL scientists made a significant and valuable contribution to the review, particularly the input to the consultation stages. Ministerial approval was given in the following year to restructure the NMS Programme Portfolio to provide a more coherent platform for developing a revised, clearer strategy with the aim of increasing economic and societal impact whilst containing or reducing spend. NPL then undertook a complete analysis and mapping of all NMS programmes and projects including an in-depth review of funding priorities and made recommendations on those areas of science where investment should be maintained or increased and others that should be reduced, closed or devolved. These priorities gained approval in 2007 to enable the new NMS programme structure to be implemented from the financial year 2007/08.

Inevitably, the identified changes would incur redundancy and asset disposal costs but as there was no funding available from DTI/DIUS the restructuring was 'phased' over a longer period to spread the cost. The planning was brought into line with NPLML's own management restructure limiting operational disruption and staff uncertainties. DIUS were, however, able to add some valuable support by maintaining NMS budget levels of between £48 - £49M p.a. until 2009 when, in the face of the economic recession and a severe austerity programme, cuts to our research programmes could no longer be avoided.

The Economic Crisis

The banking crisis and 'credit crunch' together with the resulting recession lasting from the second quarter of 2008 until the third quarter of 2009 would have a significant impact on all parties to the NSC – DIUS, Serco and NPLML. Government budget cuts amounting to more than £6M brought us close to our contractual minimum but did not start to bite until 2009/10. It would result in another redundancy programme involving 40 people although we were able to redeploy 15 staff to new roles within a restructured organisation. Continuing growth in non-NMS third party revenue would more than compensate for this decline and together with cost reductions through restructuring we were able to continue our level of investment in the Laboratory and its people.

However, like most other private sector companies who still offered their employees a defined benefit pension scheme, the crisis was to have a devastating effect. For SIRA, part of Serco's bid team and strategic partner it was to lead to its demise in 2009 although its partnership with NPL came to an end in 2006 when they ceased research and development work.

The NPL Defined Benefit Pension Scheme

The effect of the credit crunch had serious repercussions for pension schemes. It affected not only the scheme's assets with stocks and shares falling to unprecedented lows but also bond yields that were used to estimate future pension liabilities by discounting them to present day values. Very rapidly, valuations of pension schemes were to show huge deficits threatening the economic viability of many companies, so much so that at the end of 2008 the Pensions Regulator had to step in and relax rules over 'recovery' plans allowing longer periods for the deficits to be addressed – in some cases, more than 20 years were allowed.

It was a contractual obligation that NPLML maintained the NPL Pension Scheme and adhered to the funding requirements laid down by the independent actuary. Any changes to the trust deed or contribution levels needed the approval of DTI/DIUS and the agreement of the Government Actuary's Department (GAD). At the beginning of the NSC in 2004 there was a relatively small deficit in the Scheme. Bidders were all given the actuary's estimate of appropriate employer and employee contribution rates to recover this deficit. Serco adopted these advised rates for its bid and it seems reasonable to assume that all bidders would have done the same. However, in 2007, due mainly to the banking crisis, NPL's pension scheme deficit began to rise again.

NPLML were quick to act and kept DIUS closely informed. On the advice of the actuary we raised our contribution from the level that had been estimated in the bid by additional annual lump sums of £1.4M increasing in line with pensionable salaries each year. It was estimated that this cash injection would recover the deficit within 10 years. With profit margins already below 5% of turnover, NPLML's pension scheme deficit and the need for additional contributions was to become one of its major corporate risks and was to be a financial burden for the rest of the NSC.

The rules, regulations and obligations surrounding defined contribution pension schemes are involved but being a GOCO organisation added further complications. Serco/NPLML were responsible for the pension scheme during the period of its tenure (or franchise period as it was known for accounting purposes) and then all obligations reverted to DIUS unless the Contract was extended or re-let. It was therefore imperative that DIUS was kept fully informed of all the decisions of the Pension Scheme's trustees and the Company. By October 2008, as the recession deepened, the deficit had increased by £10M since the valuation the previous year so the Company and Trustees agreed that a further increase in the annual lump sum contribution to £2.255M was necessary. After consultation with the Union and members, the trustees also agreed increases in members' contributions (or reductions in their future accruals) phased over 3 years. A new funding policy and investment strategy which would reduce volatility and risk over time was also agreed.

The levels of pension scheme deficits suffered by all schemes in the UK were unprecedented and together with Serco we put forward a number of options for DIUS to consider as they would be a party to Scheme's on-going funding at the end of the NSC. The overriding assumption was that the Scheme should continue to be supported and not closed. (Closing the Scheme would crystalise the deficit immediately). Reducing members' benefits was also considered but not progressed. One attractive option was to merge the NPLML Scheme with Serco's. This had been offered in Serco's 2004 rebid. It could still be 'ring fenced' for future transfer and there would be savings through significant economies of scale. For the merger to be acceptable to the trustees of the Serco Scheme there would need to be a cash injection so that its value was not affected post transfer. This would be determined by Serco's scheme actuary but was likely to be considerably less than the existing deficit.

Serco/NPLML had acted swiftly but could see little respite from the economic turmoil in the short to medium term. Serious damage had been done to both the global and UK economy which would take decades to fully repair. We therefore put forward a strong recommendation to DIUS to consider the merger option but as a minimum, before its Year-End, explore the possibility of setting up a 'reserve' in its Balance Sheet to reflect the estimated net liability in the Scheme at the end of the NSC in 2014. This was consistent with accepted accounting practice and the value would be based on independent actuarial advice agreed by GAD. The reserve could then be potentially translated into cash injections to the Scheme or merger with Serco's. Of course, all this was dependent on some additional funding being identified within DIUS at a time of austerity and strict budget control.

The benefits of such a course of action were enormous for the Scheme and its members and the future financial security of NPLML. It would also potentially save DIUS many millions of pounds of future pension liabilities. Unfortunately the required funding to enable the Scheme to be merged or the deficit reduced was not forthcoming and NPLML continued to pay the additional £2.255M p.a. inflated by pensionable salary increases until the end of the NSC. We would revisit these options several times again and our proposals to extend the NSC also contained an attractive offer to merge the Scheme with Serco.

Defined benefit pension schemes are no longer financially viable for the majority of companies in the private sector. For example, at the beginning of 2016 there were only 11 'open' schemes remaining in the FTSE 250.

Customer Changes

One of the many key challenges of operating a 10-year Contract is the constant need to update and communicate with customers in an ever changing world. Governments and Science Ministers come and go and even those Government Departments and their representatives overseeing the Contract changed regularly, necessitating a new round of familiarisation and education. From the mid-2000s a number of changes occurred to the Government Department responsible for NPL.

In 2007 the Technology Strategy Board (which had been formed as an advisory body in 2004) became an executive non-departmental public body (NDBP) and took responsibility for most of DTI's innovation budget and the associated delivery activities. Shortly afterwards the team responsible for NPL and the NMS programmes transferred with the residual innovation policy team into the newly created Department for Innovation, Universities and Skills (DIUS). Other parts of DTI which transferred into this new Department included the Intellectual Property Office, the British National Space Centre, the teams responsible for science funding and the research councils and the teams supporting the Government Chief Scientific Adviser. These were joined from the Department for Education and Skills by teams responsible for skills, higher education and some aspects of further education. The remainder of DTI became the Department for Business, Energy and Regulatory Reform (BERR).

DIUS was a small department but controlled significant budgets. Its focus was therefore very much on the partner organisations on the front-line of spending these budgets and on the research/higher education landscape. In April 2009, the team responsible for NPL and the NMS programmes joined with the National Weights and Measures Laboratory (NWML) to form the National Measurement Office (NMO). This model was very much in line with the DIUS philosophy of only retaining functions within the core Department which could not be delivered from a partner organisation. DIUS was short-lived and, in June 2009, it merged with BERR to form the Department for Business, Innovation and Skills (BIS).

From NPLML's perspective, however, NMO was remote from the corridors of power in Westminster and it was seen as a backward step from the progress made over the years, bringing the capabilities of NPL to a far wider audience within Westminster and Government. Senior staff at NPL were far better connected and engaged with Government and the science community than NMO. It was therefore reasonable to expect that its remit would have been better served and more effective by continuing to embrace a partnership approach to the management of NPL and agree a practical and complementary modus operandi which supported both the development of the NMS Strategy and that of the Laboratory as a whole. Unfortunately, NMO did not have the benefit of past experience of a GOCO partnering arrangement and appeared to be suspicious of private sector involvement in NPL (in particular, Serco's management fee and extent of the 'reach-back' arrangements). Indeed, given our recommendation of the incorporation of NWML within NPL at their quinquennial review in 2000, they might have seen us more as a threat. Regrettably the partnering principle (see Chapter 1: Best and Final – the Last Hurdle) agreed and adopted right from the start of the original Term Contract in 1995 had been consigned to the annals of history.

For the most part therefore, NMO followed a more rigid arm's length customer/contractor management style with a higher degree of 'supervision' of the NSC and our interactions with stakeholders that felt to us very outdated and unnecessary. In practice, NMO had neither the resource nor expertise to become too involved in the operation of a complex organisation like NPL which had 10 times its staff numbers and nearly 20 times its turnover. The approach tended to add more administration and inevitably, at times, frustration and friction. We were no longer pushing against half open doors and the difficult road ahead became even more of an uphill struggle to make progress in an increasingly challenging economic environment.

The Second-Half Success and Challenges (2009 to 2014)

With the recent events of the banking crisis and economic turmoil conspiring against us it might have been reasonable to expect NPL's business to decline and our science mission to be adversely affected. This was by no means the case!

The Mid-Term Contract Review

It was common practice within Serco that a mid-term Contract review would be presented to senior members of our customer's team, demonstrating achievements and progress towards our joint objectives, raising issues and gaining valuable feedback. We felt this was particularly opportune as the new Managing Director, Dr Brian Bowsher had just joined NPLML in March 2009, BIS had delegated day to day supervision of NPL to Peter Mason at NMO in April 2009 and both the Public and Private Sectors were feeling the full repercussions of the banking crisis and recession.

Understandably, we were, extremely concerned about the future of NPL and the sustainability of our Contract during these uncertain times. Although our presentation was very up-beat about the significant progress made in the first half of the Contract, we did not pull any punches about our concerns over the level of our NMS funding, the economic down-turn and its effect on our commercial business and the increases in pension contributions and energy costs. With hindsight it was not what our customer wanted to hear at this time, having just been given oversight of NPL and under enormous financial pressure itself. I fear it might have set the tone for the future and gave greater weight to NMO's continuing distrust of us and Serco rather than our desire to work closer together in partnership to resolve these issues.

To a certain extent our fears were justified as there were cuts in the NMS Research budget. From 2009 and over successive years, funding was reduced to virtually the Minimum Research Commitment in the NSC and contributions to the NPLML Pension Scheme did rise dramatically. However, against all the odds, we continued to grow third party revenue and, together with continuing efficiency initiatives and cost reductions, investment in NPL's business and science was able to be maintained until the end of the Contract.

There was no silver bullet but it is my belief that the Company's extraordinary resilience was a result of the cumulative effect of past actions and new initiatives which not only sustained but continued to have a positive impact on the performance of the Laboratory. As always, the contribution of our staff was key. The very deliberate and painstaking inclusive approach taken when reviewing our shared vision and objectives for both NPL's science and business had a very positive response. Each member of our staff understood the importance of the part they were playing to secure NPL's future development and growth. There is no doubt that the shock of the banking crisis followed by recession and Government austerity programmes also helped galvanise our staff's resolve not to let the considerable progress made over the first half of the Contract be derailed. It certainly focused attention on efficient programme delivery and, with the support and direction of the sales function, maximising new opportunities for additional revenue.

The Introduction of 'Matrix Management'

In September 2008 Stephen McQuillan resigned from NPL to return to the manufacturing sector.

This photographic portrait of Steve McQuillan with Avatar hangs in Bushy House

He is pictured holding his Avatar as NPL was investigating the world of virtual measurement at that time. Under his leadership we had seen great progress in fulfilling DIUS's wishes to promote and improve NPL's interface with industry, and third party revenues had grown steadily.

His successor, appointed in March 2009, was Dr Brian Bowsher who had formerly been on the Executive Board of the Atomic Weapons Authority (AWE) initially as Director of Research and Applied Science and then as Director, Systems Engineering. He brought with him a wealth of knowledge and experience in the management of science and engineering in complex research environments.

The day to day oversight of NPL was now the responsibility of NMO whose advisors included the RSRAE Group for feedback on NPL's quality of science and the Measurement Board who reviewed the content and relevance of proposed NMS research projects. NMO was nonetheless reliant on NPL, as experts in measurement science, to provide a major part of the interface with academia and industry and formulate strategies and programmes of research. In order to be able to demonstrate an appropriate level of 'independence' in programme formulation, Dr Brian Bowsher took the next step in the evolution of NPL's organisation structure by the introduction of matrix management. The 2 Operational Directorates were reduced to a single one with 6 Divisions having sole responsibility for the delivery of science. The main driver for this was to strengthen a 'one-lab' approach. At the same time a new Programmes Directorate was formed. Simplistically, Operations looked inwards at internal delivery, whilst Programmes looked outwards to engage with stakeholders so that these were formulated to meet the needs of the UK. The International Directorate provided further input and advice to ensure that our European and overseas interests were fully represented. It was designed to give BIS and NPL's stakeholders a greater degree of confidence in our ability to remain outward looking when reviewing the UK's future needs for measurement standards and metrology research and 'pick winners' – those most likely to have the greatest economic and social impact – from the large number of potential research projects.

Although this matrix management structure caused some tension and, at time, heated debate within NPL (quite rightly so!), I believe it did result in more robust challenge to the content of our research programmes and, over time, improved the relevance and quality of our science. The new, dedicated Programmes team interfaced with the Chief Scientific Adviser and International Director, senior scientists from within NPL's Operations, BIS advisory groups and other customers and stakeholders. They used well developed and sophisticated mapping and modeling methodologies to predict the likely scientific impact of our research to enable 'ranking' of the various proposed projects. For all but the most sceptical of our stakeholders, the structure helped dispel the perception of self-interest and NPL 'feathering its own nest'!

Science Strategy and Standing

NPL played a major role in formulating the long awaited refresh of the NMS Science Strategy which was published by NMO in July 2011 and covered the period to 2015. Having a coherent, deliverable but challenging science strategy reflecting the wide consensus of our stakeholders was essential. It was the basis of longer term thinking on the future requirements of metrology and enabled us to align once more our own business strategy to these prioritised areas of science. In a limited number of areas we identified gaps in NMS funding that we felt justified in committing our own investment.

One such area was Biotechnology. We had made strong representations to NMO for an NMS Biotechnology Programme to be introduced but there was a reluctance to prioritise any further funding over and above that already made available to the Laboratory of the Government Chemist. We had long since directed funding to 'pump prime' this area of science through our own internal Strategic Research Programme and now specifically formulated a research project to demonstrate the importance of new standards in biotechnology.

We had also identified a future need and demand for the establishment of standards in the area of carbon measurement. A 'Carbon Conference' was organised and funded by NPLML and attended by a large cross-section of interested parties from government, academia and industry. It confirmed the necessity for a coordinated approach to carbon reduction in the UK. As no funding was available from NMO, a business case was considered for NPL to be the 'hub' of a newly formed Centre for Carbon Measurement representing a large number of interested parties with the potential to generate income from significant new research. This augmented NPL's other work on low carbon technologies and emissions reduction which was already estimated to save 2% of the UK's annual footprint over the projects' lifetimes.

The NMS Strategy formed the basis of a more forward looking vision, *'Metrology for the 2020s'*, published in May 2012. It was an NPL initiative, led by Dr Kamal Hossain, involving extensive discussion and input from NPL scientists, government partners, academic institutions and representatives from industry. The document was well received internationally and feedback was invited from a much wider audience via NPL's website. Strategic thinking does not remain static and the document remained actively used as part of NPL's longer term science strategy well beyond my tenure, demonstrating how well it continued to meet the challenges of the 2020s.

In one of the boldest moves by a scientific institution, Prof John Pethica, NPL's then Scientific Advisor and member of the Royal Society, set out on an international science benchmarking exercise with reviews of NPL's science output against appropriate peer groups. An international review panel was formed drawn from over 50 senior colleagues from NMIs, academia, industry and other expert groups. It published its results in 2011 and confirmed overwhelmingly:

- 'there was compelling evidence that NPL is operating as one of the world's top NMIs both in terms of its achievements and impact of its work'.
- 'NPL holds an internationally leading or competitive position in 80% of the areas in which it has chosen to participate'
- 'NPL clearly provides strong support to the industrial base and delivers significant benefit relative to cost'
- 'NPL provides excellent value for money'.

The International Science Benchmarking Exercise together with the publication of *'Metrology for the 2020s'* demonstrated that NPL's scientific and technical standing and influence in the world of metrology had not diminished over NPLML's years of operation but, within reduced budgets, had been enhanced.

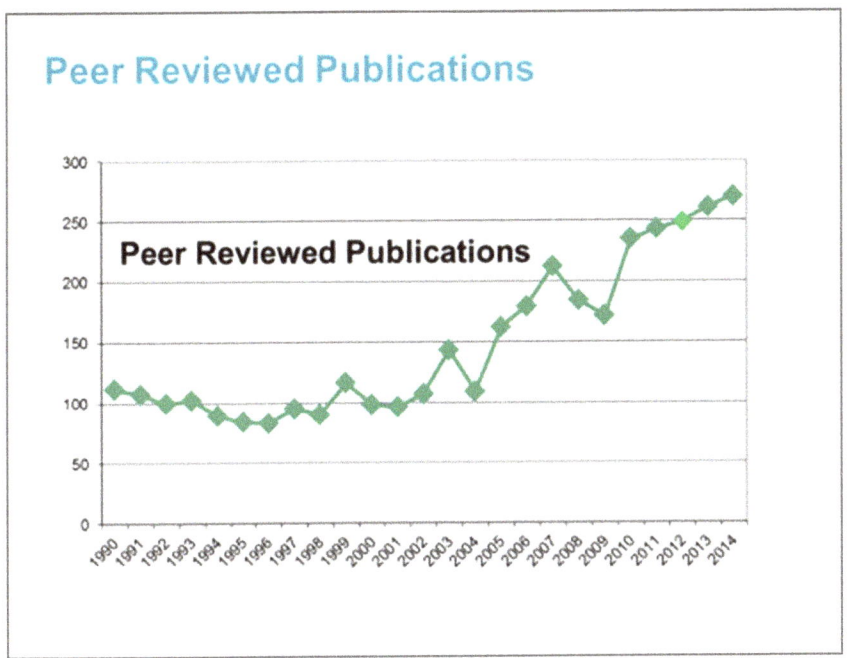

From a purely commercial perspective this was a powerful vindication of the Government's GOCO policy for NPL and, as we thought, came at the right time to support our case for an extension to the NSC or even rebid.

Business Development

NPLML continued to invest heavily in the Laboratory. One particular area where the benefits were particularly apparent was in our growing business development capability. In 2009, Keith Dobson joined NPLML as the Head of Business Development. He reviewed the function's strategy, carried out an in-depth market sector analysis and allocated resource with specific agreed annual sales targets. The Customer Relationship Management (sales pipeline) system was 'cleansed' and brought up to date and a new discipline for its upkeep was linked to an individual's sales bonus. In addition, the monthly Sales Board was given a higher profile and a more formal process introduced. Scientists and their supporting business development champion were able to pitch new opportunities and through a progressive gateway process, gain approval to submit their bids.

The Board was made up of a cross-section of the Laboratory including representatives of the finance, procurement and science community. I attended the majority of these meetings and found them extremely informative. We were able to influence and at times improve the structure and pricing of the bids making many of our proposals more attractive and commercially sound. However, I should not want to take away any credit from our scientists and business developers for the work they did to increase our 'win rate' substantially and consistently grow our third party sales revenue year on year until the end of the NSC. Between 2004 and 2014 our commercial income growth was 11% p.a. and by 2014 commercial revenue accounted for more than 40% of our total revenue and our sales order book stood at £52.2M.

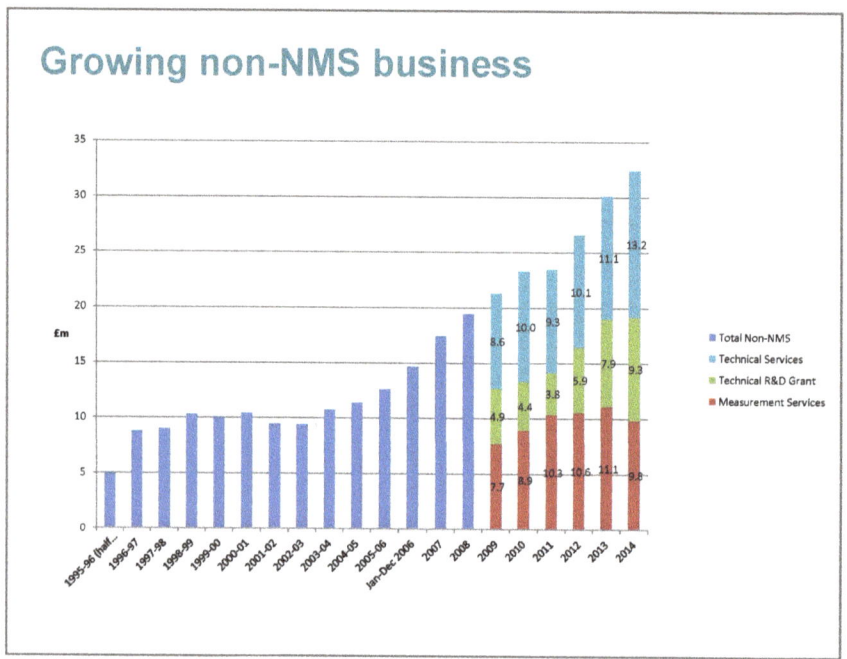

Health, Safety and the Environment (HSE)
The health and safety of our employees and the public has always been the highest priority of the Company. Although deeply embedded in the culture of the organisation, it nevertheless has to be constantly refreshed and reinforced, particularly as new scientific and technical techniques are developed and introduced. One way of raising the profile of health and safety and keeping it at the forefront of staff's awareness is to enter for the occupational health and safety awards of the Royal Society for the Prevention of Accidents (RoSPA). It is an internationally recognised organisation and an award is a much sought after accolade demonstrating an ongoing commitment to raising standards in health and safety and celebrating success. NPLML consistently entered for these awards and typically won or came second in the R&D sector.

Staff Engagement
One of the key drivers espoused by NPLML and Serco alike was the commitment to improve staff engagement in the wide variety of activities in NPL from ground breaking science to charitable work in the community. NPLML had already developed an active communication tool through its intranet showing such information as Company policies and procedures, health and safety statistics, all the latest Laboratory news and other helpful information such as accommodation available locally, social activities and much more. Although our scientists were primarily focused on their research projects we still wanted to make sure that they kept abreast of NPL's achievements, activities and other events that might be of interest. Dr Brian Bowsher, therefore, continued the practice of quarterly communications meetings in NPL's lecture theatre. In order to reach all staff these had to be repeated 3 times in the day – quite a feat of endurance – demonstrating the Company's commitment to engage staff and gain valuable feedback. Each of these meetings lasted about one and a half hours with a wide variety of content including the celebration of our many successes. The meetings were attended by the NPL executive who helped with the presentations and most importantly, were at hand to lend support to the 'Question and Answer' session at the end of each meeting.

Our Changing Staff Profile
Attracting the best of the best from the pool of available international scientific talent is challenging. We were also keen to recruit those who showed science leadership potential and shared NPL's values and behaviours – building trust and respect; fostering an entrepreneurial culture; enabling staff to excel; delivering promises. Although we set our expectations high, over the longer term it certainly paid off in terms of building outstanding world-leading teams and growing our business.

As you might suspect during the 19 years of our 2 Contracts, the staff profile changed dramatically. By 2014 there were about 100 of the original staff that transferred to us in 1995 still employed at NPL. Several of our programmes of work were fundamental to the underpinning of the NMS and of long term strategic importance to NPL and the UK. These warranted permanent employment contracts so that we could build and retain world-leading teams with long term succession planning being a key consideration. From 2004, however, we made a conscious decision to recruit more scientists on fixed term employment contracts which matched the length of the projects on which they would be working. These mirrored the terms and conditions of our permanent contracts but enabled a more flexible approach to our research and reflected normal practice within the academic workplace. Of course, these contracts could be renewed or made permanent as an individual's research developed. At the end of the NSC, between 2013 and 2014, NPL attracted more than 200 new recruits with a ratio of permanent to fixed term employment contracts of 50:50.

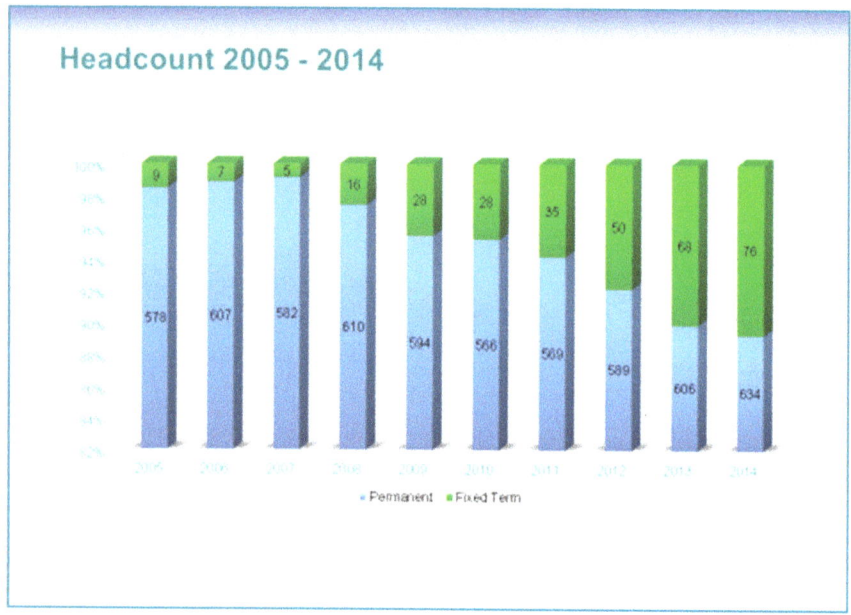

With our business growing strongly and recognising the broad spectrum of skills required at NPL, a new Apprentice School was established in 2014 covering such areas as engineering, calibration, laboratory services and business administration and bringing in up to 10 apprentices a year.

Winning the Communications Battle
The impact of NPLML's Communications function cannot be underestimated. This small group of very creative, dedicated professionals was responsible for a wide-ranging remit – public relations, NPL brand maintenance, in-house graphic design, scientific and other publications (including the NPL Annual Review), the staff quarterly communications presentations, the NPL website and intranet and management of the General Activities Programme to name but a few!

Although NPLML was a relatively small Company its outreach and stakeholder base was enormous. NPL provided hospitality of some shape or kind to more than 40,000 people in 2013. Over the 10 year Contract NPL made very substantial strides forward in taking the NPL measurement message out into all walks of life both here and abroad. The annual 'Water Rocket Challenge' engages an ever increasing number of schools and now many others, in hands on applied science and who can forget NPL's 'snowman' Christmas Greeting?

Annual Water Rocket Challenge

Even with all this success it is ironic that one of the groups who proved the greatest challenge to engage were Government Departments themselves! Perhaps it was the remoteness of NPL from Whitehall, the lack of MPs with an interest in science or the unhelpful length of reporting lines from NMO in Teddington that had to be navigated before reaching the makers and shapers within Government. Whatever the reason, we were all proud of NPL's accomplishments and constantly 'evangelical' about this jewel in the Government's research crown.

Capital Asset Refinancing

The original sale and leaseback of NPL's scientific equipment in 2000 initially released nearly £17M for DTI and the Exchequer. Our scientific equipment continued to be financed through a Tripartite Agreement between DTI, NPLML and a bank during the remainder of the Contract. The arrangement became well established, with assets of a value of £4 - £5M being procured each year by NPLML under an Agency Agreement with the bank. The cost of financing was market tested regularly to ensure we were obtaining the most competitive lease rental rates. During the banking crisis in 2008 the leasing arm of our original banking partner could no longer offer these financing facilities and similar arrangements had to be retendered and a new tripartite agreement negotiated with an alternative provider. This new arrangement proved to be equally competitive and the bank was happy to help streamline the administration behind the quarterly lease rental 'drawdown' process.

Bank of England interest rates fell dramatically during the financial crisis and by March 2009 they had dropped to 0.5%. We began to explore potential opportunities for refinancing our scientific equipment lease agreements given the significant shift in the market place. New finance leases were negotiated for both future asset requirements and those existing assets with contract terms of 5 years or longer. Although there was a 'penalty' for early termination of the agreements, this was offset by improved terms and interest rates. The new finance leases offered NPLML better value for money than the previous arrangements in terms of Net Present Value, cash flow and cost, not just in the remaining 2 years of the Contract but virtually throughout the tenure of the agreement. As the agreements were now 'finance' rather than 'operating' leases, the ownership of the assets transferred from the bank to NPLML. The transaction for existing assets was signed in March 2012 with all the contractual and administrative arrangements essentially remaining the same comprising a tripartite, lease and agency agreement.

From 2012, therefore, the value of scientific equipment appeared on NPLML's Balance Sheet together with the associated loan creditor. Asset depreciation and interest were charged to the Profit and Loss Account instead of lease rentals. As the assets were now owned by NPLML we were also able to claim 100% first year tax allowances on all purchases of scientific equipment with resulting substantial reductions in corporation tax and improvement in cash-flow.

Not all of our scientific equipment was refinanced. There was little financial benefit from changing those operating leases with a contract term of less than 5 years and they were left to continue until expiry of the agreement. An opportunity also arose for us to terminate the tranche of 'legacy' operating leases from our original banking partner who approached us to explore whether we might consider 'buying back' the assets at fair market price. Due to substantial restructuring in 2008 resulting from the banking crisis, a number of businesses within the bank were to be sold, liquidated or closed. Part of their leasing arm was one of these. The original value, remaining life and net book value of our assets were ascertained and compared reasonably with a fair market value. New loan financing was arranged with our existing banking partner and all the legacy assets were then purchased by NPLML. The 'buy-back' deal achieved the objectives of both the bank and the Company. The bank liquidated the assets and obtained the cash it desired and NPLML gained ownership of the assets with no early termination fees or outstanding interest payable.

The irony did not pass me by, however, that a bank with a majority public shareholding had to relinquish profitable leasing contracts where the ultimate owner of the asset was the Government itself. Given the sizable portfolio of operating assets that the Government owned (and still owns) across the nation and the bank's need of secured, low risk debt, I can't help thinking they might have missed a trick here!

NPL's First Spin-Out Company – AgPlus Diagnostics Limited

For an organisation like NPL, generating income from intellectual property (IP) was more involved than might first be thought. After all, NPL's primary purpose was to give access to and disseminate scientific knowledge and information from our NMS research programmes for the benefit of all UK industry and our economy. It was only on limited occasions where some specific IP was identified as a potentially valuable 'by-product' of our research that we could maximise the benefit to NPL by further exploitation. The nature of our research meant that these innovations were generally a considerable 'distance from market' and required substantial further investment usually by a specialist organisation to realise their true value. This we could achieve by negotiating licence or royalty agreements.

All IP generated by NPL was owned by and vested in our government owner. From the beginning of the original Contract, NPL had generated a small amount income from its IP portfolio and incurred considerable patents costs. NPLML had an obligation to manage IP on government's behalf and reinvest any income in its protection, maintenance and future exploitation. Until the NSC in 2004, IP had been administered within the Scientific Centres and financial information consolidated to gain an overview of performance. It had become clear that the cost of maintaining patents and administering IP was too costly, absorbing most if not all of our licence and royalty income. We therefore recruited an IP specialist to manage a new centralised process for review and control of our patents, licences and royalties. Quarterly review meetings were introduced, chaired by a member of the NPLML Board, Prof Richard Brook who had many years' experience in the field of IP exploitation. A more radical view was taken of the true value of patents to NPL and many were discontinued. A progressive 'gateway' process vetted scientists' proposals for investing time and effort in developing IP.

Once again, Science Directorates were initially concerned over losing control over their IP and the income it generated. However, licence and royalty income (and associated costs) remained within the Directorates and the review process was generally seen by scientists to be supportive as it sometimes opened up access to additional sources of funding, both internal (our Strategic Research Programme) and external. Controls were tightened to ensure that a 'virtual' Profit and Loss Account accurately reflected all IP income generated together with the patent, development and central management costs. At the same time an incentive scheme was introduced to share the profits from IP exploitation with the scientist(s) responsible for recognising and developing its potential. This not only raised awareness of the importance of IP to scientists but also ensured it was brought to the attention of the IP board early in its development. Although income generated from exploiting our IP was not large (fluctuating between £500k and £900k p.a.) its potential was maximised and exploitation costs efficiently managed.

The potential of one particular invention warranted some special attention. It was for a 'Point-of-Care' medical diagnostic device and was based on the development of an electrochemical immunoassay with silver nanoparticles as its detection system. A number of patents were filed and subsequently granted, covering the core chemistry and unique aspects of the device. Essentially the technology platform enabled the product, comprising an assay test cartridge and a handheld reader, to deliver true quantitative 'Point of Care' diagnostics against a wide range of clinical applications. Our Strategic Research Programme funding was used to develop and prove the science further but it needed considerably more investment before early stage 'seed funding' might be attracted. The scientist inventor and a business development colleague with extensive experience in this sector brought forward a proposal to the NPL Board that the innovative technology would be suitable for a spin-out company. Before taking this step NPLML engaged a specialist in the technology to review and report on the veracity of the science and its potential application. As the initial funding was substantial and the business risks for a start-up company considerable, we also had to obtain the approval of Serco and their investment committee. There were no objections from BIS/NMO as our Contract encouraged us to exploit the full potential of NPL's IP and NPLML was taking all the business risk.

After much deliberation, Serco approved an initial investment in the form of a business loan and a new company was formed called Argento Diagnostics Limited with the two NPL employees transferring to become executive directors and part owners with additional non-executive board members from NPL. An independent chair, with relevant experience of start-up companies was also invited to join the board. It began trading in 2011 and because of potential trademark issues changed its name to AgPlus Diagnostics Limited (AgPlus) soon afterwards. The NPLML Board had members who were experienced in the trials and tribulations of developing a new technology and taking it to market so we knew it was likely to be a rocky and challenging road ahead. Even then we were guilty of being over-optimistic on how long it would take to develop a 'market ready' prototype of the invention!

By the end of the NSC, AgPlus had not been able to make the all-important step of finding an investor and commercialising the technology platform and device although the potential was still plain to see. Neither, Serco nor BIS wished to retain the company following the termination of the NSC so AgPlus was transferred to Serco who found a buyer for the company. It is still trading but that illusive commercial breakthrough has not yet taken place. In September 2016, however, there was more positive news. AgPlus signed an agreement with AstraZeneca to develop a new prototype device and obtained early stage venture capital from the Rainbow Seed Fund to finance its development. Additional funding was secured from Innovate UK in June 2017 to use on a project to develop and refine the manufacturing of key cartridge components in collaboration with NPL in readiness for a commercial launch in 2018. At long last the outlook is more promising and might allow this innovative product, developed at NPL, to realise its full commercial potential.

Financial Performance – Second Half to 2014

The banking crisis, credit crunch, UK and global economic recession and resulting Government austerity programmes had the potential to impact NPL significantly. Nevertheless, throughout the second half of the Contract, NPLML demonstrated an enduring financial resilience in the face of quite considerable challenges. Our NMS budget was eventually cut by £6M p.a. almost down to the contractual Minimum Research Commitment. The market 'meltdown' in 2008 also resulted in enormous increases in the deficits and funding requirements of corporate defined benefit pension schemes. NPL's was no exception requiring additional contributions of more than £2M p.a. as part of the recovery plan. The economic environment presented a real threat to future growth in our commercial revenue and the new Laboratory's running costs, particularly energy consumption, were more than £1m above original estimates for the building. Although outside our control these business risks were our responsibility and they were to prevail until the end of the Contract.

At this critical time Government oversight of the Contract was transferred out of the 'corridors of power' in London to NMO in Teddington. It had neither the standing nor exposure within Whitehall and could lend only limited support to NPL and, with the background of austerity, assumed the primary role of defending existing budgets. This it did robustly, however, and managed to maintain budget levels in cash terms, supported to an extent by the existence of the NSC. No other part of the Department achieved this apart from the research councils. The NPLML Board and executive team also did as much as they could to promote the importance of maintaining NPL's funding and the part the Laboratory could play in supporting the UK's economic recovery and improving industrial productivity.

Baseline cost increases to NPLML especially in energy and pension scheme contributions were, as we've seen, enormous. There was also the cumulative effect of our day rate for NMS work only increasing by inflation less 0.98% p.a. requiring us to identify performance improvements of £18M over the Contract.

Our concerns about energy consumption were exacerbated in 2007 when questions were raised about the true cost of the new Laboratory's gas supply following the construction of the new Laboratory. Gas usage was tested, verified and then monitored so that metering and billing could be more accurate in future years. Negotiations over retrospective liabilities were protracted and required a year-end provision in our accounts. Settlement was finally reached and allowed a financial provision in our 2009 accounts to be released causing a 'spike' in our overall profitability in that year's accounts.

With a growing understanding of the new Laboratory's energy requirements, we worked tirelessly with NMO's Estates team to reduce consumption. Additional investment was made from BIS's limited capital budget to buy new or replacement energy efficient plant where there was a sound economic case and reasonable 'pay-back' period. The original concept of operating entire laboratory spaces within tightly specified temperature and climate tolerances was abandoned as too wasteful. Close control was driven primarily by consideration of actual scientific need. We even resorted to turning off controls completely with scientists' agreement in 'out of hours' periods. Energy efficiency also became a consideration when procuring new scientific equipment and replacing old. We were pushing against open doors here as the whole NPL community was keen to see our carbon footprint reduced to a minimum. With this heightened awareness of the Laboratory's energy consumption we were able to manage these costs more effectively and make some limited savings as far as the building design would permit.

There was little we could do to reduce the on-going cost of NPLML's defined benefit pension scheme following the banking crisis. We reviewed our investment strategy and modified the scheme's asset allocation to reduce our investment risk but as all asset classes were severely depressed it offered little shelter. Together with the scheme trustees we initially agreed a 10 year recovery plan later extended to about 15 years with additional cash contributions of £2M p.a. As the Scheme's principal employer, we were wholly liable for these additional contributions for the duration of the Contract. We had an obligation to fund it in accordance with the advice of the Scheme's actuary and the approval of the Pension's Regulator and the Government Actuary's Department (GAD). As our Contract only covered a small part of the overall lifetime of the Scheme, we had adopted a policy of 'Franchise Accounting' since the beginning of the Term Contract with DTI in 1995, first covering the initial 5-year Contract and then the new 10-year Contract. Funding past and future liabilities after the end of the Contract in 2014 would then transfer to a new contractor or back to Government. One feature of this accounting methodology meant that, in essence, additional contributions beyond those agreed at the beginning of the Contract in 2004 (i.e. the £2.225M p.a.) were charged directly to reserves in the Balance Sheet and so were not reflected in the current year's Profit and Loss Account (P&L). It explains why our P&L looked relatively healthy when viewed in isolation. Because of the annual cost of these considerable additional contributions to the Scheme we were able to include these in the Profit Share calculation so that it reflected the true extent of our annual pension scheme contributions.

In fact, the additional pension costs kept our profit margin as a percentage of sales below the 5% threshold for the duration of the NSC. As there was no prospect of our contributions to the Scheme reducing, compensating savings would have to be found from elsewhere.

In these circumstances NPLML's financial performance over the second half of the NSC has to be seen as impressive. The foundation of our success was certainly the continuing third party sales growth throughout the entire period. During the worst years of economic decline and cuts in our NMS budget, between 2009 and 2011, we were able to maintain our total annual turnover at £70 to £71M and then grow it substantially year on year to nearly £80M by the end of the Contract in 2014. Organisational, process and systems improvements all played their part. Centralisation of our measurement services business, becoming more customer focused and responsive with better turn-around times for the calibration of equipment, all helped us improve our sales offering. A more efficient and selective commercial bidding process maximised the effectiveness of our business development team increasing our win rate and margins.

Our business planning and quarterly forecasting process was well understood throughout the Company. A 'flight-path' to achieve the desired financial outcome for the year would be agreed with all areas of the business as part of the final quarter's forecast review so there was a shared responsibility for ensuring a 'soft landing' allowing our targets to be achieved consistently year on year.

Financial Performance – 2004 to 2014

	2004/05 £	2005/06 £	2006 £ 9 Months	2007 £	2008 £	2009 £	2010 £	2011 £	2012 £	2013 £	2014 £
Turnover											
NMS	47,663	50,747	34,526	50,910	50,795	49,897	47,617	46,724	46,355	47,765	47,503
Third Party	10,663	12,032	14,217	16,933	19,278	21,280	23,282	23,436	26,600	30,100	32,389
Total Turnover	58,326	62,779	48,743	67,843	70,073	71,177	70,899	70,160	72,955	77,865	79,892
Profit before Tax*	2,337	2,268	2,108	2,472	3,606	4,845	3,375	3,844	3,133	3,936	6,393
Return on Sales%	4.0	3.6	4.3	3.6	5.1	6.8	4.8	5.5	4.3	5.1	8.0
Profit after Tax	2,605	2,121	2,632	1,930	3,696	5,045	3,700	3,866	3,811	3,817	5,726

* Excluding additional NPL Pension Scheme contributions taken directly to (Balance Sheet) Reserves

The adoption of new technology together with our programmes of 'continuous improvement' helped us operate more efficiently and effectively across a whole range of activities absorbing many of the incremental costs associated with an expanding commercial business. These savings, together with economies of scale, were another essential element in maintaining and eventually improving our profit margins.

Refinancing our asset base in 2012, however, had an immediate impact on both our headline profitability and cash-flow. Finance rather than operating leases were chosen as the best value. The depreciated purchase value of the assets was now taken onto our Balance Sheet as 'additions' together with the finance lease creditor. Our P&L was charged with depreciation and loan interest each month instead of rent. The net result of this transaction was to improve our profit before tax by about £600k p.a.

and earnings before interest and tax (another important performance measure, particularly for Serco) by about £1.4M p.a. In addition, as we owned the assets, we could take advantage of 100% tax allowances on all R&D assets including the 'bulk' purchases of scientific equipment from each of the banks in 2012. This additional allowance, together with R&D Tax Credits to which we were also entitled, effectively wiped out our corporation tax liability. The resulting improvement in our cash-flow significantly helped us fund the additional contributions to our Pension Scheme and continue to finance our growing business.

Chapter 6 - 'The Writing on the Wall'

My retirement from the NPLML Board had always been planned to give ample time for my successor to be well established in post before the end of the Contract. This would help ensure a smooth handover of responsibilities and allow the new Finance Director to become an integral part of the executive team to take NPL forward to the next stage of its life. There was one final task to undertake, however, and that was the development of proposals and negotiation of an extension to the New (now old) Science Contract (NSC).

The NSC included a provision for a 5-year extension subject to mutual agreement. Dialogue between the parties was to start 2 years before the termination of the NSC to allow plenty of time for the best operational solution to be developed. In addition, it would be particularly advantageous to NMO/BIS if terms of an extension could be agreed early as it would enable a higher level of savings and investment in NPL over a longer term period of up to 7 years.

The Winds of Change

Since the day to day supervision of NPL had transferred to NMO in 2009, our business relationship had noticeably changed. A more arm's length customer/contractor approach had been adopted and it proved more difficult to engage effectively. Unfortunately there was little sign of a return to the close partnership we had formally enjoyed. Following the 2010 General Election, Prime Minister, David Cameron, appointed David Willetts as Minister of State for Universities and Science. He was to remain in post until 2014. Although not a scientist he was an academic and with his responsibility for universities there seemed to be a distinct shift in political sentiment away from prioritising industrial impact towards more fundamental science. Not surprisingly the RSRAE Group appeared to lend their support to this change in direction and perhaps hoped to attract additional funding. For NPLML, however, this was a double-edged sword since, for the past 16 years and with Government's blessing, we had been dispelling our reputation as 'the University of Teddington' and expounding the virtues of 'science with social and economic impact'. Even with this mantra, NPL's scientific reputation had still been enhanced whilst sales to third parties had grown at an unprecedented rate and would continue this increase through the final years of our Contract. At a time of austerity it seemed over optimistic to dream of increased funding for the NMS.

Perhaps the GOCO operating model had run its course at NPL. There was certainly less of an appetite within BIS to guarantee a Minimum Research Commitment for a further 5-year extension period. Serco and the executive team at NPLML were all too aware of this change of sentiment and were keen that a Contract extension should properly address BIS's strategy for NPL over this next 5 to 7 years and continue to offer exceptional value for money. We felt the rationale for an extension nevertheless remained strong. NPL was enjoying its most successful years and the GOCO business model was still working well, having had the resilience to weather extreme economic conditions and BIS budget cuts. A protracted rebid of the Contract or change of ownership would undoubtedly slow our momentum and progress in the short term. At this critical period for our economy NPL needed to support the UK growth agenda. A rebid would also be an expensive option at a time of austerity. Serco was conscious of the need to demonstrate value for money, increase its investment in science capability, both people and facilities, and provide a resolution of the pension deficit issue. It was therefore important to engage with NMO and BIS early and ensure that our proposals reflected their vision and strategy for NPL's future.

In 2011, well before the specified 2 year negotiation period, we approached NMO and BIS so that, assuming they would want to pursue and explore the possibilities of a 5-year extension, we could agree a process and timetable that was acceptable to them. Responsibility for managing the project was put in the hands of the team at NMO. They had limited resources but we believed the extension process could be dealt with effectively and efficiently by working closely with them to capture all their requirements. Our extension proposal would then reflect NMO/BIS's updated vision and strategy for NPL and ensure that their aspirations were translated into a properly costed operating solution that was affordable within their budgets with the minimum of amendments to the existing Contract.

However, NMO's approach to the management of the project was quite different and instead of giving a strong lead and working with us to develop the very best set of options an extension could offer both in terms of value for money and meeting their longer term strategy for NPL, they appeared reluctant to engage at the executive level. It almost felt as though we were already in a competitive tendering environment. Our proposals for a Contract extension therefore lacked much of their valuable input and the opportunity was lost to explore and develop an optimal solution that encompassed BIS's longer term vision beyond the extension and provided best value for the taxpayer. Even at this early stage it appeared not to be NMO's favoured option and we would have to redouble our efforts. Perhaps the writing was on the wall and NMO was already looking for an alternative to an extension to the NSC.

For its part, BIS set up a Review Group chaired by Sir Adrian Smith, Director General of Knowledge and Innovation, together with the Chief Executive of NMO and a small team supported by advisors including the RSRAE Group.

Our Contract Extension Proposal (September 2011) – 'Route to 2019'

Recognising that the BIS members of the Review Group might not have been fully appraised of NPL's successful track record under Serco's stewardship we presented our past performance and achievements together with a plan of our future vision for the Laboratory. With a lack of direction from NMO and motivated by David Willetts' desire for science capability to be further enhanced by driving even stronger partnerships with universities, we began preparing our proposal for the next 5 to 7 years of operation, hoping to translate his aspirations into practical solutions which, in turn, would lead to greater engagement and valuable feedback to ensure full alignment with BIS's aspirations.

A Business Plan for NPL covering 2012 to 2019 was produced and a set of financial options and projections were prepared. These first had to be presented to Serco's Investment Board and our financial strategy and level of investment justified and agreed. As one of Serco's most prestigious contracts and having firm confidence in NPLML's executive and management teams to deliver our proposals, they were prepared to take a higher level of business risk. This was particularly demonstrated by again proposing a solution to the NPL Pension Scheme deficit.

The first meeting with BIS's Review Group was on the 28th September 2011. Our proposal presentation had first been passed to NMO as a courtesy for comment and then distributed well before the meeting.

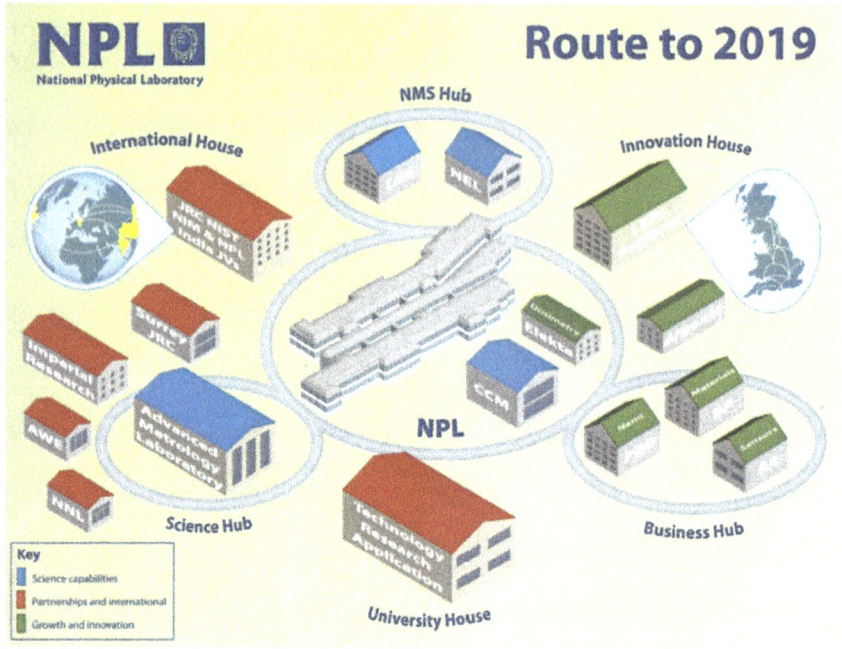

In summary, we demonstrated our track record of achievement (as detailed in Chapter 5), notably, we had: significantly increased science outputs and impact; grown partnerships and third-party revenues; delivered operational efficiencies; received awards for science and business; taken advantage of valuable and effective reach-back to Serco. We set out a clear vision to 2019 with NPL continuing to grow as a world-leading UK Science and Technology Laboratory working in close partnership with academia, industry and government and augmenting our existing regional footprint. This was put into context with an assessment of current economic, social and policy drivers together with envisaged challenges and opportunities. The next few years were considered to be critical for NPL to contribute significantly to the UK economy and a competitive re-tender of the Contract would risk disrupting this important work. Finally, we outlined our proposals for Contract extension including increased investment in science, focus on supporting growth and innovation, strengthening partnerships and ensuring the sustainability of the Laboratory.

In addition, if BIS were to accept early adoption of the Contract extension i.e. from April 2012 greater cumulative benefits would be generated with savings throughout the extension period to 2019. A new NMS Science Strategy had been published just a few months earlier in July 2011. Our proposal included an offer to finance and implement a change and investment programme starting early in 2012 and have the new NMS Portfolio in place by the beginning of April, the start of NMO's financial year. Its centerpiece would be a new Strategic Capability Building Programme that would respond to national challenges.

Our Financial Offer

From a financial perspective our proposal was far-reaching with a significant but well considered increase in business risk for Serco. For example, NPLML would be taking third party revenue risk for a further 7 years, forecast to grow 68% from 2012 to 2019. The cost of change to implement the NMS Science Strategy was estimated to be £2M. In addition, there would be a further significant investment in NPL's Strategic Research Programme and science capability of £2M that would again accelerate the alignment of resources with the new NMS Portfolio and NPL's future aspirations. Serco also committed to supporting AgPlus Diagnostics with additional loan financing that would lead to a potential trade sale benefitting both NPL and NMO/BIS. We requested a swift decision on the extension, perhaps by December 2011 for implementation by April 2012 so that these benefits might be realised as quickly as possible.

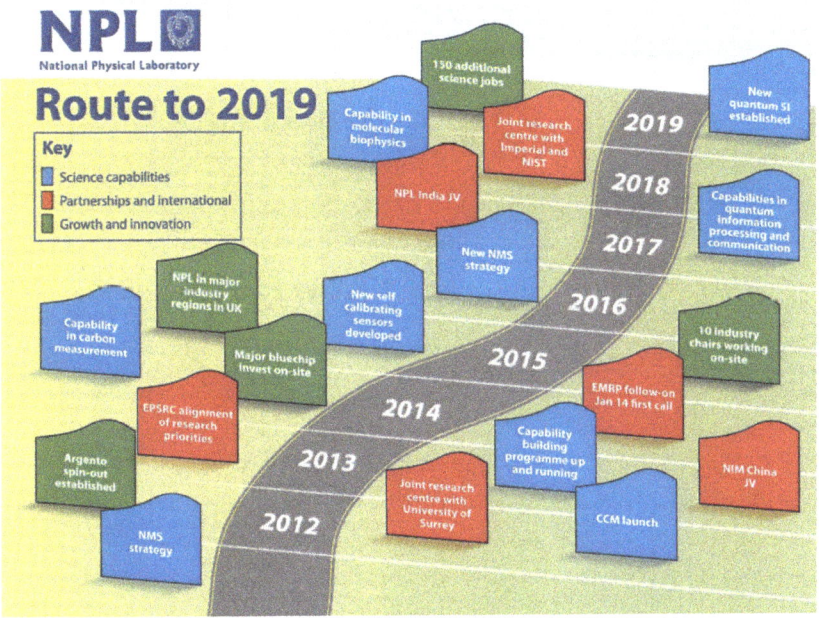

All this was additional investment over and above our on-going commitments in the NSC. Serco was also in a unique position to offer another substantial benefit to BIS should a Contract extension be acceptable. Funding the deficit in NPLML's defined benefit pension scheme had been a significant issue for the longer term sustainability of the Laboratory since the banking crisis of 2008. At the time of writing the proposal NPLML's additional lump sum contributions (over and above those agreed in the NSC) to the scheme to address the deficit had risen to £2.573M p.a. with a recovery period of 14 years to 2024. This was a huge drain on NPLML's cash resources and one of the Company's top business risks. By contrast, Serco's own defined benefit scheme was 100% funded and considerably larger, having almost 10,000 members. These economies of scale enabled operating costs to be kept to a minimum and opened up further opportunities for investment and risk management.

Taking the pension deficit liability forward into a Contract extension, although manageable, was obviously undesirable. When the banking crisis first struck the UK in 2008 causing the Scheme's modest deficit to increase dramatically we had approached DIUS/BIS with an offer to merge NPL's scheme with the equivalent Serco scheme so that further deterioration in its funding position might be avoided. It was hoped that this might be a viable option but it did require a one-off lump sum additional contribution of less than £10M to satisfy the respective actuaries that the transfer would not put either pension scheme at a financial disadvantage. (Chapter 5 – the NPL Defined Benefit Pension Scheme). At that time the offer was not taken up but it remained 'on the table' in subsequent years.

Our Contract extension proposal therefore again recommended that BIS should give consideration to the NPL Pension Scheme being merged with Serco's. The NPLML Scheme would be 'ring-fenced' and members' benefits maintained. At the end of the Contract extension period there was only likely to be a small number of 'active' members remaining who could either defer or transfer their pension entitlements if required. Merging the Schemes in 2011/12, however, would require an even more sizeable upfront lump sum of anything between £20M and £30M, depending on timing, to equalise the respective funding levels. Serco was prepared to make such a commitment and finance the bulk of the additional funding over the period of the Contract extension but with market conditions so volatile we had to seek a limited underpinning contribution from BIS estimated to be in the region of £8M. This was, however, considerably less than the outstanding additional deficit lump sums or contribution levels that would be payable by BIS beyond the extension period from 2019 to

2024. To my mind this offer warranted very serious consideration as it removed the possibility of any further downside risks and costs and addressed one of the key issues of the sustainability and competitiveness of the Laboratory. The aim was to complete the merger by April – June 2012.

There was one further benefit to the removal of the pension deficit from NPLML. If BIS were to develop plans for greater equity participation in NPLML at some time in the future, for example, as a precursor to a rebid in 2019, then the pension deficit would be a real deterrent, in fact, a 'show-stopper'. This might well have been the case in 2013/14 when I understand further equity investment in NPLML was unsuccessfully sought by NMO.

Updating the Contract for the Extension Period

The NSC had some shortcomings, particularly the new pricing mechanisms that were discussed in Chapter 4: 'A Level Playing Field' – DTI's Invitation to Negotiate. A GOCO Operating Model is only as good as the underlying contract. Unlike the original 1995 Term Contract, the commercial terms of the NSC in 2004 did nothing to support the enhancement of NPL's science but concentrated on addressing procurement issues (it was a competitive retender with a well-established incumbent) and contained mechanisms that reduced both the single day rate each year in real terms and, potentially, NPL's future funding level. From the start of the Contract we had made a conscious decision not to let this affect the quality of NPL's scientific standing in the world and this was borne out by the results of the International Science Benchmarking Exercise (Chapter 4: Science Strategy and Standing).

Working in a relative vacuum regarding NMO/BIS's views on some level of Contract modifications for the extension we set out a limited number of proposals for consideration as to how the NSC might be improved to help support the development of NPL's science capability. We assumed we would have an opportunity to discuss our proposals with NMO and BIS in the hope that their requirements could be accommodated and lead to an agreement of acceptable terms. If these negotiations did not meet BIS's future vision for NPL then there would be plenty of time to instigate a full rebid of the Contract.

With hindsight, suggesting modifications to improve the NSC in our first presentation might have been a risky strategy since we lacked a true partnering relationship with the executive of NMO. However, we still wished to demonstrate to BIS the value of an open dialogue and a partnership approach to our on-going working relationship.

We therefore highlighted 2 possible amendments to the NSC together with other recommendations as to how the existing arrangements might be improved.

Agreeing the Minimum Research Commitment (MRC) under the Contract was key to the sustainability of NPLML as this investment underpinned the capability of NPL and our ability to leverage additional funding, for example, with 'matching funds' from the European Union. However, the NSC allowed for a year on year cumulative reduction of 5% in the value of NMS Research once a key milestone had been reached in the PFI contract. This was a significant and unnecessary business risk for NPLML that seemed to fly in the face BIS's desire to enhance NPL's scientific capability. Under considerable pressure from the Treasury, NMO had started exercising its right to reduce this underpinning portion of the NMS budget in 2010/11. Because of the challenging economic environment and overall 'flat cash' settlement in the Spending Review we proposed that this funding reduction clause was removed and the current year's (2011/12) overall spend of £46M be maintained (the MRC was then £42M) with possible inflationary increases thereafter.

The NSC provided for annual inflationary (RPIX) increases in our (single) day rate *less* 0.98%. The mechanism would realise more than £18M of contractual savings for NMO/BIS over the 10 years of the Contract. Again, rather than driving a reduction in NMS funding we proposed that the deflator should be reset or removed for the extension period to enable greater investment in NPL's science capability. If this mechanism was non-negotiable (as it formed a fundamental part of pricing the NSC) then perhaps the savings generated by the reduction in the day-rate could still be reinvested in NPL (like the existing Profit Share arrangements) or in the existing Strategic Research Programme already funded by NPLML, rather than risk further NMS budget reductions.

These 2 mechanisms within the NSC increased business risk and could act as a constraint to growing investment in NPL's science capabilities over the extension period. Operational efficiency and excellent value for money could still be demonstrated effectively through existing mechanisms and there were further proposals for improvements in the way we managed the Laboratory and delivered NMS Programmes.

Annual reviews of NMS Programme and Project outputs were already in place together with the flexibility of 'light touch' rolling formulation. The NSC's pricing mechanism which aggregated all levels of research scientist and direct programme costs into one single day-rate had nothing to commend it. Nevertheless we knew this was a fundamental commercial tenet of the NSC. Rather than contemplating any changes here, we proposed maintaining the overall funding envelope generated by this mechanism but managing and operating the NMS Research Programmes using our own internal systems based on 'full economic cost' which could be broken down into scientist grades and direct costs to ensure total transparency for BIS/NMO and other stakeholders. Reconciliation to the contractual funding envelope to ensure our spend profile was maintained in line with the NSC could then occur annually or as required. We were already in advanced discussions with NMO on agreeing the appropriate process and hoped to introduce it in 2012, since the shortcomings of the single day-rate were well recognised by us all.

To add further confidence in the governance of NPLML and to facilitate a greater partnership approach to the operation of NPL, we proposed to establish a more representative board structure by again inviting senior staff from BIS/NMO and the academic sector to become members. We believed that this, together with a review of the current NMS programme management structure in collaboration with NMO, would lead to a more integrated, responsive and fit for purpose governance process.

Since the start of the PFI project for building a new Laboratory in 1998, facilities management (FM) services had been hived off from the main Term Contract under a separate agreement with DTI. Under the NSC and following the termination of the PFI contract, FM services continued to be contracted directly with our Government customer. Once the retrofitting of the new Laboratory had been completed this arrangement became less efficient and there was a need to optimise FM support to enable improved delivery of these services and facilitate the implementation of changes to the Laboratory infrastructure required by the new NMO science strategy and ultimately the Teddington site as a whole. Options were proposed that included NPLML managing the FM contract as agent to NMO and/or taking on lead responsibility for re-letting the FM contract when it was due to be renewed in 2014.

Recognising that BIS may wish to develop an alternative operational model for NPL in the longer term, we offered to work in partnership with them towards their preferred organisational structure and facilitate the transition. Options may have included changes to the scope (e.g. measurement, accreditation, standards) and nature (e.g. GOCO, mutual, JV etc.) of NPL's business model. As a final valuable and far-sighted gesture of goodwill and with Serco's blessing, we also confirmed that we would be supportive should NMO/BIS wish to consider an amendment to the NSC during the extension period to facilitate post 2019 operations.

It was hoped that our presentation would generate genuine interest and facilitate a better understanding of BIS's requirements and priorities for the future of NPL so that a mutually acceptable operational solution could be identified. It might then be used as a benchmark against which other business models could be judged either at the end of the existing Contract or the extension.

Our Follow-Up Proposals (November 2011) – 'A Site Strategy'

The presentation, I believe, was well received but it became clear that Sir Adrian Smith was looking for a more expansive vision for NPL covering the whole site and how this might impact on NPL's role as an NMI in the national innovation system. This, of course, went well beyond our remit under the NSC and the scope of our extension proposals. BIS and NMO themselves had responsibility for the NMS and NPL site strategy for the development of the estate so it would require input from them.

With capital budgets that barely covered the costs of maintaining the existing NPL buildings, NMO's site strategy was limited to the potential development of an Advanced Metrology Laboratory subject to the availability of sufficient future funding. Nevertheless, in anticipation of a closer working relationship with NMO, we agreed to return to the BIS Review Group at a later date with a vision for the Teddington site.

The presentation was updated to include additional information on NPL's role in delivering science excellence and supporting UK growth and quality of life covering the next 5 to 7 years together with a new section which incorporated an ambitious vision for the development of the Teddington site.

We concluded our presentation by reiterating the case for Contract extension and the opportunity it provided for consideration of long-term (post 2019) solutions and our willingness to work together with BIS to position NPL for their vision of the future.

A Strategy for the NPL Site

Our strategy for the Teddington site was to transform NPL into a Research and Innovation Hub to realise its full potential and significantly contribute to the UK's growth agenda through accelerating the development of new products and services. This development would go hand in hand with expanding our regional footprint where we already had strategic partnerships and shared facilities with the University of Surrey, Edinburgh and Oxford, Huddersfield University and St Mary's University College. Our extensive interface with customers and stakeholders from Government, academia and industry enabled us to ascertain potential demand for different types of facilities. We were then able to identify possible locations for them on the current site. These developments would be phased over a number of years and would depend on their strategic importance, availability of funding/financing and the acceptance of detailed investment appraisals and/or business cases.

Additional facilities to deliver this vision of a Research and Innovation Hub on the NPL site included:

An Advanced Metrology Laboratory (AML)

Our Metrology 2020s vision had outlined emerging challenges for metrology science in areas such as new quantum technologies, climate change, large scale research in Big Science and measurement frontiers from atom to large scale and at a far greater level of complexity and integration. This was already part of NMO's longer term strategy for the site and the possibility of additional BIS funding had been identified. Our aim was to establish such a centre in long-term partnership with leading academic institutions such as Imperial College and University College London to develop a Centre of Excellence that furthers the understanding of underlying scientific principles as well as providing a reference point for industry in these newly emerging technologies.

Unique Test Facilities
As technologies are pushed to their limits and new ones are developed to operate at the leading edge of our understanding, companies require new unique facilities to test and validate them. The site at Teddington with its state of the art measurement laboratories and associated infrastructure was ideal for companies to invest in such facilities, with the added benefit that some might be made available to the whole of UK industry as national capabilities. Enquiries had already been received from the energy sector around housing facilities on site to assess the performance of materials, coatings and sensors in extreme and harsh environments.

Demonstrator Capability
A growing requirement from industry and government was for the experimental design and testing of prototypes and demonstrators to ensure new technologies and products were properly validated and their benefits fully quantified and realised. NPL was already active in this market in areas such as thermal performance of building structures, smart infrastructure and wireless sensor networks and structural health monitoring of large civil structures.

Light Industrial Units
Through a network of regional centres and our Technology Innovation Fund, NPL already aimed to support over 3,000 companies in our customer base to gain access to our knowledge, expertise and facilities. A feasibility study undertaken by external consultants for BIS and NPL had identified 'strong demand' for an innovation centre on the Teddington site. This need could be most efficiently met by building a small number of flexible light industrial units to accommodate both small to medium enterprises (SMEs) to larger companies looking to house niche divisions or research.

Knowledge and Innovation Centre
To support NPL's role as a Research and Innovation Hub, there would be a requirement for additional conference, visitor and learning facilities. It was therefore proposed to build dedicated conference and collaboration space as well as a teaching lab that could be used by children, students and teachers alike, enabling knowledge exchange and skills development.

As well as these new facilities, our site development included proposals for modifying and extending the main Laboratory and some of the existing buildings to provide further space for the organic growth of our business.

It can be seen that our site strategy was not a 'pipe-dream' but based on our understanding of available additional funding from BIS and real revenue generating demand or alternative funding for these new facilities in close proximity to NPL's on-site expertise and services. Of course, a Research and Innovation Hub would, in itself, be an outstanding marketing and sales tool raising interest and awareness in our products and services and generating additional income for NPL.

Funding the NPL Site Development
These ambitious, (perhaps too ambitious), plans for the development of the Teddington site would however require a significant level of additional capital investment. Our site strategy included an outline of the likely capital expenditure required and, equally important, the programme funding and additional revenue streams needed to finance the operation of the facilities once constructed. Key to this was a real commitment from BIS to maintain and increase whenever possible the funding of NPL to ensure it remained one of the leading NMIs in the world. It would allow us to leverage and attract additional funding from other Government Departments, universities and the private sector. If securing sufficient new money became an issue then the existing buildings on the Teddington site (and a portion of the land) were Government owned, giving an opportunity to raise additional loan financing at historically low cost. Alternatively, there were a number of other funding or financing options through grants and the European Investment Bank, again with low, long-term rates.

If such an expansion plan were to be adopted it would be advantageous for BIS to have direct reporting lines to NPL giving that all important 'gateway' to Whitehall again. The strategy would recognise (at long last) NPL as a lucrative investment in UK's industry and quality of life that contributed to the economy and GDP, improved the efficiency and profitability of individual companies and created thousands of new skilled jobs.

Sir Adrian Smith and the BIS Review Group, advised and assisted by NMO and with input from the RSRAE Group, now had an opportunity to consider in detail the value of our proposals. We were expecting this to be a critical period when negotiations would finally commence. Serco and the NPLML executive team had set aside time to field clarification questions, respond to further requests for information and update the NPL Business Plan to 2019. It was expected that this would be an opportunity to ensure our proposals fully reflected BIS's future vision for NPL and incorporated their feedback and any further requirements.

The expected round of negotiations did not, however, materialise, confirming that the writing was indeed on the wall for the NSC. Perhaps the GOCO model or Serco itself were out of favour with the Minister. The Chief Executive of NMO displayed little liking for the power and management responsibilities that the Contract delegated to the Managing Director of NPLML. Of course, this was precisely what had attracted government to the model in the first place with its commercial freedoms, flexibility of operation and swift decision-making that was so important in a competitive commercial world.

With no approaches or negotiations it was therefore easy to come to the conclusion that NMO/BIS were already working to an alternative agenda for the future of NPL and perhaps looking into other possible operational models. It was also a long-standing view of the RSRAE Advisory Group that the commercialisation of NPL through the GOCO model detracted from the science. Although there was no evidence of this being the case, this sentiment, if used selectively without reference to the robust safeguards within the NSC and our successful track record in both science and business, could have cast doubt on the effectiveness of the model. In fact, with BIS funding for NPL decreasing in real terms over the Contract period, the growing income generated from our commercial business had been an essential element in generating a substantial level of additional investment in science.

The Ministerial Decision

Although there was some high level dialogue in January 2012 between members of NPLML's Board, Sir Adrian Smith and John Dodds, Director, Innovation at BIS, there was only limited follow up on our extension proposal. A phone call was received from the Minister, David Willetts, supported by Peter Mason, NMO's Chief Executive, on Tuesday 13th March, explaining their decision for the future operation of the National

Physical Laboratory. He acknowledged that we had already presented our proposals for running NPL under a Contract extension to Sir Adrian Smith and the BIS Review Group and that he had also reflected on the findings of the RSRAE Advisory Group assessment of the quality of science and other feedback from stakeholders. His principal objective was that 'NPL remained in the premier league of national measurement institutes' and considered that there might be 'better ways for getting the most from the significant assets we have at Teddington'.

In his follow-up letter he also explained that he had set in train work to explore alternative options for the operation from or before 31 March 2014 but did not expect these to include 'running a competition along the lines of the 2004 exercise'. At that stage, however, he had not ruled out some form of extension but wanted to consider 'other governance and contractual models'. There were a number of options to explore and their aim was to find a solution which:

- Strengthened the quality of science;
- Made better use of the existing facilities by sharing and collaborating with the academic community;
- Made better use of the site, on which there was spare capacity, by attracting synergistic partners; and
- Facilitates more involvement and interaction with business.

This was a deeply disappointing outcome, particularly as our proposals had highlighted exactly how we would address all of the Minister's aims and continue to build on our proven track record of success. Even if he had been fully appraised of our successful track record and the value of our proposals, we had not managed to convince him of the advantages of an extension to the NSC. It may still have been considered too much of a constraint to the Minister's aspirations and not offer the desired scope for change. Perhaps returning NPL to the public sector with some sort of partnering arrangement with universities was becoming a more attractive option. I understand that during this process, in July, Serco did offer to include a university partnership as part of the Contract extension, potentially with a modest equity share but by that time the die was probably cast.

The delivery of this project was delegated to NMO who did not have the management experience, expertise and skills in-house and would have to call upon considerable input from outside advisors and consultants (including NPL staff). At this stage there was no indication of the likely status of 'new' NPLML within Government. This could potentially have a major impact on the commercial and operational freedoms the new entity might be able to exercise. To address the issue and keep NPL as far from the Department as possible but retain some safeguards which full privatisation would not offer, an equity partner, perhaps a university, was considered. This would not, of course, be possible without addressing the NPLML pension fund deficit, a fact probably still not fully appreciated by NMO at this time and a major error of judgment. A move back into Government would again rekindle concerns over such issues as the adverse impact on commercial income and operational efficiencies gained over the past several years, state-aids and access to grant funding; constraints on staff recruitment/remuneration and marketing/selling expenditure; the imposed use of shared services and how Government accounting and procurement would affect the viability of the Company. Stepping away from the established GOCO model would be a major project!

If NMO was seriously considering the sale of an equity share in NPLML then this 'exercise' was likely to escalate into the production of a full-scale 'prospectus' for an organisation that was far more complex than might have been assumed from its modest turnover of over £70M in 2012. NPL was involved in a wide spectrum of activities. Its income was diverse – not-for-profit, research grant, EU matching funds, low value calibration services, long term research contracts, imports and exports. Expenditure was also spread over a large number of specialist suppliers and NPLML owned a considerable asset base of leading edge, specialist and unique scientific equipment which could be valued in various ways. The tax affairs of a Company within the research and development environment were not straight forward and as NPLML was the principal employer of the Pension Scheme there would be significant implications for the contributions associated with the recovery plan for the deficit and accumulating future liabilities.

In addition, there was a conflict of interest in NMO acting on behalf of BIS in determining the future of NPL. On 2 previous quinquennial reviews, with the blessing of Government, NPLML had reviewed the possibility of merging with NWML which had become part of an enlarged NMO. Latterly, a working party which included non-executive members from both NMO and NPLML had looked favourably on the benefits of combining their respective measurement operations. In these circumstances it would be difficult for NMO to demonstrate that it was being even handed and, indeed, its own future was likely to be dependent on the outcome of the project. No feedback was received on the considerable financial benefits potentially running to more than £25M that had been offered in our proposals (particularly the removal of the Pension Scheme deficit and on-going funding risk) and no attempt had been made to explore in more detail what a final extension agreement might look like.

However, with a heavy reliance on consultants and other specialists (and extensive input from NPL), NMO nonetheless set about exploring alternative options for the operation of NPL.

Chapter 7 - End of an Era

Contract Termination

A number of contractual obligations and constraints came into force in the last 2 years of the NSC. These had been highlighted and discussed at our monthly management meetings with representatives of NMO. Following the Ministerial 'decision' that other options were to be considered for running the Laboratory in the future, we drafted a formal side letter to the NSC confirming our understanding of the requirements and processes together with other related issues and this was signed on 11th April 2012. It covered the period to the 'Transfer Date' when the Contract terminated on the 31st March 2014. The requirements were grouped under various themes:

- Contract Management – NMO had to be notified of any sales or purchase contracts exceeding £30k which would not be completed by 31st March 2014.
- Assets – Authorisation of procurement was already covered by the Capital Planning process and disposals were notified quarterly under the existing asset management procedure.
- Employees – The NSC stated that we should cease the recruitment or dismissal of senior employees. This was fundamentally in conflict with handing back the Laboratory as a going concern at the end of the Contract. We therefore clarified that the definition of a senior employee would be based on a certain grade rather than an actual salary amount and agreed that we would continue to recruit, manage and reward these staff members under our normal business processes provided that NMO was kept informed of our intentions.
- Trade Unions and Representative Bodies – Day to day management of the Laboratory before the Transfer Date might also require NPLML to amend, vary or abrogate collective agreements and, again, NMO were simply content to be kept informed.
- Changes to the Undertaking or Business – All the services offered by the Laboratory formed part of the undertaking and so this did not present an issue. The only possible case would be the potential sale of AgPlus Diagnostics Ltd. which would need NMO's approval anyway.

- Accommodation – Any issues would be handled between the NMO Estates Manager and the NPL Estates team as part of their normal business.
- Legal Proceedings – NMO acknowledged that sensible management of the Laboratory might require NPLML to become involved in legal proceedings and in these cases we would agree with them beforehand the aims and objectives of each action.

There were other additional contractual requirements which, until a final decision was made on the future operation of NPL, we agreed were inappropriate to commence, namely, that NMO did not require us to start the preparation of a Transfer Plan or form a 3-person 'Co-Operation Project Team'.

While NMO were exploring alternative options for the future operation of NPL, Serco and NPLML were kept entirely in the dark about their timetable, process and project plan. Indeed, their 'unannounced' approaches to some of our customers and other stakeholders caused unnecessary concerns which had to be dealt with tactfully as, often as not, these were commercially sensitive. At this stage, NMO had not addressed key fundamentals for achieving a new sustainable NPL organisation structure. It is difficult to see how these early discussions with potential partners or other interested parties could have informed the eventual decision making process but it did, perhaps, help NMO gain a little more understanding of the workings of universities, industry and NPLML's business itself.

The Final Ministerial Decision

NMO's progress was slow and it was not until the 28th November 2012 that Sir Peter Williams and Dr Brian Bowsher at NPLML received a telephone call from David Willetts. The Minister had decided not to extend or re-compete the Contract and therefore it would terminate on the 31st March 2014. The new organisation would move back into Government ownership and include 'strategic partners'. NMO was again assigned the task of delivering the project by the NSC termination date. There was nothing left for us to do but to accept the Minister's decision and support BIS and NMO in making the transfer of NPLML as smooth as possible and provide all necessary background information to them so a workable, sustainable solution could be found.

It was the end of an era for NPL after nearly 20 years of being run as a Government Owned Contractor Operated organisation. For me, it was a sad note on which to step down from the Board of NPLML but I had fulfilled my final task of supporting the production of our Contract extension proposals. It was time to hand over the reins to a new, very capable Finance Director, Nicola Anson, who would take on the role from the 1st January 2013. I was retained by NPLML in a part-time consulting capacity to assist in the production of NPLML's and AgPlus's 2012 Statutory Accounts and, as I had an in-depth knowledge of the NSC, lead the preparation of the NPL Transfer Plan required by the NSC.

The transfer would mean a significant increase in our workloads but we were determined to keep disruption to NPL's science to a minimum. It was Serco's policy always to 'exit with excellence' when Contracts came to an end. NPLML mobilised the 3-person Co-Operation Team supported by a number of other function heads so that a smooth and timely transfer to Government ownership could be achieved. NMO secured additional funding from BIS to engage a firm of consultants initially to ensure that the necessary Government procurement rules were followed and ensure the successful unwinding of the Serco Contract but they were soon to realise that the project, which also included the selection of strategic partners, was far more complex and onerous than first thought. Over the extended Transfer Period, the consultants' remit was continually expanded and probably eventually cost more than a full rebid of the Contract.

Value of Existing GOCO Operating Model – Was it Under-estimated?

Given nearly two decades of successful operation, it was difficult to understand the Minister's decision. Certainly the GOCO business model was no longer favoured politically. Without a well-founded partnership between NMO and NPLML, it is not surprising that the NSC might have been considered too inflexible and difficult to revise, acting as a constraint to the Minister's aspiration of possible university equity partners. Joint ventures, perhaps with mutual or not-for-profit organisations were in the ascendance at that time. However, these organisations, by their very nature, were extremely risk averse and unlikely to participate in an equity partnership. Other organisational models like companies limited by guarantee or ownership by a professional body, if allowed by their articles of association, would suffer from the same financial and operating constraints.

NMO initially held out hopes of securing an equity sale to demonstrate long term commitment and 'glue' in the partnership. This, and the possibility of a cash 'windfall', although unlikely, might have helped to support a case not to extend the Contract. We were convinced, however, that this outcome was extremely remote, at least until some of the 'show-stoppers' had been resolved like the Company's pension deficit, NPL's status within Government and its future funding. It was our view that the financial risks and obligations associated with NPL would therefore revert to BIS together with an increasing requirement for additional funding to ensure the Laboratory's future sustainability. A measure of the business risk Serco was prepared to bear was reflected in their contractual guarantee to indemnify BIS against any potential losses up to a figure of £50M. Risk transfer was, and still is one of the key tests of value for money but seems to have been discounted or not fully appreciated in NPL's case.

Given NPL's enviable track record it might have been easy for NMO/BIS to come to the conclusion that there was little left to extract from the NSC in terms of further efficiencies and therefore the organisation structure no longer represented best value for money. After all, Serco had transformed NPLML into a very successful National Laboratory and a thriving business which, with the same executive and management team (as all but the managing Director had employment contracts with NPLML), might be run just as effectively and efficiently within Government. NPLML's profit margin, part of which was distributed to Serco as dividends, could then be retained by BIS (hopefully for the benefit of NPL). A proportion of Serco's management fee charged to NPLML might also be saved but most of these reach-back benefits would have to be sourced from other suppliers. Of course, protection from the costs and future liabilities of the pension scheme would be lost as would the commercial drivers of a private sector company but perhaps this might have been welcomed by the RSRAE Advisory Group. However, maintaining value for money and operational efficiency in an increasingly competitive commercial environment requires continual improvement – it is a 'race' without a finishing line!

There were still uncertainties over NPLML's new status under Government ownership which might impact operational freedoms and access to the funding and financing enjoyed in the private sector. It also seemed to me that the significance and magnitude of Serco's unique and generous offer to take over the NPL Pension Scheme liability might not have been fully explored and considered by the BIS Review Group. Without the GOCO model and Serco guarantees, significant additional BIS funding would have to be found before NPLML would be a viable, sustainable 'going concern' within the public sector.

David Willetts was keen to strengthen the quality of science. In our extension proposals we had shown how this could be achieved with the minimum of modifications to the NSC by underpinning existing funding and we had shown our willingness to work in partnership with NMO/BIS towards their preferred organisational structure and facilitate the transition during the extension period. Our world-class science had been validated by the International Science Benchmarking Exercise published in 2011 and we could also point to the near tripling of our peer-reviewed publications and citations since 2004. We already had strong working relationships with 70 universities (45 in the UK; 25 international), 20 NPL staff held visiting appointments and we had participated in 321 joint papers with 'top 10' partners in the previous 5 years. These achievements were delivered in spite of reduced funding. Our extension proposal had made a commitment to further investment in science capability funded by continual improvements in operational efficiency and growth in commercial revenue.

As far as improved utilisation of existing facilities and the expansion of the Teddington site were concerned, our proposal to NMO and BIS had shown, with the support of Serco, how the Minister's aims might be achieved. NPLML had made a commitment to increase its efforts to share resources both in Teddington and regionally with universities and industry. We already had an 'industrial hub' at the University of Huddersfield and had commissioned a study to establish an 'NPL Scotland'. Serco was better placed than most of the other viable options to take advantage of funding and financing opportunities from both public and private sector partners.

NMO must have underestimated the cost, time and complexity of delivering the task assigned to them as, for example, the NSC had to be extended by a further 9 months to the 31st December 2014. The project was reliant on support from advisors and consultants covering a number of work streams including transfer arrangements, selection of an equity partner or partners, negotiation of beneficial terms and assessment of the viability of new organisation structures. It involved the production of a detailed 5-Year Corporate Plan or 'prospectus' including a financial and funding forecast at a time when many fundamental questions remained unanswered about the impact of the transfer on NPLML's future sustainability.

By contrast, the cost of a Contract extension would have been minimal and relatively easy to implement and, of course, given NMO/BIS the time to resolve outstanding questions and explore fully the options open to NPL.

Alternatively, although under pressure to deliver the Minister's assignment by the end of the Contract, it might have been easier for NMO to implement the Transfer Plan first as most of this work was resourced by NPLML and Serco and could realistically be delivered within that timescale. The selection of a strategic partner could have followed towards the end of the NSC when there would be greater clarity on how the Pension Scheme deficit might be addressed, the estimated level of future funding for the NMS, the eventual status of NPL within Government and additional guarantees that might need to be in place. As soon as it became evident that a solution to these issues was likely to be protracted and there would be no prospect of raising cash through an equity partner, much of the nugatory work undertaken by NMO, their consultants and NPLML might have been avoided. The process of selecting a university partner or partners could then have been conducted from a position of greater knowledge about NPLML's future science aspirations and business. With fewer uncertainties, a larger number of universities might have shown interest in partnering with NPL and the selection of the best strategic fit could have been completed in a much shorter time scale.

Within NPLML, however, our main task was to make sure that NMO and their consultants had all the information necessary to support them throughout the project in order to gain a full appreciation of the implications of their decisions as a new organisational structure for NPL was developed.

Developing a New Sustainable NPLML Organisation

The transfer of NPLML back into Government ownership was well specified in the NSC. There were 2 options within the Contract, either a Share Sale Agreement (SSA) where the entire equity of NPLML was returned to BIS at the value of its Consolidated Net Assets, or an Asset

Sale Agreement (ASA), valued in the same way but with the 'shell' Company remaining with Serco.

The Minister's decision also included possible equity partners. They would want to understand BIS' future vision and objectives for NPL as an NMI and the part they would be expected to play in the new organisation. This would inevitably lead to more detailed discussion of the respective risks and rewards for the new shareholders. Initially NMO did not have answers to even the most fundamental questions that future investors in NPLML would be seeking. However, it was still decided to open exploratory dialogue with universities and other prospective partners whilst, in parallel, progressing the SSA, their preferred option.

A Menu without Prices

The need for a 'prospectus' or 5-Year Corporate Plan therefore soon became a priority. NPLML's existing Business Plan produced as part of the Contract Extension proposal was a sensible baseline. However, we were not party to NMO's project plan and little was known about its vision for NPL beyond the end of the Contract so we set out a number of initial fundamental assumptions upon which the validity and robustness of a forecast would have to be based until these outstanding issues were resolved. This would also make sure that all parties, NMO, its advisors and NPLML had a shared understanding of the available information.

A fundamental assumption was that NPLML would continue to operate as a single stand-alone entity and not be subsumed into a Government Department or Agency. As such, the Company would still apply commercially accepted International Accounting Standards and continue to adopt the principle of a 'full economic costing' (FEC) model.

Under the existing model NPLML's integrity and independence had been of the utmost importance. The introduction of equity partners could limit this independence and mechanisms to manage potential conflicts of interest would have to be incorporated into the new organisation structure so that the Company could continue to enjoy unencumbered development of its business, products, services and intellectual property. Moreover, it was assumed that the status of the new Company would not place an unreasonable restriction on NPL's business and trade, for example, limiting its calibration services, international collaborations or selection and recruitment of new employees, their remuneration packages and salary increases.

There were a number of other important basic factors that were still unknown and so NPLML's existing forecast remained the best starting point for producing a prospectus or 5-Year Corporate Plan. For example, BIS would have to undertake to continue funding the capital requirements of NPL's existing building infrastructure, its maintenance, repairs and alterations. This would include any additional budget for the Advanced Metrology Laboratory or similar development and associated programme costs not shared by the new partners. There was an assumption BIS would continue to fund the NMS Research Programmes at the existing level of around £45M p.a. with an annual inflation increase and that the Company's new status would not reduce NPL's access to European grants and co-funding amounting to more than £7M p.a.

Until an indication of the new cost base of the Laboratory was confirmed it was also assumed that the pricing of all NPL's business, both NMS and third party, would remain the same. Any variation could potentially affect the competitiveness and therefore volume of our work. Another significant cost discussed in our contract extension proposal was the contribution to the NPL Defined Benefit Pension Scheme and additional payments as part of the deficit recovery plan. Its removal would have a very beneficial impact on the Company's cost base. Without a solution the Company's going concern status would be in jeopardy. Similarly, the insurance premiums paid under the NSC amounting to more than £1M p.a. might be avoided if BIS were to be permitted to self-insure NPL.

Under the NSC, BIS would be required to pay to Serco the consolidated net assets valuation of NPLML on the Transfer Date. In addition, the Company would require enough cash to provide working capital for its forecast investment in double digit sales growth. Serco was prepared to be flexible in its dividend policy for NPLML as it approached Contract termination, allowing the net assets valuation, cash and dividend position to be managed to meet BIS's requirements. At this stage, it was reasonable to assume that the Corporate Plan would include sufficient working capital to finance the Company's cash forecast and BIS would therefore have to set aside new cash to settle the transfer price.

With this level of uncertainty surrounding NPL's Corporate Plan, it is not surprising that the production of a new, robust operating model for presentation to potential partners was fraught with difficulty. Project delivery was inevitably delayed, requiring the Plan to be continually updated.

University Challenge

We were now fast approaching the end of 2013 and the Transfer Date. Much time had been lost pursuing the unrealistic goal of attracting equity partners. NMO was therefore forced to change its policy and begin its search again for strategic university partners without the requirement of equity investment. Throughout the remainder of the bid proposal period NMO had to modify its requirements and 'goal posts' were moved. One by one, many interested universities and other potential partners dropped out of the selection process. As the project faltered, BIS became more involved, led by its Director, Innovation. The NSC was extended to 31st December 2014 to give more time for the negotiations to be concluded, the project plan and its objectives were re-established and progress finally made towards the selection of preferred bidders and their proposals.

In July 2014, David Willetts announced a partnership of the Universities of Surrey and Strathclyde had been identified as a preferred bidder to enter into a new strategic partnership with BIS and NPL. Both these universities had been consistent and strong contenders throughout the long and often difficult process. The proposals of the 2 universities brought together their track record of working with business and industry and their complementary academic strengths. Working with BIS and NPL they aimed to establish a Postgraduate Institute to train up to 300 high-calibre PhD students providing a pipeline of skilled researchers and expand the number of regional 'hubs' which reflected local expertise and business needs like the already successful University of Huddersfield.

David Willetts, Minister for Universities and Science, stated that the new partners' proposals provided:

> 'the best opportunity to meet the aims set at the beginning of the process. The partnership will help boost NPL's and the partners' scientific excellence, will strengthen engagement with business, and will make more of the facilities and the site'.

NPL was to retain its role, status and international standing as a world-leading National Measurement Institute, meeting the needs of UK industry.

Brian Bowsher, NPL's Managing Director, said:

> 'We already have strong links with both universities and see exciting opportunities to broaden NPL's science, develop our regional footprint and continue the growth and impact of our work for UK industry'.

In January 2015, NPL transferred back to Government and was 100% owned by BIS. At that time many of the original issues still remained unresolved. These included the exact form of the university partnership agreements, NPL's business classification within Government, the level of NMS funding, the future of the NPLML Pension Scheme and deficit, the building or site rent, scientific asset financing, grant eligibility and the Company's position on 'State Aids'.

A Partnering Agreement was finally concluded between BIS, now the Department of Business, Energy & Industrial Strategy (BEIS), NPL, the University of Strathclyde and the University of Surrey on the 1st April 2015. It included a commitment to maintain NPLML as an appropriately capitalised going concern.

Transition and Transfer Plans

As soon as the Minister decided not to extend the NSC, Serco mobilised the necessary resources to implement and support BIS in the delivery of the Transfer Plan. The process was governed through the Serco Exit and Transition Board with 3 members from our parent company led by Ian Downie, Managing Director of the Strategic Partnerships Division, and 3 members from the NPLML executive led by Dr Brian Bowsher. In my capacity, now, as an Internal Consultant my responsibility was to prepare the draft Transfer Plan assisted by other managers within NPLML. There were 2 major elements to the Plan:

- Execution of the Share Sale Agreement (SSA), transferring NPLML from Serco to BIS in compliance with the provisions of Schedule 25 of the NSC.

- Transition of services and reach-back benefits provided by Serco so that NPLML could continue to operate as a 'going-concern' on hand back.

The requirements were specified in the Contract but as the agreement was 10 years old it needed to be updated and agreed with NMO to ensure a smooth transfer. Rather than have 2 sets of lawyers pouring over the agreement, Serco offered to use their own legal counsel to review, mark up and agree any changes with NMO and this was duly accepted.

Delivering a Going-Concern

Under the GOCO arrangement NPLML was largely self-sufficient but it did benefit from a number of services and contracts managed by Serco. These were delivered at arm's length either through contracts with Serco Shared Service or external providers managed by Serco. In addition, further important reach-back services were provided by Serco's own central functions. In order to maintain a going concern at the point of transfer of NPLML, all of these functions and services had to be identified, requirements and options analysed, new providers sourced, procured and implemented before or by the Transfer Date. The activity was led by NPLML's Infrastructure and Support Services Manager, Dennis Yates, who was responsible for NPLML's Contracts and Purchasing teams. This was managed as a separate 'Transition Project' within the overall Transfer Plan.

Where possible, Serco contracts with external providers were novated to NPLML. These included pension administration, actuarial services and management, and contracts for IT software and hardware. Where novation was not possible alternative solutions had to be sought through open tenders and subsequent implementation of a new service provider. These were in areas such as payroll and HR benefits, insurance, utilities, business travel support and fleet management for company and pool cars. Other functions and services provided by Serco also had to be replaced either by external advisors or resourced in-house by NPLML. These included specialist accounting, finance and tax services, HR administration, central procurement, health safety and environmental advice and company secretarial services. During this process Serco supported negotiations with existing suppliers, facilitated the procurement of new contracts and were flexible in the timing of implementation during 2014.

The Transfer Plan

There were a number of key requirements in the NSC dealing with the return of NPL to BIS. These covered the specifics of the 'Transfer of Shares in the Contractor'; 'Co-operation' in preparing the Transfer Plan; 'Disclosure' including NPLML's Annual Reports and Financial Statements and a Schedule of Warranties; and the form of the 'Share Sale Agreement' defining the process and terms of the transfer of the shares in NPLML (and its subsidiary, AgPlus Diagnostics Limited) including the Completion Accounts, Payment of Price, Deed of Tax Covenant, Warranties and other Disclosures.

Our Transfer Plan covered these activities in detail with proposed completion dates and responsibilities and was subsequently agreed by NMO by the end of 2013 without amendment. In addition, a Risk Register was drafted noting potential issues and how these might be mitigated to ensure our work with NMO was properly co-ordinated and deadlines achieved.

In early 2014 NMO/BIS took the inevitable decision to extend the existing NSC and on the 12th February they obtained Cabinet Office approval for up to 1 further year. Previous side letters to the NSC were also rolled up into the extension including our agreement with NMO on adopting multiple rather than a single day rate and how AgPlus was to be treated on transfer. Subsequent advice from the Shareholder Executive, however, recommended that AgPlus should no longer form part of the undertaking on transfer and, rather than closure, Serco offered to source prospective buyers. Although the expectation was initially that NMO would choose to take the full 1 year extension to the Contract, a 9 month period to the 31st December 2014 became the preferred Transfer Date.

I had agreed to retire at the end of April 2014 and saw no reason to delay my departure any further. I had agreed the Transfer Plan with NMO and supported Serco and the NPLML executive team as best I could during this difficult, complex and often frustrating period. By this time, Serco had still not received formal notification of the actual method of transfer of NPLML; whether it would be a share or an asset sale. NMO/BIS were probably waiting for the outcome of proposals from the university bidding groups before confirming their final decision but with near certainty that there would be no equity sale to partners, the SSA still seemed the more likely option and I assumed that an alternative Transfer Plan to cover an asset sale would not be necessary! My retirement was short lived as in September 2014 I was asked by Serco to continue my (very) part-time consultancy under contract to them in an advisory capacity only and cover the actual transfer process and completion accounts of AgPlus Diagnostics following its sale.

The NPLML Share Sale – 'Payment of Price'

As soon as the new Transfer Date was known, NPLML's financial forecast was revised including, most importantly, the Company's net assets valuation at the end of the Contract. This value, however, could be reduced depending on NPLML's dividend policy during 2014. NMO/BIS were kept informed of this value as it represented the sum payable to Serco (subject to retention sums) on completion of the share sale. No dividends had been declared by NPLML in 2013 as the auditors, in the absence of a future funding commitment from BIS, were already concerned about NPLML's status as a going concern when operation passed to Government. The Serco Exit and Transition Board was still happy for BIS to determine the level of dividends, if any, to vary the net assets position in the final year whilst making them aware that some form of guarantee acceptable to the auditors would need to be in place. BIS therefore not only had to give careful consideration to the level of working capital required by NPLML on transfer but also the quality of the 'guarantee(s)' to give sufficient comfort that the business would be a sustainable going-concern in the future.

NMO had first expressed a preference for the net assets value to be kept to a minimum but realising that sufficient working capital could be an issue on transfer, subsequently requested that NPLML should be left with enough working capital in the short term to avoid additional funding having to be sourced by BIS. In addition, NMO, through BIS, began preparing a case for presentation to Treasury for guarantees to be put in place that supported NPLML's Balance Sheet in the early years of Government ownership. From the 1st January 2015 NPLML would be liable for the full extent of the pension scheme deficit rather than only the period of the Contract term (under the GOCO model's 'franchise accounting') and this together with the bank loans for operating assets would create a negative net assets position and considerably weaken the Balance Sheet. Needless to say, no cash dividends were paid by NPLML in 2014 and a further cash injection from BEIS would be required sooner rather than later.

Key Areas of Accounting 'Judgment'

Pension Scheme Contributions

On the assumption that an acceptable BIS guarantee or asset would be in place enabling NPLML to offset the pension deficit, there remained the issue of ongoing Company contributions to the Scheme following the independent, formal 2013 triennial valuation. This took place every 3 years and had to be agreed by the scheme trustees, the Government Actuary's Department (GAD) and, of course, NMO/BIS. Global markets were still fragile and the deficit had increased by a further £10M since 2010 even after the substantial additional annual contributions. As BIS had not accepted our Contract extension proposal to merge the Scheme with Serco's, a new strategy had to be formulated to address the deficit issue and the future of the Scheme. From 2015 funding the deficit recovery plan and future accruals for pension payments would effectively become the ultimate responsibility of BIS. In the meantime, all the parties accepted that any further increase in the Company's contributions would be detrimental to its financial stability and that maintaining the existing level of contributions (including the additional payments) and extending the recovery period was the most acceptable solution at that time.

GAD was also asked to carry out a valuation based on its own financial assumptions. It served as a possible precursor to transfer to the Government's own 'classic' Principal Civil Service Pension Scheme (PCSPS) perhaps with the deficit being reimbursed over a period of time if permitted. This did not prove to be a viable option in the remaining timeframe and so the necessary Government funding assurances (effectively guarantees) were put in place including a 5-Year Corporate Plan for NPL approved by BIS, pending a more permanent solution.

On the 30th March 2016 BIS made an equity investment in NPLML of £59M to reduce the pension deficit by £30M, the loan balance (for scientific equipment) by £20M and to provide further cash reserves. This additional funding increased net assets, recapitalised the Balance Sheet and finally dispelled any continuing going concern issues, allowing the 2015 Annual Report to be signed off and the agreement with NPL's university partners to be honoured. In March 2017 a further equity injection of £37M was made which enabled the NPLML Pension Fund deficit to be removed and the Scheme to be placed on a 'self-sufficiency basis' (i.e. the expectation that no further funding would be required from BEIS in the future).

AgPlus Diagnostics Valuation

In 2011 NPLML had set up a subsidiary company, AgPlus Diagnostics to take an innovative diagnostic technique to market and later the following year it was agreed with NMO that there should be an independent 'open market' valuation of AgPlus each year as the Contract end date approached. A firm of accountants was engaged to carry out the valuations based on the company's 3 year rolling forecasts with additional benchmarking against 'comparable' start-ups'. BIS, on advice from the Shareholder Executive, no longer wanted the risks and financing responsibilities associated with AgPlus. An agreement was finally negotiated that transferred the 86% shareholding from NPLML to Serco at the end of the Contract by a dividend 'in specie' valued at £3.6M offsetting the outstanding loan funding in AgPlus. The valuation of the investment in NPLML's accounts of £4.2M was written off against the revaluation reserve.

Tax Position

As a research organisation NPLML could take advantage of the generous tax advantages granted by the Exchequer and was entitled to claim R&D Tax Credits for its programme work and 100% first year allowances on its purchases of scientific equipment. Being a wholly owned subsidiary it could also pass any unused tax losses to its parent company. NMO/BIS did not confirm in writing that they intended to trigger the sale of NPLML until the middle of 2014, enabling full annual group relief to be claimed up to the Financial Year 2013. After this, special tax rules came into play called 'Arrangements in Place' which removed this utility. The savings in corporation tax (CT) were particularly valuable as they improved NPLML's cash flow and provided essential working capital to finance year on year investment in the Laboratory, grow its business and finance the substantial additional contributions to the pension scheme of £2.3M p.a.

The Final Curtain

On 1st January 2015 NPLML returned to Government ownership after 20 years as a private company. NPL was to continue its life as a Public Corporation. The classification owes much to the significant and growing proportion of its total revenue generated from third party customers under the GOCO business model. As a Public Corporation NPL can continue to benefit from at least some of the freedoms and a level of autonomy previously enjoyed. A key strength of NPL is that it straddles both public and private sectors. It was fully recognised by BIS that the board and executive members in the new corporate structure would play a critical role in ensuring the continuation of this essential bridge to NPL's stakeholders both in the UK and internationally.

Up until its final day the GOCO model was robust and still operating effectively and efficiently, the NPL executive team and staff were reaping even more success and our international standing remained high. The third party (non-NMS) business had continued to grow even through the difficult economic climate since 2008 and the last 3 years of uncertainty and increased workloads caused by the transition. It was testament to the Serco/NPLML transition team that the transfer was completed smoothly and effectively with the minimum disruption to NPL's science and business. Dr Brian Bowsher had maintained the trust and high regard of BIS throughout the process and was asked to stay on as Managing Director of NPLML over the initial transition period while a new Chief Executive Officer (CEO) was recruited. At the end of June 2015 NPL finally bid him a fond farewell after serving the Company as Managing Director for 6 years.

Dr Brian Bowsher with his portrait in the Globe Room of Bushy House on the occasion of his retirement

NPL was managed on a temporary basis by Dr Martyn Sené until replaced by Dr Peter Thompson as CEO on the 3rd September 2015. Although this was the final curtain, it is salutary to reflect on NPLML's final year of operation as a GOCO, its commercial and scientific achievements and legacy.

The highlights are summarised in the Foreword to NPLML's Annual Report for the year ended the 31st December 2014, the details of which are included below.

> *'It was another very successful year for NPL both commercially and in science. Total revenue was £79.9M, an increase of over £2M from the previous year and £21.6M since 2004/05. Most of this growth came from competitively won third party work which amounted to £32.4M. By contrast this was just over £10M at the start of the NSC (after the transfer of the TTI contracts to Serco valued at £3M) and so represented a sustained growth rate of more than 10% p.a. over the 10 year period. At the same time NPL's commercial sales order book stood at a record high of £52.2M with major new contract wins to manage the €600M European Metrology Programme for Innovation and Research (EMPIR) on behalf of the EU and a £7M contract from the Defence Science and Technology Laboratory (Dstl) to lead developments in quantum technologies.*
>
> *Growth in NPL's business was vital to sustain increasing levels of investment in the Laboratory's science and infrastructure against a background of flat funding from BIS. Our over-arching strategy remained constant through the Contract and comprised 4 key elements: excellent science, international status and influence, demonstrating social and economic impact, and growing a sustainable business.*
>
> *Excellent science was demonstrated by our scientists producing a record 280 peer-reviewed publications, many in the most prestigious journals. Our Centre for*

Carbon Measurement continued to go from strength to strength and 3 new Centres were also established: the National Centre of Excellence for Mass Spectrometry Imaging (with the University of Nottingham and the pharmaceutical industry (notably GSK); the Quantum Metrology Institute with partnerships with DSTL, Innovate UK and the Research Councils; and the Global Sensing and Satellite Centre (GloSS) in partnership with Surrey University.

Our international status and influence flourished with major projects with sister measurement institutes in China, India and Thailand all delivered to time, cost and technical specification as well as being trusted to manage the prestigious EMPIR Programme as part of our work for the EU.

Demonstrating impact whether social or economic has been at the core of our science strategy for a decade. Each of our NMS Programmes included (and hopefully still do!) a deliverable to measure its beneficial impact and we supported Government in producing econometric analyses showing the significant value of science and innovation to the UK, so important to boost competitiveness, increase productivity and create skilled jobs.

Growing a sustainable business underpinned investment for the long-term and supported the recruitment of 110 people enabling greater strength in depth in key and developing technologies. The greatest priority of the NPLML Board, executive and staff is to ensure the Laboratory operates safely and at the end of the final year we had achieved over 2.5 million hours without a 'loss-time' accident'.

'Transformation' has become an over-used word these days often denoting change programmes that are soon forgotten till the next time! I believe, in NPL's case, the adoption of the GOCO business model as a stand-alone private limited company encompassing all the activities of the Laboratory, met, and probably exceeded, the Government's original political and economic aspirations. Of course, it is impossible to tell what NPL might have looked like today if it had remained a Government Agency but with decades of Government budget cuts, austerity programmes and economic turmoil it is hard to see how it could have grown into the successful research organisation it is today. Real transformation has to include a significant shift in the organisation's culture and this we undoubtedly achieved whilst maintaining its core values of scientific independence, integrity, and a strong service ethic.

These firm foundations have created a legacy upon which NPLML can continue to move forward now as a Public Corporation and fulfill the aspirations of a new Government and political order in a world that will be very different. But one thing remains certain and that is the importance of supporting the UK's science and technology in an ever more competitive global market place.

Some of NPL's Highlights 2004 – 2014

2007
NPL time signal moves
The antenna that broadcasts the time throughout the UK on behalf of NPL is moved from Rugby to Cumbria in a change of contract.

2010
Graphene and the Nobel Prize for Physics
The Nobel Committee cited NPL's pioneering work in the metrology of graphene to illustrate the scientific background for the 2010 Nobel Prize for Physics.

2011
The world's most accurate clock

NPL's caesium fountain atomic clock, known as NPLCsF2, is revealed to be the most accurate long-term timekeeper in the world as it would lose or gain only one second over 138 million years.

The clock is used as the primary frequency standard for the measurement of time in the UK and contributes to the worldwide timescales used for global communications, satellite navigation and time stamping of financial transactions.

2011

TRUTHS

The Traceable Radiometry Underpinning Terrestrial and Helio-Studies (TRUTHS) is a benchmark satellite calibration system. The proposed mission would provide the data needed to reduce uncertainty in climate forecasting and its realisation is one of the long-term objectives of the Centre for Carbon Measurement at NPL.

TRUTHS has the potential to position NPL and the UK as the go-to source for the most accurate spaceborne climate data.

TRUTHS will also provide policy makers with the confidence to take quick, decisive and 'fit for purpose' action, encouraging the world's governments to take critical decisions on appropriate mitigation and adaptation strategies.

2012

Launch of the Centre for Carbon Measurement at NPL

The Centre for Carbon Measurement is launched to reduce uncertainties in climate data, provide the robust measurement required to account for, price and trade carbon emissions, and help accelerate the development of low carbon technologies. The Centre brings together academic and business partners with government and builds on NPL's capabilities in environmental measurement and low carbon projects.

2012
World's first room-temperature maser

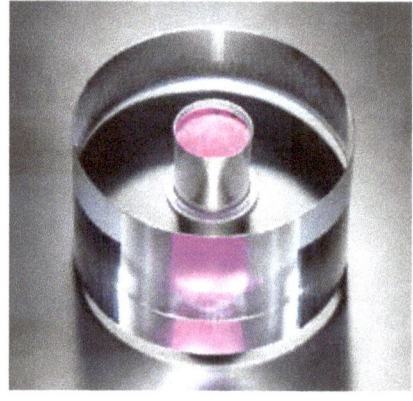

Scientists from NPL demonstrate, for the first time, a solid-state 'MASER' (microwave amplification by stimulated emission of radiation) capable of operating at room temperature, paving the way for its widespread adoption. The team from NPL and Imperial College London has demonstrated masing in a solid-state device working in air at room temperature with no applied magnetic field. This breakthrough means that the cost to manufacture and operate MASERs could be dramatically reduced, which could lead to them becoming as widely used as LASER technology.

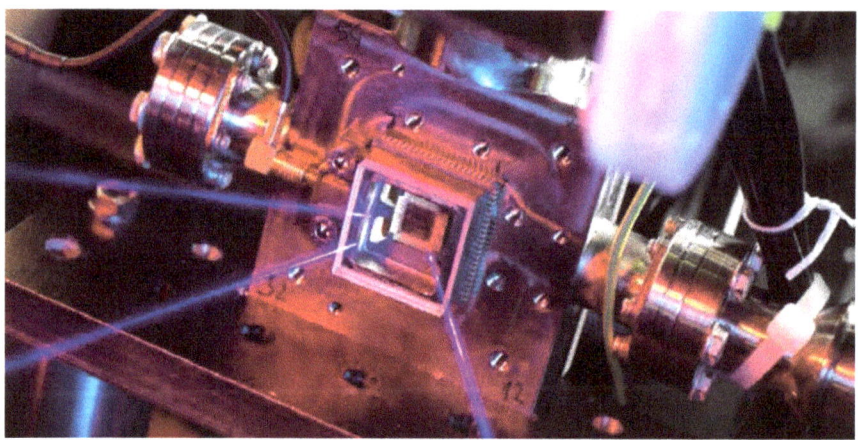

2012
Trapping ions on a chip

A ground-breaking device, demonstrated for the first time at NPL, could help usher in the era of quantum computing. Quantum algorithms can perform certain calculations exponentially faster than classical systems and quantum cryptography could improve data security to an almost unbeatable level. This technology is based on the use of entangled particles known as qubits to perform calculations.

NPL's novel device is a 3D ion microtrap array made from a silica-on-silicon wafer using a scalable microfabrication process. Scientists were able to confine individual ions, as well as strings of 14 ions, in a single segment. The microfabrication process will enable the creation of more complex devices which could handle even larger numbers of ions, while retaining the ability to control individual particles.

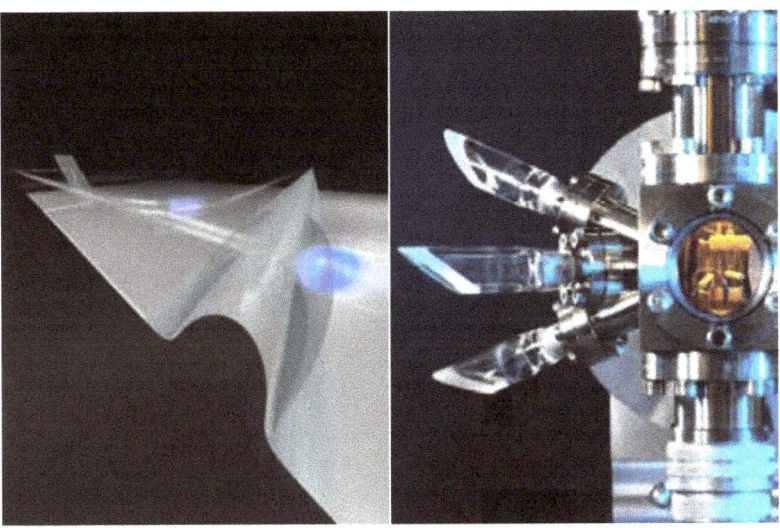

2013
NPL*Time*®

A new service called NPL*Time*® was launched, offering the financial sector a certified precise time signal, directly traceable to Coordinated Universal Time (UTC) and independent of GPS.

This removes susceptibility to problems such as jamming and solar storms.

2013
World's first graphene single electron pump

The present definition of the SI unit of electric current, the ampere, is vulnerable to drift and instability, and is not sufficient to meet the accuracy needs of present and future electrical measurement.

An innovation from NPL and the University of Cambridge could pave the way for redefining the ampere in terms of a fundamental physical constant. The team successfully produced the first single electron pump made from graphene, which creates a flow of individual electrons, emitting them one at a time at a steady rate. Exploiting the unique properties of graphene enables fast operation of the pump, overcoming the Achilles' heel of metallic pumps, slow pumping speed. This provides the electron flow rate needed to create a new standard for electrical current based on electron charge.

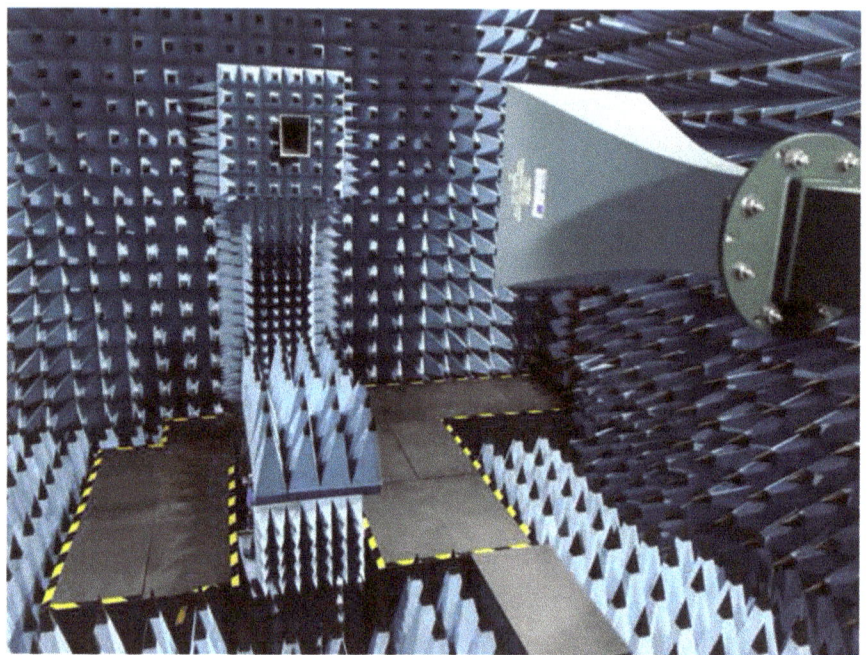

2015

Official opening of NPL installed antenna range at NIM China

Following two years of design, construction, installation, validation and training, an NPL project to install an antenna extrapolation range at the National Institute of Metrology (NIM) in China was officially opened in April 2015.

Since opening a new campus in Changping, north-west Beijing, NIM has been keen to improve its microwave antenna measurement facilities through collaboration with NPL. Over the course of the project, the NPL team made multiple site visits, produced over 300 design drawings and manufactured and tested hundreds of parts. In addition to the hardware supplied, the project also included the provision of software, procedures, validation and training.

Chapter 8 – Back to the Future

NPL as a Public Corporation

At the time of writing, NPL had only been a public corporation for just over 2 years so it is much too early to judge whether the change in operating model will deliver the hoped for objectives. However, within Government ownership, the public corporation classification offers NPL the greatest opportunity to maintain a reasonable degree of commercial freedom, grow its third party (non-NMS) turnover and continue to deliver the hugely beneficial industrial impact so vital for the UK economy.

Serco achieved its objective of 'exiting with excellence' and NPLML transferred to 100% BIS ownership on 1st January 2015, no doubt with the customary 11th hour rush. Its public corporation status was confirmed in March and the Partnering Agreement with the Universities of Surrey and Strathclyde was signed on the 1st April.

Extra Government Funding

Other issues, particularly those concerning funding would take longer to address. The Universities Partnering Agreement had committed BIS to funding NPLML as an appropriately capitalised going concern and, as noted in the previous chapter, on the 30th March 2016 BIS was able to access the necessary budget and make an equity injection of £59M into the Company. This allowed NPLML to reduce the pension scheme deficit by £30M, clear much of the loan liability for the scientific assets of £20M and provide a reasonable level of working capital. NPLML's Balance Sheet then returned to a positive net assets position, addressing any remaining going concern issues.

A Pension Scheme can be valued in a number of ways. From the 1st January 2015, NPLML adopted the Financial Reporting Standard 102 (FRS102) for small and medium sized companies based on International Accounting Standards. It specifies the valuation convention to be used in annual statutory accounts so as to maintain consistency and comparability between companies. This is different from the valuation basis used by the Scheme actuary which is updated every 3 years and takes into account a greater number of variables. It is known as the 'on-going' basis and tends to be a more realistic, 'member centric' view of the Scheme's assets and liabilities and inherently has indicated a far larger deficit than the appropriate accounting standard. The independent actuarial valuation as at 31st December 2015 showed a deficit of £22M on the accounting standard basis and £51M on the actuarial on-going basis. The NPL Pension Scheme was allocated £30M so it was likely that additional lump sum cash contributions would be necessary.

In March 2017 a further equity investment of £37M enabled the NPLML Pension Scheme to be placed on a 'self-sufficiency' basis leaving the option open for its eventual transfer back into the appropriate Civil Service Scheme.

The NPL Laboratory Buildings

At the same time that NPLML was transferred to BIS, the Laboratory buildings and plant, valued at £194M, moved to its balance sheet as a fixed asset with costs being defrayed through a property lease 'rental' charge to NPLML as before. The buildings were re-valued but with little change. However, the rental charges were reviewed and revised, increasing considerably from £7.8M to 12.1M p.a. leading to a knock-on rise in NPL's prices, primarily recovered through the NMS Programmes so that it was cost neutral to the Company. Although this is a 'circular' movement of funds, it does maintain the principle of NPL charging 'full economic cost' for its services. As an observation the annual rise in NMS turnover shown between the 2015 and 2016 Annual Accounts was therefore mostly due to price increases rather than a greater volume of work.

The Strategic Partnership

It will take time for the benefits from the partnership with the Universities of Surrey and Strathclyde to manifest themselves. Whilst the growth of third-party income seems to have slowed as the Laboratory assimilates its new structure, the university interactions seem to have catalysed the development of NPL's Post-Graduate Institute and also aided the growth of regional activity. Research programmes cannot be switched on and off quickly and they will have to be formulated or re-aligned to ensure they remain relevant to all parties. It is, however, likely that individual 'side' agreements will have to be concluded as appropriate on such things as apportionment of investment, funding and returns together with resource commitment and sharing IP outputs and exploitation.

Value for Money – Return for the Taxpayer

As NPLML required an additional amount of cash funding of £59M after transfer to BIS and an additional lump sum contribution of £37M to the pension fund the following year, it might be easy to question the original decision to move NPLML back into Government ownership and not take advantage of the Contract extension proposals. After all, with hindsight, Serco's offer to merge NPL's Pension with its own defined benefit scheme could have saved the majority of the £67M paid by BIS/BEIS. Although a comparatively small lump sum contribution would have been required from BIS, the case for an extension could not have been sufficiently strong or appreciated for the necessary funding to be released at that time. Whatever the reason, Government budgets can seem very inflexible when 'spend to save' opportunities arise.

Given the success of NPL over the Contract term, it might be questionable whether, at that time, a 5-year extension to the Contract would have been too higher price to pay. Practically speaking, within a research environment it takes a good 3 years to reallocate funding to new programmes (without incurring additional costs). Serco had been well-disposed to introducing new (possible equity) partners to NPLML during the extension period as part of a well-planned future strategy. Aligning research programmes and agreeing investment opportunities with partners takes time and these arrangements could have been put in place before termination of the extension to facilitate a seamless transfer to the envisaged new operating model.

The recapitalisation of NPLML through additional equity also enabled the loans from the leasing company for scientific equipment amounting to £20M to be extinguished. The rationale was that, as a public body, borrowing from the Treasury should represent better value for money. Going forward NPLML's newly acquired assets will be financed through BEIS who will be paid a capital charge of 3.5% p.a. and the debt will build up over time to a 'steady state' eventually matching their net book value. This interest rate (or 'cost of capital') will be reflected in the full economic cost calculations for pricing purposes and I understand that BEIS will be 'recycling' the interest received, back into the NMS research programmes. For comparison, under the tripartite leasing agreement between NMO, NPLML and the lender, the average interest payable was 3.36% in 2014. With the relative freedom of a public corporation and effective asset management, the previous strong arguments for private finance no longer prevail providing, of course, BEIS can continue to provide the necessary capital funding for NPL (see Chapter 3 – Investment in New Facilities and Capital Assets). Ultimately, with sufficient free cash available, it might be feasible for NPLML to purchase assets outright but there are likely to be other demands with greater returns or political expediency, to take precedence.

It can often be very misleading to look simply at costs or inputs and this is particularly true of research and development. Indeed, I (together with so many others) spent a good deal of my time at NPL extolling the virtues of the quality of the outputs as being the best measure of value. Within a Civil Service budgetary regime it seems to me that there will always be a conflict between 'inputs' vs. 'outputs' and 'cost' vs. 'return on investment', the former, a short-term and finite measure, the latter, longer term and more open to judgment. Only time will tell whether NPL's move back to Government ownership does turn out to be better value for money for the taxpayer in the longer term but this will be another measurement challenge with too many uncertainties! Hopefully the future for NPL will continue to be bright without any detrimental effect on the great scientific outputs that NPL produces year on year.

What of NMO?

Responsibility for NPL transferred back to BIS on the 1st April 2015. The case for synergies and savings resulting from a merger with NPL were not strong enough to sway Ministers' opinion and it was decided that NMO's existing legal metrology, technical and enforcement work should continue under a new name, the National Measurement and Regulation Office (NMRO). A year later, the Better Regulation Delivery Office (BRDO) and NMRO were brought together into a single directorate within BIS to focus on regulation and enforcement, with uncertainty on any future occupancy of the Teddington site.

Serco's Rise and Fall

Serco's business and contract portfolio continued to grow throughout the NSC. At its zenith in 2013 turnover reached over £5bn. Although the NPL Contract had become a very small part of Serco's global portfolio it was still considered to be one of its most valued assets. It was an outstanding example and showcase of Serco's successful management and operation of a complex Government facility of world renown.

Since the beginning of the original Term Contract Serco had been keen to demonstrate its commitment to protect and maintain NPL's independence, integrity and reputation. The Board of Directors included independent, non-executive members from academia and industry and since 2002 Sir Peter Williams had been the Chair. There was also an open invitation for Government representatives to join the Board or attend its meetings. Although a wholly-owned subsidiary of Serco, NPLML was nevertheless operated as a separate stand-alone entity whilst still benefitting from its management, professional expertise and support.

As we operated effectively 'at arm's length' from Serco's mainstream divisions, my understanding of Serco's changing fortunes over the latter years of the Contract is limited. The banking crisis and subsequent collapse of market confidence had a devastating impact on businesses world-wide. Economic recession and Government austerity programmes affected most organisations. As the majority of Serco's contracts were in the global public sector, its prospect of continuing 'double-digit' sales growth and improving profit margins were obviously threatened. Nevertheless, from the start of the economic crisis, there was a genuine motivation across Serco's contracts to support the various Government Departments and identify improved ways of working and budget savings. Opportunities were found to vary or extend existing contracts for the benefit of all parties but others were cut back or cancelled.

The share values of companies throughout the world dropped significantly as the severity of the crisis unfolded. With its strong order book and secure mainly government backed cash flow Serco fared better than many and was promoted to the FTSE 100 in December 2008 somewhat earlier than expected. However, with the prospect of severe cutbacks in government spending, Serco's own growth prospects came under intense scrutiny from the City. To support its share price dividends were increased but this could only be a short-term remedy and a change in operating model and business strategy became vital. Serco embarked upon a much greater drive to attract business from the private sector and acquisitions in business process outsourcing were seen as an opportunity to achieve diversification and critical mass rapidly in a fiercely competitive market-place. Serco's own support services were further standardised and centralised with more processes performed 'offshore'. For a company that had such a diverse portfolio of contracts a 'one size fits all' operating strategy often did not sit comfortably with operating managers who were also put under greater pressure to do everything they could to protect or improve margins whilst maintaining levels of service. This was easier said than done and I do wonder whether maintaining growth and the status of a top 100 company to satisfy City expectations began to be given undue emphasis in some parts of the business to the detriment of its founding principles and values.

Within NPLML, our corporate structure buffered us from the worst vestiges of these pressures and by the General Election of 2010 our reporting line into Serco had changed and the 'special' status of NPLML and other entities like us were properly recognised under a new Division called Strategic Partnerships.

On the election of the Coalition Government in 2010, Francis Maude became Minister for the Cabinet Office. He formed the Efficiency and Reform Group (ERG) to work with H M Treasury with the aim of making Government Departments more efficient, stopping wasteful spending and improving the way goods and services were procured. I understand that commercial negotiations were even opened with major Government suppliers to secure reductions in contract prices and 'rebates'. As future business was at stake, refusal was not an option. These were desperate times!

In July 2013 news broke that there was to be an inquiry into Serco's (and G4S's) contracts with the Ministry of Justice over their charges for operating tagging schemes. Serious failings in the management of these contracts were uncovered. By then Serco had grown its turnover to £5B and perhaps the values espoused by the executive team had become too detached from the day to day realities and responsibilities of contract management in this particular business area. Although Serco was subsequently cleared of fraud allegations in December 2014 it had suffered an 18 month suspension from fresh Government work, undergone a full audit of all its Government contracts and suffered considerable damage to its reputation. Serco made due reparations to Government and, through a major project, provided them with evidence of a full review of the Company's processes and procedures together with proof of implementation of all the necessary improvements in its management and control of contracts. As a separate entity, NPLML itself underwent a full audit of its NMS Research Programmes and a review of its annual Statutory Accounts all of which were accepted without issue.

The enquiry into Serco's affairs did not, however, affect the outcome of Ministerial decision about the future of NPL as this was made in 2012, well before these contractual issues had come to light. It did no doubt help vindicate the decision not to extend the NSC as it neared termination.

For Serco, the reality check came early. As the outsourcing market adjusted to austerity, competition became fierce and prices fell. Private companies were often far too optimistic in their assessment of business risk, margins were squeezed and government far too willing to accept the lowest bids for the most sensitive of public services. Although at the time of writing the outsourcing industry is facing a crisis the model is by no means broken and painful lessons are now being learned by all parties.

Many contracts work well and the NPL GOCO agreement is an outstanding example of how a complex national facility can be managed effectively as a true partnership offering long term sustainability, value for money and sharing of benefits for the public good. The GOCO model is discussed in more detail below and later in Appendix B – the NPLML Business Model.

GOCO or No-Go?

A number of important fundamentals need to be in place if the benefits of the GOCO business model are to be optimised for all the parties to the contract (and stakeholders including the taxpayer and society at large). The lessons are all too apparent for those who have lived through the experience.

Political Will

Before anything can happen, of course, there has to be the political will for change. As we have seen in Chapter 1, during the early 1990s, an immense head of steam had been building to cut public spending and improve the delivery of science within Government owned laboratories. When Michael Heseltine was appointed President of the Board of Trade in 1992 he quickly proceeded with 'prior options' reviews of all DTI's laboratories and for NPL, the GOCO business model enabled HMG to maintain ownership and ultimate control of this valuable national asset but introduce private sector management and commercial practices which had a number of significant benefits. Greater commercial freedom would enable new sources of income to be generated from selling a larger proportion of NPL's expertise and services to third party customers resulting in improved asset utilisation and economies of scale. Better value would also come from reductions in government bureaucracy, a greater emphasis on operational efficiency and more effective delivery of its programmes of science, allowing real reductions in its science and technology budget to be made immediately and in subsequent years without loss of scientific outputs.

Another benefit of the process is that it forces Government to think through in some detail what they want from their assets in terms of future vision, mission and objectives and how these are best achieved. In NPL's case it gave the NMS Research Programmes a valuable long-term contract commitment which was hugely welcome.

The Government seemed to have been deterred from emulating the NPL GOCO model across other public bodies, perhaps in early days because of the cost of the bulk transfers of members' civil service pension entitlements to private sector 'look alike' schemes. Nowadays, this obstacle has been removed as there is no longer a requirement for members to transfer out of civil service schemes if their work moves to a Government contractor.

The Underlying Contract

The effectiveness of the underlying contract comes right at the top of the list of essentials. This is illustrated by our original 1995 contract which was extremely well crafted and certainly stood the test of time. It cleverly balanced the interests of both DTI and Serco and emphasised the partnering approach to the management and operation of NPL. A separate entity with independent members on its board as well as an invitation for Government representation cemented that principle together with open book accounting and the transparency of an overall profit share arrangement independently certified by the Company's auditors. As we have seen, unfortunately the 2004 Contract changed some of the pricing mechanisms which tended to undermine the principles of putting excellent science first although NPLML/Serco continued to strive for this outcome.

A Partnering Approach

It is also essential that a GOCO arrangement is managed and operated as a true partnership based on mutual trust. Of course, there still needs to be a well-drafted and 'watertight' contract but all parties have to sign up to delivering a shared strategic vision and set of objectives. For the vast majority of our tenure this modus operandi prevailed but regrettably diminished as day to day supervision was handed over to NMO. Even then, the trust was such that, except where we needed clarification or mutually agreed changes, the NPL contract was consigned to the bottom drawer and stayed there!

For their part, Government Departments must be willing to extend the maximum operational and commercial freedom to the contractor so as to gain optimum benefit and be prepared to accept a reasonable but modest profit return to be charged commensurate to the level business risk and perceived benefit. Serco was content to accept a return of 5% on turnover in return for a long term Government contract with secure and transparent future cash flows whilst always ensuring performance guarantees were met. DTI could be reassured further by Serco's partnership approach, unfettered access to NPLML's business and financial information and the innovative cumulative profit share arrangement, a proportion of which could be ploughed back into funding additional NMS projects.

Despite some poor publicity surrounding certain Government contracts (and privatised industries), I still believe that it is possible to combine a successful commercial business with a strong public service ethic and social purpose but the organisation structure has to be right (see Appendix B). I would like to think that the Government Departments responsible for NPL over Serco's tenure always thought of the Company as their own but without the management and operational worries and commercial risk!

Long-Term Strategic Commitment
For a contractor to take full responsibility for business risk where there is a large proportion of national 'mission driven' work involved, Government needs to commit to an agreed level of annual funding for the duration of the Contract together with long term strategic objectives so that a robust business and financial plan can be produced. In NPL's case, as the UK's National Measurement Institute and an essential part of the country's metrology infrastructure, guaranteeing an appropriate level of funding over the initial 5 and then 10 years was not seen as an issue but as time went on, making a long term commitment seemed to be more of an obstacle. Certainly, one of the key advantages of the GOCO arrangement for NPL

over, say, a public corporation, was the Government's long term guarantee of a minimum research commitment.

'Reach-Back' to Parent

Although NPLML was set up as a stand-alone entity and operated at arms-length from Serco, it was essential to have reach-back to a financially strong parent with access to all their skills and expertise. In 1995, at the beginning of the Contract, NPLML's turnover amounted to about 25% of Serco's! When Dr George Gray, the then Chief Executive of Serco was asked by the DTI tendering team what assurances he could give them of his commitment to the GOCO Contract he simply said that he would put all the resources of the entire company behind it if he had to – and he meant it! As Serco grew we were able to reap the considerable benefits of the economies of scale it offered and take advantage of its continual development of best operational practice (rather than reinventing the wheel for ourselves). For example, it meant that NPLML could not only secure the considerable insurance cover required by the Contract but also enjoy the savings resulting from Serco's purchasing power. It allowed us to rely on Serco's expertise in setting up a new defined benefit pension scheme for transferring NPL employees and benefit from much reduced management and advisory fee structures. As a wholly owned subsidiary of Serco, from day 1 of the Contract we could trade normally, with suppliers extending 30 day terms of credit to NPLML. For DTI and subsequent Government Departments there was the overarching contractual guarantee indemnifying them from potential losses of up to £50M.

Proximity and Connectivity to Government Decision-Making

Just as reach-back is important, being at the heart of Government is essential especially for organisations like NPL with its enormous social and economic impact. NPL, of course, is evangelical about its research and the services it can offer and has an excellent professional marketing and communications team. It is also essential that NPL benefits from a direct reporting line into a Government Department with wide-ranging intelligence of the many initiatives relevant to NPL and well-established links, access and proximity to those decision-makers to enable timely interventions where the Laboratory can make a positive contribution and difference to the many national challenges. As a public corporation, NPL is now enjoying a noticeable renaissance in its status as a full Government partner; influencing, shaping and contributing to strategic decisions for improving UK industry and the economy. This partnering approach and connectivity into government thinking is essential to maximise the impact and benefits to be derived from a national institution like NPL.

Private Sector Management and Commercial Practice
Much has been written previously about the benefit of introducing private sector know-how into a public sector organisation. Ministers were determined to see real change and lasting reductions in Government expenditure. I believe that the original rationale for adopting the GOCO model and entrusting Serco with the stewardship of NPL for nearly 20 years did deliver the desired outcomes. We managed the substantial business risk associated with running NPLML. We grew NPL's science and impact and increased value to our Government owners by optimising opportunities for business growth and cutting costs so that the considerable infrastructure overhead could be spread over a far greater customer base. Using innovative approaches, we delivered the NMS Research Programmes, managed the operating assets more effectively and efficiently and shared the surplus profits of the Company with our Government customer.

It is unlikely that NPL as a public corporation will operate as efficiently as a private company. The equity injection of £96M will help reduce costs, especially in the short term. Being a more integral part of Government should help generate more publicly funded work and grants but will private sector engagement and revenue suffer? The organisational structure seems more complex but might serve to generate more opportunities to expand the business in the future. It is noticeable, for example, that the numbers of administrative staff reported in the accounts have increased by about 15% from 2014 to 2015 and a further 8% between 2015 and 2016. As a percentage of total staff they appear to be trending towards 25%. It will be interesting to see how the new operating model progresses – but that's another book!

Operating and Commercial Freedom
In 1995 it seemed like a courageous step for Government to entrust the operation of a National Laboratory and NMI to the private sector. In those pre-PFI days Serco/NPLML was responsible for both the delivery of the science and maintenance of the Teddington site and buildings. In my opinion, maximising these freedoms gave the greatest opportunity for Government's strategic objectives to be realised and long-term

transformation to be achieved, always providing the underlying contract is well structured (as was ours in 1995).

At NPL some of these freedoms were to be eroded somewhat when, in 1998, the estates and facilities management services had to be split from the NPL Term Contract as required by the PFI for the new Laboratory. Although necessary, it did create additional contractual boundaries with both DTI and the new FM contractor and inevitably affected some of the flexibility previously enjoyed. Likewise, the changes to the pricing mechanisms in the 2004 NSC failed to reconcile the financial and scientific aspirations of our Government customer making delivery more challenging, particularly as 'higher science' became more of a Ministerial priority in later years.

GOCOs can come in many different forms. Perhaps the simplest is the insertion of a private sector management team into a public sector organisation to drive transformational change. This was successfully demonstrated at the National Nuclear Laboratory (NNL), when a consortium of Serco, Battelle and the University of Manchester, carried out a change programme from April 2009 to October 2013. These arrangements are nevertheless inherently more limited in scope and short-term until a more permanent operating solution can be found.

Full privatisation can be an option if a long-term commercial business case can be developed and sufficient investment attracted. The Laboratory of the Government Chemist (LGC) was successfully privatised in 1996 on the back of significant growth prospects from increasing regulation and outsourcing from both the public and private sectors. In 2001, the Defence Evaluation and Research Agency (DERA) was split into 2 organisations. QinetiQ took on the commercial business and was floated on the stock exchange. The renamed Defence Science and Technology Laboratory (Dstl), retained research capabilities best delivered as a trading fund within Government. Privatisation always has the challenge of negotiating and agreeing a fair deal for the taxpayer, a notoriously difficult task with potential for undervaluation and windfall profits for management, staff and shareholders.

For NPL, as a National Measurement Institute of growing importance to the UK research and innovation infrastructure, particularly now that we are destined to leave the European Union, full privatisation has never been considered a viable option. The NPL Contracts (1995 and 2004) had many advantages which I have waxed lyrical about on numerous occasions but, perhaps, the formation of a single, ring-fenced private limited company to manage and operate the Laboratory has proved to be one of its greatest strengths. It provided the assurance, checks and balances of an independently constituted board and cemented the partnering approach with Government; gave them full unfettered access to our business information including bespoke systems for monitoring their NMS Research Programmes and offered a share in the overall profits of the Company. Although there were Government rules concerning state aids and anti-competitive behaviour we were actually afforded a great deal of operational and commercial freedom enabling us to be flexible and adaptable as an organisation and weather the storms of economic recession, cuts in our NMS budget and decant to a new Laboratory whilst further developing scientific research. The Company still continues to operate, now as a Public Corporation – long may it prosper!

Epilogue

Although perhaps the GOCO model is currently not favoured within Government, public attitudes and political policies do change over time. I still believe for organisations with similar attributes to NPL, it is an important tool in the Government's arsenal where private sector management and commercial practices can be successfully employed to transfer risk and bring about transformational change often beyond the capabilities of Government. In fact, we see constantly within the media, public services are under great strain as, for example, the demography of our population changes and the UK's political and economic position on the world stage evolves. Surely it is incumbent on Government to ensure that there is a pool of private sector companies that have the competencies and social purpose to support them in their change agenda and deliver value for money to the taxpayer.

I am certain of one thing at least and that is how extraordinarily successful NPL Management Limited and the GOCO model have been over the last 2 decades and although biased, I have set out the achievements and will let them speak for themselves!

Appendix A

NPLML MANAGING DIRECTORS: 1995 – 2014

Name	Tenure
Dr Peter Clapham	1990 – 1995 (under DTI)
Dr John Rae	1995 – 1999
Dr Julian Hunt	1999 – 2000 (Interim)
Dr Bob McGuiness	2000 – 2005
Steve McQuillan	2005 – 2008
Dr Martyn Sené	2008 – 2009; 2015 (Interim)
Dr Brian Bowsher	2009 – 2014 (and 2015 under BIS)
Dr Peter Thompson	2015 – present (under BIS/BEIS)

National Physical Laboratory | Board of Directors – 2014
From left: Ian Downie, Nicola Anson, Richard Brook, Martyn Sené, Peter Williams, Brian Bowsher

Appendix B

THE NPLML BUSINESS MODEL – AN ORGANISATION STRUCTURE TO SUPPORT GOVERNMENT PARTNERING

Our Partnering Legacy

For 20 years NPL Management Limited (NPLML) was a wholly owned subsidiary of Serco Group plc operating the National Physical Laboratory (NPL) on behalf of government. The Company served both the public and private sectors in the UK and globally. During this time it demonstrated that a partnering arrangement between a private company and government department could work extremely well to their mutual benefit and for a wider circle of stakeholders including the UK taxpayer.

With reach back to its parent company it was able to bring efficiencies, investment, innovation and much needed change to the culture and management of NPL to deliver the government's strategic vision for the UK's Measurement Institute. In doing so, it continued to improve NPL's impact within the world of measurement science and consequently UK business and industry. This can be traced back not only to improving the UK's GDP but also increasing the profitability of individual companies using its services including many small to medium sized enterprises (SMEs) as well as attracting overseas investment. It also supported the government's agenda for raising UK citizens' quality of life, for example, improving the treatment of cancer and monitoring air quality. All this was achieved through a partnering arrangement which ensured mutual trust, public accountability, sharing of returns and the transparency that it offered value for money to the taxpayer.

The business model need not be and, in my opinion, should not be confined to a narrow GOCO arrangement. It has many attributes which could serve government, the public and private sectors extremely well and win back confidence in private companies to deliver real and sustainable benefit and value for Government and the UK citizen.

Challenges Limiting Success

Background

GOCO or similar partnering arrangements like the 1995 NPL Contract have unfortunately not been emulated or developed over the years as our original government sponsors had hoped in their discussion paper, 'The contracting out of NPL – partnering in practice' (Chapter 1: Best and Final).

This has not been helped in recent years by a number of high profile cases where the private sector has been found wanting in its delivery of public infrastructure contracts, and the media, quite rightly, has been quick to highlight their shortcomings as has the parliamentary opposition of the day. Success stories generally remain unsung.

Partnerships with private companies, however, can and have been a powerful catalyst for delivering the innovation and continual improvement so vital for our public services. Apart from NPL, my own experience extends to the National Nuclear Laboratory where a partnership of Serco, Battelle and the University of Manchester worked extremely well and successfully turned around a failing organisation by introducing more able leadership and management practices so that now, back in government ownership, it continues to operate effectively. Successful partnerships require strong leadership, mutual respect and trust with well-defined responsibilities and clear policies or strategy for all parties to embrace and work towards. Regrettably, this has not always been the case and challenges remain.

Challenges

The banking crisis and ensuing reductions in government spending adversely affected the outsourcing market. Fewer new opportunities meant greater competition, increased business risk and downward pressure on growth and margins. After the election of the Coalition Government in 2010, the Cabinet Office formed the Efficiency and Reform Group to work with H M Treasury to reduce waste and improve government procurement. Commercial negotiations with major suppliers resulted in price reductions and 'rebates' from existing contracts. (See Chapter 8 – Back to the Future: Serco's Rise and Fall).

In these circumstances, perhaps it was inevitable that, sooner or later there would be repercussions on standards of service, and contracts (or even companies) would fail. Perhaps government departments as well as boards of private companies should shoulder some of the responsibility for these costly failures or issues with contract performance. This more adversarial approach to procurement and arm's length contract supervision still seems to prevail in sharp contrast to the partnering principles of NPL's GOCO arrangement. Some government contracts still require companies to take on 'uncapped' financial risks. How can this be seen as anything other than counter-productive to a good working relationship and shared values?

Perhaps government departments would actually be better served by considering a partnering approach to a wider range of contracts as a more constructive and sustainable means of delivering the service improvements they and the public desire. Properly contracted and managed, partnering arrangements will engender shared values and could offer greater flexibility of resources and value for money over the medium to longer term. It would create a pool of government contractors – companies or subsidiaries of companies both large and small, perhaps with expert partners from the charitable sector or universities etc. Private companies delivering these services or running part of the UK's national infrastructure for the domestic market would then have an organisational structure that better reflects their public responsibilities and ethical priorities together with business objectives that are better understood and accepted by their shareholders and the City.

Even from within the relative 'insulation' of the NPL GOCO I was very much aware of the change occurring in the outsourcing market. With this background, it was not surprising that civil servants remained cautious when working with the private sector. There was a tendency to treat companies as arm's-length contractors rather than trusted partners. The impact on working relationships was often compounded by the rapid turnover of government sponsors who could lose sight of the history, benefits and initial reasons for putting partnering arrangements like the NPL GOCO in place.

Now that NPL has transferred back to the public sector, and no doubt with the hard work of the new chief executive and his team, it appears once again to be treated as a true partner and this has enabled it to be better positioned to play an effective part in supporting government (and also to be the beneficiary of considerable but much needed cash injections). However, as a public corporation NPLML has lost some of its commercial freedoms, flexibility and agility. This in time will impact the growth of third party income streams, operational efficiency and, with government constraints on senior salaries, attraction and retention of staff might also prove a greater challenge.

By the same token, private companies must do more to address their tarnished reputation for feathering their own nests at the expense of public service delivery or being too greedy, expecting a 'fee' that is not commensurate with business risk (assuming a 'fair' contract). In the US, where there are many more examples of GOCO arrangements, contractors generally expect a lower fee. The US Department of Energy, for example, has for many years successfully employed a GOCO approach to managing the majority of its 17 national laboratories and it still remains the favoured choice. Government contracts, well-crafted and performed, can offer companies long term, predictable cash flow with transparency of earnings and sustainable returns.

The NPL Contract made it clear that we should work in the best interests of the Laboratory (and government) at all times. Although the further integration of NPLML's support activities with Serco might have generated greater efficiencies it would not have represented best value to the customer particularly where there may have been a dilution of capability or key skills and a threat to the 'stand-alone' principle. Moreover, speedy access to a contractor or its parent for support or expertise is a vital resource for government departments. Good communication between both customer and contractor is essential but can sometimes be neglected after a contract is let or won.

None of these challenges is insurmountable and can be overcome with the right leadership in place, well-structured and fair contracts, a commitment to service with excellence and a positive shift in ways of working. Indeed, a Cabinet Office 'Code of Good Practice' already exists for partnerships between departments and arm's length bodies. John Manzoni, Chief Executive of the Civil Service and Cabinet Office Permanent Secretary stated in his introduction:

> 'Arm's-length bodies represent an extension of the department's delivery, so really we should think about a

> *department and its arm's-length bodies as a total delivery system. For the system to work well, the relationship between a department and its bodies cannot be just about oversight. An effective partnership must be based on trust, clarity of accountability, and a shared understanding of purpose and outcomes'.*

This echoes exactly the sentiment and practice of the original NPL Contract and is a theme that emanates throughout this entire book. If a similar code were to be extended to companies within the private sector who were prepared to accept the obligations of a partnering contract and make the necessary cultural and organisational changes then a much more favourable environment would be created to help improve and add value to our public services. This has been emphatically demonstrated by NPLML's partnering agreement which spanned 20 years with an outstanding track record.

A Proven Structure to Support Partnering

Key Attributes of the NPLML Business Model

Partnerships with the public sector must obviously uphold a strong service ethic and all interested parties must appreciate the importance and purpose of the contract and be comfortable with the level of risk and return. As has been seen a successful partnering arrangement needs a whole range of attributes. (Chapter 8 – GOCO or No Go). However, an NPLML business model can facilitate a change of culture both within the public and private sectors alike and positively challenge existing values and beliefs.

After all, Serco's investors accepted these very values for NPLML over many years!

Formation of a Separate Entity

Firstly, it all revolves around the formation of a separately identifiable entity (or entities) within which a contract(s) or undertaking is managed or operated on behalf of government. It has several advantages:

- It may include various organisational structures, for example, joint ventures or partners from the public or charitable sectors.

- There is a Board of Directors which could include independent, perhaps government member representatives with specific experience and expertise together with a clear remit to ensure the correct level of (public) oversight. As a subsidiary of a larger company, the board can act as a 'buffer' (or even a deterrent) against unwelcome interference from a parent company and will be protected from any structural changes within the group that may occur over time.
- An Annual Report and Accounts has to be produced and independently audited. The amount of detail within the report can be specified ensuring an appropriate level of scrutiny whilst safeguarding commercial confidentiality or additional certified annual statements can be commissioned on key items like profitability, pensions or internal controls against fraud etc.

A myriad of contract terms and requirements can be specified but as a separately identifiable entity there are some that are essential and far easier to monitor, verify or enact.

- Open book accounting allowing independent scrutiny by authorised parties including the National Audit Office or relevant government department. In NPLML's case, full access to all the company's business information was available giving an even greater level of transparency. Such access should alert stakeholders to operational or financial performance or conformance issues and facilitate early resolution.
- Well documented government 'step in' rights on contract termination or default specifying the agreed process to be followed and identifying the exact basis of valuation of the company or its assets on transfer, ensuring continuation of the operation, a smooth, seamless move to another contractor or back to government.
- Simple 'bottom line' profit sharing arrangements that can be independently certified by a firm of accountants, incentivising both the government and contractor to work in partnership for the benefit of the operation and create savings to be reinvested in the entity. (See below).

Disclosure as part of the Partnering Approach

I have recounted how, on bidding the first NPL Contract, Serco decided to disclose in full its 5-Year Business Plan and Financial Forecast – Profit and Loss Account, Balance Sheet and Cash Flow Statement. In doing so, it showed the company's desired contract profit margin. This was a radical departure from Serco's usual approach to bids where operational solutions and pricing were a closely guarded secret, as perceived unique selling points and margin risk assessments were extremely valuable.

However, full disclosure of a company's business plan does lay the foundations of a relationship based on trust. It enables the customer to gain a full understanding of the structure of the bid and an appreciation of the risk premium that the contractor attaches to various aspects of the contractual requirements. For example, penalties that are too onerous might increase the pricing (and risk) of a contract well beyond any benefit to the customer or taxpayer. In essence, the approach facilitates negotiation of the optimum contract price without unduly prejudicing the robustness and sustainability of the contract or level of service.

Of course, 'cost-plus' contracts already require disclosure of margins together with agreed labour rates and direct costs together with specified allowable overhead rates. Before this type of contract is granted the company generally has to undergo a stringent vetting process to satisfy compliance with quality procedures and value for money criteria. However, these contracts are generally only suitable and used for well-defined project work.

Knowing a company's business plan and forecast profit margins will also allow the customer to make a more in-depth financial evaluation of a cost verses benefit analysis, for example, that will provide a clear rationale of the advantages offered by contracting to a private sector company. If this is coupled to a profit sharing arrangement any possible adverse media or political criticism can be dealt with far more effectively.

Profit Sharing

Profit sharing can take several forms but a separate entity or subsidiary formed to deliver a contract or contracts to government presents the freedom to offer a very simple and transparent arrangement based on the company's 'bottom line' profit, normally pre-tax, as a percentage of total turnover.

It can be further enhanced if a financial forecast is disclosed since this can be used as the basis of calculating the profit share accumulated over the longer term and thus smooth out any year on year fluctuations in the company's results. In the NPLML Business Model this was known as a 'cumulative profit share'. The initial forecast was for 5 years and the pre-tax profit threshold had been agreed at 5% of turnover with any surplus shared 50:50. As the contract unwound, actual certified annual results replaced forecasts and revealed potential profits to share. The mechanism is particularly beneficial where there is exceptional expenditure in one year, perhaps on a reorganisation of part of the business, followed by the desired improvements in performance in future years. Agreement with the customer on the appropriate amount of shared profit to be released for additional projects can then be reached during the normal contract review process. If the contract is extended or is 'open-ended', financial forecasts will continue to be rolled forward and the process can be repeated for as long as necessary.

Surpluses generated by profit share arrangements can, of course, be returned to the Exchequer, but, as they generally fall outside annual budgets, they can more readily be invested in new or existing projects where direct funding is not available.

Total Facilities Management
Contracting out the management of an entire facility like NPL has, in my opinion, real advantages over letting individual contracts on a piecemeal basis. The benefits have been discussed and extolled throughout the book. The approach allows management of a service or operation to be fully integrated with resulting efficiencies and economies of scale. It can offer greater agility and flexibility to meet unexpected demands or emergencies. The amount of administration and contract supervision is reduced so staff can be redeployed to more productive work. For government it can offer greater value and access to the contractor's expertise to support the ongoing delivery of its longer term plans and strategies; for companies it gives transparency of earnings and the potential to optimise the operation of a facility and share savings with the customer.

The Service Ethic

Without getting into a debate about exactly what 'service ethic' is, I would suggest that it has more to do with the organisation's leadership and shared values together with well-trained people and efficient systems and procedures so that customers' satisfaction remains high and companies can demonstrate excellent performance through transparency of information.

Although in practice there has to be a balance between the different interests of the customer, employees, taxpayer, company and shareholders/City, the principle objective of an organisation working for government should always be to deliver the contracted service to the highest standard possible. The NPLML Business Model creates an organisational structure to support this whilst providing opportunities to 'add-value'.

There was a great clause in NPLML's first Term Contract regarding the Laboratory's scientific endeavour and our service ethic:

> 'If there [is] a conflict between maximising impact of our knowledge, and commercial benefit, we [NPLML] will always choose the former.'

I believe this sums it up nicely!

Alan Mann
June 2017

Glossary

Abbreviation	Description
AEAT	AEA Technology Limited
AgPlus	AgPlus Diagnostics Limited
AML	Advanced Metrology Laboratory
ASA	Asset Sale Agreement
AWE	Atomic Weapons Establishment
BEIS	Department of Business, Energy & Industrial Strategy
BIPM	Bureau International des Poids et Mesures
BIS	Department of Business, Innovation and Skills
BNFL	British Nuclear Fuels Limited
BRDO	Better Regulation Delivery Service
BSI	British Standards Institute
CIPM	International Committee for Weights and Measures
DERA	Defence Evaluation & Research Agency
DIUS	Department of Innovation, Universities and Skills
DSTL	Defence Science and Technology Laboratory
DTI	Department of Trade and Industry
EIB	European Investment Bank
EID	Engineering Industries Directorate
EMPIR	European Metrology Programme for Innovation and Research
EMRP	European Metrology Research Programme
EPSRC	Engineering and Physical Science Research Council
ERG	Efficiency Reform Group
EURAMET	European Association of National Metrology Institutes
FEC	Full Economic Cost
FM	Facilities Management
FTSE	Financial Times Stock Exchange
GAAP	Generally Accepted Accounting Practice
GAD	Government Actuary's Department
GDP	Gross Domestic Product
GloSS	Global Sensing and Satellite Centre
GOCO	Government Owned; Contractor Operated
IP	Intellectual Property
ITN	Invitation to Negotiate
ITSU	Information Technology Support Unit
ITT	Invitation to Tender
JV	Joint Venture
KT	Knowledge Transfer
KPI	Key Performance Indicators

LGC	Laboratory of the Government Chemist
LIMS	Laboratory Information Management System
MoD	Ministry of Defence
MProMS	Milestone Progress Management System
MRA	Mutual Recognition Agreement
NAMAS	National Measurement Accreditation Service
NMI	National Measurement Institute
NMP	National Measurement Partnership
NMO	National Measurement Office
NMRO	National Measurement and Regulation Office
NMS	National Measurement System
NMSPU	National Measurement System Policy Unit
NNL	National Nuclear Laboratory
NPL	National Physical Laboratory
NPLML	NPL Management Limited
NPLX	NPL Executive Team
NSC	New Science Contract
NWML	National Weights and Measures Laboratory
PFI	Private Finance Initiative
RDA	Regional Development Agency
RoSPA	Royal Society for the Prevention of Accidents
RPI	Retail Prices Index
RPIX	Retail Prices Index excluding mortgage payments
RSRAE	Royal Society and Royal Academy of Engineering
SME	Small and Medium-sized Enterprises
SSA	Share Sale Agreement
TCD	Teaching Company Directorate
TSB	Technology Strategy Board (now Innovate UK)
TTI	Technology Transfer and Innovation
TUPE	Transfer of Undertakings, Protection of Employment
UKAS	United Kingdom Accreditation Service

Bibliography

Title	Author
LAB REPORTS: FROM THE PUBLIC TO THE PRIVATE	Rebecca Boden (Middlesex University Business School) Deborah Cox Philip Gummett Kate Barker (PREST: University of Manchester)
The Appliance of Science? New public management and strategic change	Rebecca Boden (Bristol Business School, University of the West of England) Debbie Cox (PREST: University of Manchester) Maria Nedeva (PREST: University of Manchester)
Management of Scientific Institutions NPL 1995 to 1998 The transition from Agency to Government Owned Contractor Operated (GOCO)	Dr R C Whelan Lambda Research, Cambridge (December 1998)
SUCCESSFUL CONTRACTORISATION - The Experience of the National Physical Laboratory	Dr Andrew Wallard (Deputy Director)
R & D EFFICIENCY Volume 8 Issue 2 Dec 1998 RAE OF NPL MANAGEMENT	David Fishlock
A CENTURY OF MEASUREMENT An Illustrated History of the National Physical Laboratory	Eileen Magnello
Getting better value from Public Sector Research Establishments	Quentin Maxwell-Jackson (CENTRE:FORUM)

The Termination of the PFI Contract for the National Physical Laboratory	National Audit Office (LONDON: The Stationery Office May 2006)
Increasing the Productivity of Government-Supported Research and Development Conclusions from the Experience with the U.S. Model	Jeffrey Wadsworth (President and Chief Executive Officer, Battelle November, 2009)
NPL Management Limited Filing History Full Accounts 1995 – 2016	Companies House www.gov.uk/government/organisations/companies-house
NPL ANNUAL REVIEWS NPL Archive	National Physical Laboratory www.npl.co.uk
National Measurement Office Annual Report and Accounts	Department of Business Innovation and Skills www.gov.uk/government/organisations/national-measurement-office
Inflation and Prices Indices	Office of National Statistics www.ons.gov.uk/economy/inflationandpriceindices
Industrial and Domestic Energy Price Indices	Department of Business, Energy & Industrial Strategy www.gov.uk/government/statistical-data-sets/industrial-energy-price-indicies
Cabinet Office	Classification of Public Bodies: information and guidance – Partnerships between departments and arm's-length bodies
NPL's History Highlights	www.npl.co.uk/history

CPSIA information can be obtained
at www.ICGtesting.com
Printed in the USA
BVHW060820030719
552582BV00026B/1155/P